Graphics
for the
Performing
Arts

Graphics
for the
Performing
Arts

Harvey Sweet

University of Northern Iowa

Deborah M. Dryden

Contributing Author

ALLYN AND BACON, INC.

Boston   London   Sydney   Toronto

Color Plates C-1 through C-8 courtesy M. Grumbacher, Inc.
Color Plate C-9 courtesy Jay Jagim.
Color Plates C-10 and C-11 courtesy Katy Lyness.

Copyright © 1985 by Allyn and Bacon, Inc.,
7 Wells Avenue, Newton, Massachusetts 02159

Library of Congress Cataloging in Publication Data

Sweet, Harvey.
    Graphics for the performing arts.

    Bibliography: p.
    Includes index.
    1. Performing arts.   2. Graphic arts.   I. Dryden,
Deborah M.   II. Title.
PN1590.G73S93   1985   792′.025′0221   84-28411
ISBN 0-205-08301-3

Printed in the United States of America

10 9 8 7 6 5 4 3 2 1   90 89 88 87 86 85

Contents

Preface

This book addresses artists working in drama, dance, opera, and musical and variety shows, whether performed live before an audience in a theatre or recorded on film or for television. Although each of these arts and performance modes has a distinct aesthetic, they also bear many similarities, not the least of which is the use of scenery and costumes.

Designers working in the performing arts are responsible for determining the appearance of the scenery and costumes that will be used for a production. Designers' concepts must first be approved by producers and directors and then translated into actual settings and clothing by artists and technicians in the scenery and costume shops. During the period between conception and realization, the designer must explain the design idea to all members of the production staff. This communication is achieved with sketches, renderings, and technical drawings.

Thus these graphics—the instruments by which specific, detailed information is communicated—are a step in the process between conception and realization. Sketches and renderings are not the design, but a means to represent the design idea; technical drawings are not the scenery and costumes but instructions on how to create the scenery and costumes. Designers must know how to design, craftsmen must know how to build, and both must understand how to draw and "read" the graphics which guide the work.

The drawing style used in the theatre is based upon a set of standards adopted by the United States Institute for Theatre Technology. Scenic drafters for film and television primarily use architectural graphic standards. While numerous graphic styles to represent lighting and sound design have been published, at this time neither designers nor technicians of lighting and sound have adopted a graphic standard, nor can a "best practice" be determined based on current work.

This book has been arranged to provide the novice with an orderly learning program. An early understanding of the skills, materials, and modes of mechanical drawing serves as a foundation for developing the freer forms of sketching and drawing used by designers. The book begins with a discussion of the materials and equipment used for drafting and progresses through mechanical drawing techniques, procedures, and views used to make working drawings. The drawing skills that prepare the artist for the task of design are treated next. These skills include perspective and figure drawing, the drawing of highlight and shadow, the use of color, and selected rendering materials and techniques. Each chapter concludes with a series of exercises that provide the artist an opportunity to practice the techniques covered in the chapter. The book concludes with two appendices: a complete set of design and technical drawings for a sample production, and the United States Institute for Theatre Technology's "Standard Graphic Language in Scenic Design and Technical Production."

Although the book begins with basic explanations of the equipment and materials used in drafting and drawing, each chapter progresses to a discussion of more advanced drawing techniques which should be of value to the experienced technician and artist as well as to the novice. Studying this material can give the reader a great deal of information about the use of graphics, but of course the highest level of skill will be achieved through experience and practice. The graphic artist, just like the musician, must practice regularly to attain proficiency. With drawing skills firmly developed, the artist can then concentrate on developing abilities as a technician or designer.

In preparation of this book I have been assisted in many ways. I must express special thanks to Deborah M. Dryden for contributing Chapter 5, "Figure Drawing and Costume Rendering." She was aided by Michael Olich and Lynn McLeod. I would like to thank the United States Institute for Theatre Technology for their assistance with the research project that preceded this book and for permission to publish the "Standards" document included in Appendix B. Also providing materials for inclusion in the book were Koh-I-Noor Rapidograph, Inc.; Teledyne Post; Hunt Manufacturing Company; Vemco, Inc.; and M. Grumbacher, Inc. The University of Northern Iowa has been especially supportive of this project, notably the Graduate College and the Department of Communication and Theatre Arts. Individual thanks must go to Lee Watson, J. Randy Earle, Thomas Beagle, Richard Devin, Tom and Tony Nicol, Dr. Jay Edelnant, Dr. G. Jon Hall, Becky Burns, and Ruth Petersen. I also must thank my students who both wittingly and unwittingly challenged me to write this book. To Superscript Associates, my gratitude for handling the myriad production tasks throughout the production process. Most of all, I wish to thank my wife, Pat, for her encouragement and perceptive criticism throughout this project.

Introduction

Graphics is a means of communication that uses pictures rather than words to transmit information. In the performing arts, drawings and paintings are used to express design ideas and to explain construction processes. These graphics are the means by which designers and technicians communicate with each other and with other members of the production staff.

Scene designers and art directors prepare drawings and paintings to express the general atmosphere of the production's settings; costume designers create sketches and paintings to indicate their visualization of the garments to be worn during performances. These design drawings are artistic conceptions that answer general questions about the period, style, mood, and the overall atmosphere of a production. The design drawings also answer specific questions about the treatment of details and design elements.

These graphics are more than artistic renditions of an idea. They serve practical functions as part of the planning and communication process leading to performance.

Design drawings inform the director of the designer's resolution of the issues and ideas that were discussed during planning meetings. The graphics are concrete statements of the designer's intentions which allow the director to assess whether the design is congruent with the director's concept for the production.

Performers also benefit from design drawings. An actor may obtain an impression of the environment the character inhabits and understand the clothing the character wears. This knowledge can provide valuable information to aid the actor in the development and portrayal of the character and help determine specific business for a scene.

Renderings of a production's setting inform the lighting and costume designer about the scene designer's treatment of the environment, and renderings of the costumes inform the scene and lighting designer about the nature of the wardrobe for the performance. This information allows all the designers to coordinate their work and to achieve a visually harmonious production.

Finally, design drawings are essential to the designer. The completed graphics not only provide a means by which the designer communicates with colleagues, they also provide a means by which the designer can solidify design ideas. During the rendering process the designer completes the design concept for a setting or a costume. Choices regarding color, texture, line, and a myriad of other details are made at this time.

Renderings are only some of the graphics required of the scene designer. This artist must also create floor plans, elevations, and sectional drawings to indicate the specific arrangement of each scenic element. Floor plans and elevations are among the technical drawings that must be made to guide the construction of scenery. These drawings provide specific information about the layout, dimensions, materials, and means of construction. They are similar in style and purpose to the architectural plans used to guide construction of a house or office building. Many architectural drawing techniques are used in the performing arts, especially television and film, which also use architectural construction techniques. However in the theatre, these techniques are adapted to the specialized needs of theatrical scenic construction.

In contrast to design drawing, which is a relatively free artistic mode, technical drawing requires a highly regimented use of lines, symbols, and drawing media. Rather than giving an impression of the setting, these drawings explicitly state the specific shape, size, and placement of each component of scenery.

All of the graphics prepared for a production, whether in theatre, film, or television, are drawn by artists and drafters for the purpose of communicating information. Communication, however, is only effective if both the maker and the "reader" of the drawings understand the graphic language. Although the different groups of artists involved in a production may need different levels of expertise, it is a common assumption in the performing arts that the best artist has at least a basic understanding of the work of collaborators. Thus producers, directors, technical directors, performers, technicians, and camera operators are better able to coordinate their own efforts with those of their colleagues. Graphics that are clear, meaningful, accurate, and comprehendable by all members of the production staff will result in a more effective performance. This is the goal for which all workers in the performing arts strive.

Graphics
for the
Performing
Arts

CHAPTER 1

Mechanical Drawing Equipment and Materials

INTRODUCTION

Drawing is a process of communication that uses pictures rather than words to present ideas. A picture may be created as a freehand sketch or with the aid of drafting guides. Drafters prepare drawings with the assistance of straightedges, scales, and drafting instruments which assure precise lines and accurate dimensions. Although mechanical drawings may be created on almost any surface with most any equipment and materials, a number of specialized drafting instruments have been developed that improve efficiency, accuracy, and clarity. Drawing surfaces that reduce hand and eye strain, guides that assure accurate lines, and drawing instruments that meet the specific needs and personal preferences of most drafters have been created. In addition, a variety of papers and drafting films have been developed that enhance the appearance and reproducibility of drawings.

DRAFTING EQUIPMENT

Work Surfaces

Mechanical drawings are prepared on **drawing boards.** These large, flat surfaces are constructed from wood, metal, plastic, or composites of these materials. Drawing boards must be sturdy, flat, and smooth with distortion-free edges to guide drafting instruments. A board should be large enough to hold the biggest drawing that the drafter may need to make, yet also provide space around the drawing for reference materials. Drawing boards are available in nine standard sizes, from 12″ × 17″ to 36″ × 48″. Most scenic drafters work on large layouts requiring one of the bigger drawing boards.

A **drafting table** is a drawing board mounted on a stand (Figure 1–1). The table may be a simple base that supports a standard drawing board at a fixed angle, or it may be quite elaborate with a built-in pencil trough, bookshelf, desk, file, rear-illuminated work surface, automatic height and tilt adjustments, or electric outlets. The working surface may be a standard drawing board, or it may be constructed with a special frame and top. The angle of the board should be adjustable from 0° to at least 20° above the horizontal plane. Drafting tables are available in sizes ranging from 20″ × 26″ to 54″ × 120″. The drafter may work at any of these units standing or seated. It is imperative that the table be sufficiently sturdy so as not to wiggle or vibrate while the drafter is drawing or erasing. All areas of the table should be comfortably accessible.

FIGURE 1–1
Drafting table. (Courtesy Teledyne Post.)

The surface of a drawing board or drafting table may be improved by installing a **drawing board cover.** A board cover provides a smooth, distortion-free work surface that reduces eye and hand fatigue and eliminates minor imperfections in the surface of the board. Vinyl covers and heavy paper covers with tinted surfaces or printed grid lines are available. Both types of cover are attached to the drawing board with double-sided tape or thumbtacks. Vinyl covers may be cleaned with a damp cloth or solvent cleaner.

Guides

A **T-square** (Figure 1–2) is a companion to the drawing board. The head of the T-square rests firmly against one side of the board. The blade crosses the entire drawing surface to provide a consistent horizontal base line. The blade of the T-square should be equal in length to the width of the drawing board. T-squares up to 48″ long are constructed from wood, plastic, stainless steel, or composites of these materials. The edges of most T-squares are made from clear plastic, so the drafter can easily see the work, and are designed to maintain a space between the blade and the drawing surface to reduce smudges and prevent ink from creeping under the guide.

FIGURE 1-2
T-squares. (Courtesy Teledyne Post.)

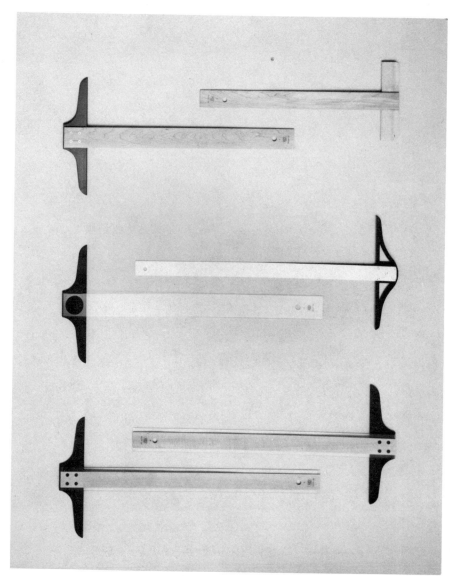

A **parallel bar** (Figure 1–3) performs the same function as a T-square. However, rather than guiding the straightedge off one side of the drawing board, a system of cables and pulleys keeps the guide aligned as it travels up and down the board surface. A variety of parallel bars are available with different styles of control systems and blade compositions.

A **30-60 triangle** and a **45 triangle** complete the basic set of drawing guides. Each of these triangles has one 90° angle; the other two angles are 30° and 60°, in the first case, and 45° at each corner of the second triangle. These triangles are used with a T-square to draw lines at 15°, 30°, 45°, 60°, 75°, or 90° (Figure 1–4). A triangle may also be used independently as a simple straightedge to draw lines not

FIGURE 1–3
Drawing board with parallel bar. (Courtesy Teledyne Post.)

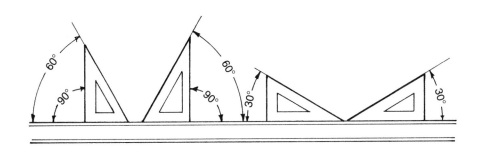

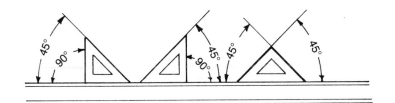

FIGURE 1–4
45 and 30–60 triangles may be used separately as straight edges; with a T-square to form 30°, 45°, 60°, and 90° angles; or in combination to form 15° and 75° angles.

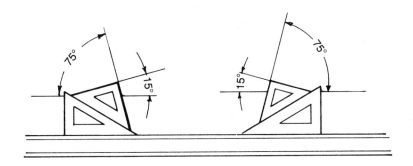

5

located on one of the measured angles. An **adjustable triangle** (Figure 1–5) may replace both a 45 and 30-60 triangle. This instrument combines a moveable hypotenuse with a compass. Any angle between 0° and 90° may be drawn.

Curves, arcs, circles, geometric shapes, and various symbols may be drawn with the aid of a template. A **template** (Figure 1–6) is a thin piece of plastic with a pattern forming its edge or cut into its body. In addition to geometric shapes, templates with standard ar-

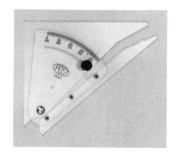

FIGURE 1–5

An adjustable triangle may be set to any angle between 0° and 90°. (Courtesy Teledyne Post.)

FIGURE 1–6

Templates. Hundred of additional architectural, engineering, general theatrical, and special-purpose templates are available. (Courtesy Teledyne Post.)

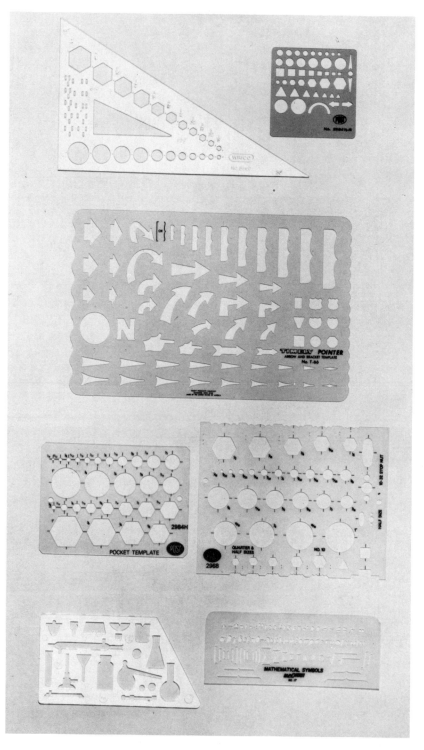

chitectural, mechanical, structural, electronic, engineering, and theatrical symbols, lettering guides, and furniture plans are available. They are designed to exacting standards with openings adjusted for narrow lead or pen points to achieve the proper size on drawings. **French, railroad,** and **ship curves** are used to draw asymmetrical arcs (Figure 1–7).

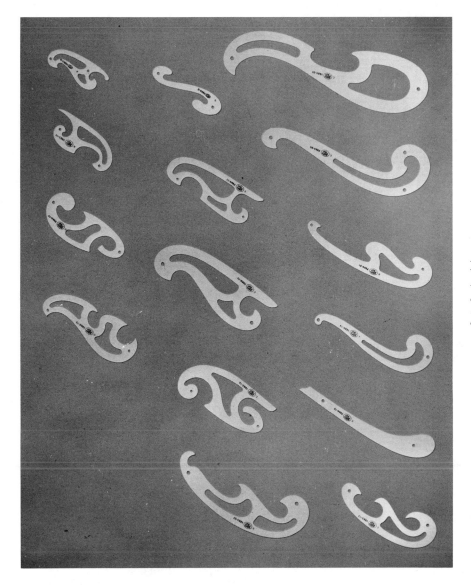

FIGURE 1–7
French, railroad, and ship curves are available in a variety of sizes. (Courtesy Teledyne Post.)

Scales are precision instruments used to determine measurements on drawings. They are available in shapes and increment patterns designed to meet the needs of either architects or engineers (Figure 1–8). The handiest scale for most scenic drafting is a triangular architect's scale which combines ten different degrees of gradation on a single instrument (Table 1–1). These scales are open-divided with the main unit of each scale graduated through the length of the instrument; however, only one major unit at one end is subdivided into inches. Architect's scales are also available in metric dimensions substituting meters and centimeters for feet and inches.

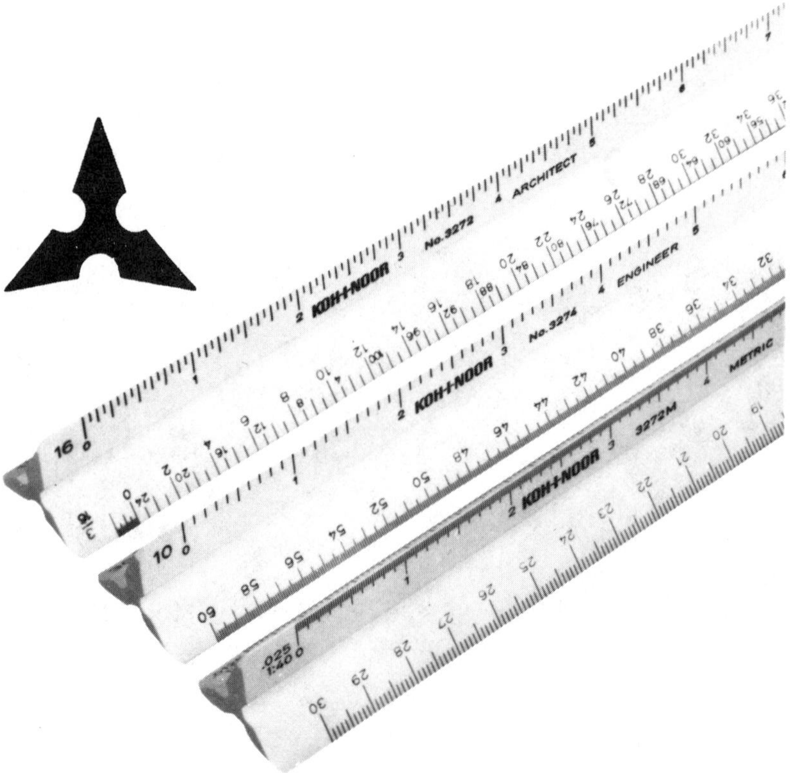

FIGURE 1–8
Triangular scales. (Courtesy Koh-I-Noor Rapidograph.)

TABLE 1–1
Scales to represent feet and inches on a triangular architect's scale.

3/32	1/2
1/8	3/4
3/16	1
1/4	1½
3/8	3
FULL	

The minimum equipment needed for mechanical drawing includes a drawing board, T-square, set of triangles, and a scale. With the exception of the drawing board, all of this equipment may be replaced by a drafting machine. A **drafting machine** provides a set of drawing arms located 90° apart on a moveable handle or head. The arms are engraved with two fully divided scales which also function as straight-edges for drawing. Interchangeable drawing arms are available in both engineer's and architect's scales. The head of the machine that holds the drawing arms may be set at any primary angle, usually square to the drawing board. The arms may be rotated to the right or left, where they may be locked in place to draw lines at any desired angle. A compass is contained in the head of the machine to indicate the position of the drawing arms.

There are two styles of drafting machines: track drafters and arm drafters. A **track drafter** (Figure 1–9), requires both a vertical and horizontal track to guide the drawing head. The drawing head is mounted on a vertical track that allows the head to move the full height of the drawing board. The vertical track travels the width of the board in a horizontal track that is attached to the top edge of the board. The head may be moved up, down, or across the board to any location, where it may be locked in place, rotated, or hinged off of the drawing surface. An **arm drafter** (Figure 1–10) is similar to a track drafter; however, rather than being guided along tracks, the head is mounted at the end of a hinged arm with an "elbow" near the center. The head may be located in any position on the board but may not be locked in place or hinged off of the drawing surface. Track drafters require almost the entire top edge of the board for mounting; arm drafters

FIGURE 1–9
Track drafter. The horizontal track attaches to the top edge of the drawing board and guides the vertical track as it moves across the width of the board. The vertical track guides the drawing head, which may be located anywhere on the drawing board. The drawing head carries two interchangeable drawing arms with engraved scales that form a 90° angle. The drawing head may be rotated to any angle and locked in place. (Courtesy Teledyne Post.)

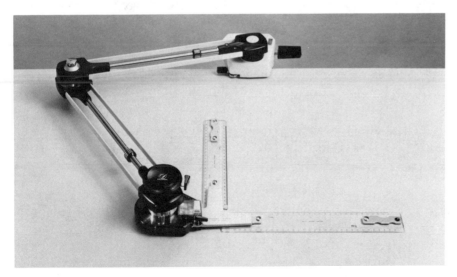

FIGURE 1–10
Arm drafter, also called band and pulley drafter, is mounted at the top edge of the drawing board. The head, at the end of an arm with an "elbow," carries two interchangeable drawing arms with engraved scales. The drawing head may be positioned anywhere desired on the drawing board and the drawing arms rotated to any angle. (Courtesy Teledyne Post.)

may be mounted in a small area at the top edge of the board. Although this equipment is relatively expensive, the convenience and efficiency that either drafting machine provides the advanced drafter is well worth the investment.

9

Drawing Instruments

Pencils

Most scenic drafting must be performed quickly; because permanency is of little concern, the work is usually done with pencils. Some drafters prefer to draw with ink; however, their preparatory work is still done with lead. Drafting pencils are available in three basic forms: wood-clad pencils, mechanical lead holders, and automatic pencils.

Wood-clad drafting pencils are similar to wooden school pencils. However, they are made with a better grade of lead and usually have no eraser. As the lead is consumed, the pencil must be sharpened. As a result the pencil becomes shorter, altering the relationship between the fingers and the instrument. This factor can be overcome with mechanical lead holders (Figure 1–11). These instruments are metal or plastic sleeves that hold replaceable leads. As the lead is consumed,

FIGURE 1–11

Mechanical lead holders. (Courtesy Koh-I-Noor Rapidograph.)

additional lengths are advanced out of the holder; the holder remains a constant length. When the lead is not in use it may be retracted into the holder to protect it. **Automatic pencils** (Figure 1–12) are similar to mechanical lead holders. However, they use thin leads from 0.3mm to 1.0mm in diameter. A separate holder is required for each diameter lead. The same size lead is used as the width of the desired line, so

FIGURE 1–12

Automatic pencil. (Courtesy Koh-I-Noor Rapidograph.)

it is not necessary to point those leads. When the button on the top of an automatic pencil is depressed, a very short length of lead is advanced out of the holder; repeated depressions of the button will advance more lead. A narrow sleeve protects the end of the lead as the pencil is moved along drawing guides.

Leads are manufactured from graphite and clay compositions in seventeen degrees of hardness (Table 1–2). The hardness of a lead is printed at one end of a wood-clad pencil or on the surface of the refill leads for mechanical lead holders. Lead hardness determines the darkness of lines that may be drawn—softer leads draw darker lines; they also have larger diameters which give added strength. Leads for automatic pencils are available in fewer degrees of hardness, usually B through 4H. An HB lead in most brands is equivalent to the hardness of a Number 2 school pencil. Most drafters use a variety of leads for their work. Thin and very light lines are drawn with 2H, 4H, or 6H leads, and heavier, darker lines are drawn with softer leads. The soft leads tend to smudge easily but deposit solid dark lines. Harder leads form crisp lines but may dent the paper, making complete erasure difficult. Leads with special compositions are necessary for drawing on polyester drafting films. These leads are numbered with an alphabetic prefix, such as E, F, K, or P. There are five degrees of hardness of leads for film, from 1 (soft) to 5 (super hard). Leads may be sharpened on a sanding block or with a lead pointer (Figure 1–13). Automatic pencils do not require pointing.

TABLE 1–2
Degrees of lead hardness for drafting pencils.

6B	SUPER SOFT
5B	
4B	VERY SOFT
3B	
2B	
B	SOFT
HB	
F	MEDIUM
H	HARD
2H	
3H	VERY HARD
4H	
5H	
6H	SUPER HARD
7H	
8H	
9H	

FIGURE 1–13
Lead pointer. (Courtesy Koh-I-Noor Rapidograph.)

Ruling pens (Figure 1–14) are infrequently used in contemporary drafting. These instruments consist of a pair of blades that may be adjusted to any reasonable line width. India ink is placed between the upper portion of the blades with a dropper. The ink is held in place by capillary attraction. As a line is drawn, gravity pulls the ink from

FIGURE 1–14

Ruling pen. (Courtesy Teledyne Post.)

between the blades to form a sharp opaque line. For the most part, more convenient technical pens have replaced ruling pens. A **technical pen** (Figure 1–15) holds ink in a cartridge that automatically feeds the pen tip. Up to seventeen different point sizes are available. They are identified numerically, from 6x0 (0.11mm) to 14 (6.0mm). In addition, a broad range of accessories such as lettering sets and compass adaptors may be used with these instruments. As with pencils, the abrasive

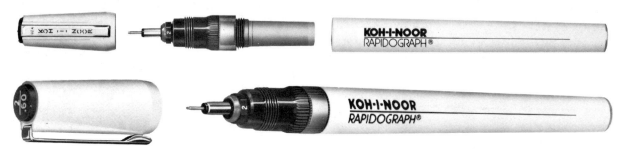

FIGURE 1–15

Technical pens with replaceable point and refillable ink reservoir. (Courtesy Koh-I-Noor Rapidograph.)

surface of drawing media will wear out pen points. Occasional replacement of the tips is necessary. Stainless steel, tungsten, and jewel pen points are available. Reasonable care must be taken to keep pen tips clean.

A compass is used to draw circles and arcs. A **bow compass** (Figure 1–16) has a threaded cross-piece between its legs to allow

FIGURE 1–16

a) Large bow compass, b) Dividers, c) Small bow compass. (Courtesy Koh-I-Noor Rapidograph.)

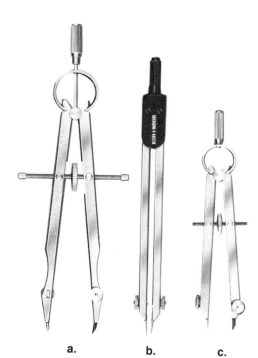

a.   b.   c.

precise adjustment of the centering pin and drawing tip. These instruments are used to draw small- and moderate-sized circles. A **beam compass** (Figure 1–17) is used to draw large circles and arcs. The centering pin and drawing leg are adjusted to the proper radius on the beam, which may be extended up to 36″. The drawing leg of most compasses may be equipped with a pin point, lead holder, or inking tip.

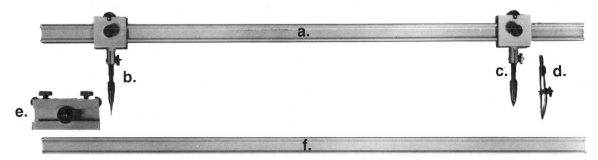

FIGURE 1–17
Beam compass. a) Beam, b) Centering pin, c) Interchangeable lead holder, d) Interchangeable inking tip, e) Beam extender, f) Beam extension. (Courtesy Koh-I-Noor Rapidograph.)

A **divider** (Figure 1–16) is similar in appearance to a bow compass. It is equipped with a friction joint that allows fingertip adjustment of the legs and has two pin points rather than a drawing tip. This instrument is used to transfer dimensions on a drawing or to make trial measurements without marking the page.

Accessories

Drafting erasers are used to remove either pencil or ink from a drawing. A good eraser will remove lines without damaging the drawing surface, staining the paper, or leaving a shadow where the lines have been removed. Erasers of different compositions are available for lead, ink, and general cleaning. Some ink erasers are designed to be used with a solvent, and others are impregnated with a solvent to aid cleaning. Electric and cordless erasing machines (Figure 1–18) are time-saving devices utilized by many drafters. Kneaded rubber erasers

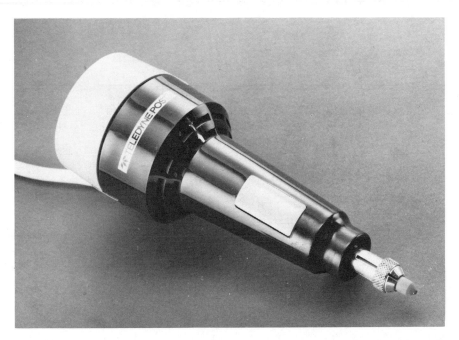

FIGURE 1–18
Electric erasing machine. (Courtesy Teledyne Post.)

and art gum erasers are used to clean drawings and for other art applications. An **erasing shield** may be used to mask all but a small section of a drawing where erasing will be done. The shield is a very thin piece of stainless steel with holes and slots of various sizes and shapes cut into it. A **dusting brush** is used to whisk erasure residue off the drawing without smudging lines.

Drafting tape attaches papers and films to the surface of the drawing board. This material is very similar in appearance and feel to masking tape. It holds the paper firmly in place, yet allows it to be easily removed without tearing or leaving any residue on either the board or the drawing. The tape is available in widths from 1/4″ to 1″.

A myriad of accessories are available to the drafter, including paper and tool holders, files, adhesives, guides, pointers, cleaners, lights, easels, lettering guides, tapes, and knives. A visit to a professional drafting-supply store will reveal the vast array of equipment and materials that are available.

DRAWING MEDIA

Characteristics

Drafting may be done on any surface that will accept lead or ink; however, most drafting surfaces must meet additional requirements. There are several qualities that should be considered in the selection of papers, cloths, and films.

Physical strength describes the ability of the material to withstand erasing, cutting, tearing, cracking, fading, and aging. Strength is dependent upon the composition of the material, its thickness or weight, and the physical effects of coatings.

Stability describes the ability of the material to resist temperature and humidity changes without warping.

Transparency describes the ability of light to pass through the paper during the reproduction process. Transparency is dependent upon the composition and density of the material and the effect of resin impregnations and coatings.

Color describes the whiteness or tint of the material. Some media are tinted to reduce eye fatigue and glare.

Tooth describes the coarseness of the drawing surface. This will affect the ability of the medium to accept pencil or ink, the quality of line that can be achieved, and the ease of erasing a line.

Media acceptance (related to tooth) describes the ability of the drawing surface to accept pencil, ink, or other drawing materials. Some types of surfaces are designed explicitly for use with one or another drawing tool, and others will accept all materials equally well. Drafting films, for example, require inks and leads with special compositions.

Sidedness describes whether the drawing surface can receive drawing marks on one or on both of its surfaces. Most modern papers are suitable for drawing on both sides; however, because of manufacturing processes, one side of the paper is usually preferred for its tooth and erasability.

Printed media are available with preprinted borders and with standard or custom title blocks. Most media may also be purchased with nonprinting grid lines in various scales. These assist the drafter during the drawing process but do not appear on prints or in photographs.

Size describes the standard dimensions of a drawing surface. Papers and films are available in cut sheets and in rolls. Standard dimensions are listed in Table 1–3.

Media Categories

Drawing Paper

A very heavy-weight paper that is colored white, buff, or green. This kind of paper used to be used for preliminary drawings from which tracings were made. It is infrequently used in contemporary drafting.

Tracing Paper

A low-density paper that is naturally transparent. No coating or impregnations are added to the paper to improve its physical strength, tooth, or transparency. These papers are used for making temporary transparent overlays, for working out rough ideas, or for sketching. This material is relatively inexpensive, physically weak, and unstable.

Vellum

A 100 per cent rag paper that has been treated with coatings or resin impregnations to enhance transparency, tooth, stability, and physical strength. Most contemporary drafting is done on vellum. Vellums are treated to accept pencil, ink, or both on either one or both sides. Vellums can also be tinted to reduce eye strain or printed with borders, title blocks, or nonreproducing grids.

Tracing Cloth

A finely woven cotton fiber that has been treated to enhance transparency and to accept either pencil or ink. The material is highly transparent and durable; however, it is reactive to temperature and humidity changes and deteriorates with age. Formerly, tracing cloths were used for permanent drawings. They are seldom used in contemporary drafting due to stability problems and high cost. The material is definitely sided, and drawing is done on the matte surface.

Paper Size	Cut Sheets	Rolls
8½ × 11	18 × 24	Either 20 or 50 yards in length
9 × 12	22 × 34	24″
11 × 17	24 × 36	30″
12 × 18	34 × 44	36″
17 × 22	36 × 48	42″

TABLE 1–3
Standard sizes of drafting media.

Drafting Film

This material has replaced most tracing cloths and is replacing the use of vellum in some industries. Film is manufactured from thin polyester (plastic) sheeting similar in appearance to the plastic drop cloths used by painters; however, one or both sides of the material has a matte finish that will accept special leads or inks. Drafting film is stronger, more stable, and more transparent than any other drafting medium. It is virtually unaffected by temperature or humidity changes and is almost totally transparent. Film has also been known to last over thirty years without curling, cracking, discoloring, or showing any other signs of age. The material is available in thicknesses from 1.5 mils (.0015 inches) to 7.5 mils (.0075 inches). Film 3 mils thick is considered medium weight and is most similar in feel to vellum. Film 4 mils thick and greater is used for precision drafting, computer applications, and electronic engineering. The thinnest film, 1.5 mils, is considered satisfactory for original drawings that will receive minimal handling. Although it is significantly more expensive than vellum, many industries consider film to be the most practical drafting medium because of its strength, transparency, and stability. Films are available with tinted bases, printed forms, and nonreproducing grids. Due to expense and the minimal need for archival preservation of drawings, drafting film has only limited application in the performing arts.

Reproduction Processes

Most drawings prepared by drafters, designers, and technical directors are reproduced for distribution to other members of the production staff. This allows each staff member dealing with blocking, for instance, to have a copy of the floor plan. As many copies as may be needed are also produced for other designers or the shops. When a drawing goes into the shop it usually receives fairly rough treatment; an original drawing would be quickly destroyed. Duplication of drawings preserves the original so that additional copies may be made or revisions drawn without starting the drawing over.

Drawings are reproduced on printing machines. Printing is a two-step process: exposure and development. An original drawing on a transparent medium such as vellum is placed right-side-up against paper treated with light-sensitized diazo chemicals. This open-faced sandwich is fed into a printing machine where it is exposed to ultraviolet light. That portion of the sensitized paper covered by lines is protected from the light. After exposure, the original drawing is separated from the sensitized paper, and the exposed paper is put into a developer where it is passed through an ammonia atmosphere. The portion of the sensitized paper that was protected by lines during exposure will now appear as dark lines on the print. The remainder of the exposed paper will appear nearly white.

Prints may be made on opaque papers, transparent papers, or transparent polyester films. They can produce blue, black, or sepia (rich orange-brown) lines on a white background, depending upon the print medium used. Print papers and films are rated as to thickness or weight, development speed, and color. Older printing processes produced prints with white lines on a dark blue background. This is the origination of the term "blue print."

Commercial reproduction services exist in most communities. They are normally equipped to make any variety of prints in small or large quantities. Charges are based on a cost per square foot of printed materials. A good printer is usually able to obtain satisfactory copies from average-quality drawings. For reasons of convenience, cost or time, many studios acquire their own reproduction equipment. Large machines are capable of producing quantities of high-quality prints at reasonable cost, but purchasing or leasing these machines is fairly expensive. In addition, the machines must have regular maintenance, moderately large floor space, and a vented atmosphere to control the buildup of ammonia fumes. Tabletop printers, which are smaller and less expensive, are used by many theatres. These machines are available in printing widths up to 48″. They are capable of producing prints similar in quality to the larger machines. Some tabletop machines do not use an ammonia developer. Nonammonia machines can be operated in a standard office without special ventilation or air filtering. The nonammonia machines can reproduce on most print media; however, they are not as efficient as the larger machines for reproduction on films.

Modern printing equipment and materials are capable of producing **intermediate copies** which make it possible to preserve the original drawing yet allow a copy to be altered and reprinted or attached to another original for additional printing. Intermediate copies are called "**sepias**" because the lines are colored a rich orange-brown on a transparent background. Drawings on sepias may be altered by simply adding lines or removing information with an eradicator fluid. Erasable sepia papers are also available. Polyester films may be used to make intermediate copies which serve the same purpose as sepias. The films produce very high-quality prints with physical characteristics similar to drafting film.

Sepia papers are definitely sided. If a "second original" is desired, the print is made in the normal manner with the drawing facing away from the sensitized paper (toward the operator). If the sepia is to receive additional drawing, the original is placed face down on the sensitized paper; the resultant print is upside-down. The drafter adds any information on the nonprinted side of the sheet. Lines are erased or eradicated on the printed side.

Intermediate copies can be used effectively by the designer, technical director, and the drafter to make minor adaptations of design or technical drawings or to reproduce drawings of mirror images that are adapted on one side of the centerline. Technical directors and drafters may produce intermediate copies of design drawings and add technical notations for construction. The marked-up sepia is then printed for the shop. Drafters may also use intermediate copies to show various levels of construction by drafting a single plan of a unit, for instance a revolve, then drawing the substructure on an intermediate copy of the plan. Another intermediate copy may be used to show the layout of decking materials. Intermediate copies may also be used as bases from which standard drawings can be developed, such as a centerline section or a hanging section for a particular theatre. Creative employment of reproduction processes and media can aid the drafter throughout the drawing process. Proper use of drawing tools and drafting media can also help save time and create efficient, neat, and accurate drawings.

HANDLING THE EQUIPMENT AND MATERIALS

Before starting work, prepare the equipment and work area. Begin by removing all unnecessary clutter from the work area, especially any food or beverages. Dust the drawing board and be sure there is no accumulation of graphite on the work surface or on drawing instruments. After a period of use, drafting equipment will accumulate deposits of graphite. If these are not removed they will cause smudges on the paper. Occasional cleaning of drafting equipment with the suds of a mild detergent will alleviate this problem.

Drawing tools should be laid out in an orderly manner and in a location convenient to the work area. Right-handed drafters would place tools on their right, left-handed drafters on their left. The instruments should be placed off the drawing board, out of the path of the T-square.

Lay out the paper on the drawing board (Figure 1–19). The sheet should be placed several inches above the bottom edge of the board and parallel with it. The left edge of the paper should be located within 3″ of the left edge of the drawing board. Left-handed drafters should locate the paper closest to the right edge of the board. The paper should lay smooth and be firmly attached to the board at each corner with a piece of drafting tape approximately 1½″ long.

Place the T-square on the board. The head of the T-square hangs over the edge of the board on the side opposite the drawing hand (to the left for right-handed drafters, to the right for left-handed drafters). Holding the head of the T-square firmly against the edge of the board, slide the instrument up and down the drawing surface. If movement of the T-square is impeded by curled tape, replace the tape causing the problem. The head of the T-square must rest firmly against the edge of the board each time a line is drawn. *The top edge of the T-square is the drawing guide;* it also supports the bottom edge of triangles and templates. A 30-60 triangle is used to draw most vertical lines. The T-square and triangle in combination allow the drafter to draw

FIGURE 1–19

Preparing the work area. The head of the T-square is located on the side opposite the drawing hand. Tools and drawing instruments are placed on the drawing hand side of the board. Drawing paper is taped to the board near the bottom and head-of-the-T-square side of the board, with drafting tape placed diagonally across each corner.

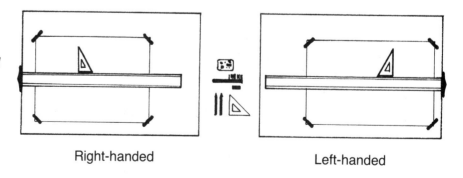

Right-handed   Left-handed

true horizontal and vertical lines relative to each other and to the edge of the drawing board. It should be possible to move the pair of instruments freely around on the working surface and to draw a vertical or horizontal line anywhere on the sheet.

Leads must be kept well sharpened to obtain precise lines. They may be pointed with a sanding block or lead pointer. To point a wood-clad pencil with a sanding block, a ⅜″ length of lead is exposed by carving the wood away from the lead with a knife. Lead in a holder is simply extended ⅜″ beyond the end of the holder. The sanding block is held in one hand, and the lead is wiped across the length of the sandpaper while the pencil is twirled between the fingers. The angle between the surface of the sanding block and the lead determines the shape and length of the point. Consistent pressure, angle, and rotation of the pencil will form a point terminating in a symmetrical conical tip (Figure 1–20). Pointers to sharpen both wood-clad pencils and leads in holders are available. Depending upon the style of pointer, approximately ⅜″ of lead is exposed. It is placed in the opening on the top of the pointer, which is rotated several turns to shape the lead. After pointing, the lead should be wiped clean of all residue. Do not sharpen pencils over the drawing board.

A drafting pencil is held between the fingers in the same manner as any other pencil. One technique is mandatory to achieve consistent lines and even wear on the pencil: the instrument must be slowly twirled between the fingers as each line is drawn. The pencil should always be rotated in the same direction. This practice causes even wear on the point which results in lines of consistent appearance. Even pressure must be maintained on the pencil to obtain a constant degree of darkness and line width.

Almost all lines are drawn with the aid of a guide. The orientation of the pencil against the guide is critical: *the pencil must be perpendicular to the edge of the guide at all times* (Figure 1–21). If the point is allowed to tip away from the guide, a wavy line will result; if the point tips toward the guide, graphite will accumulate on it and smudge the drawing. The top of the pencil leans at an approximate angle of 60° in the direction that the hand moves to draw the line. Lines are drawn

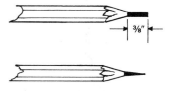

FIGURE 1–20
Pointing the lead. A properly pointed drafting lead is approximately ⅜″ long and tapers to a conical point.

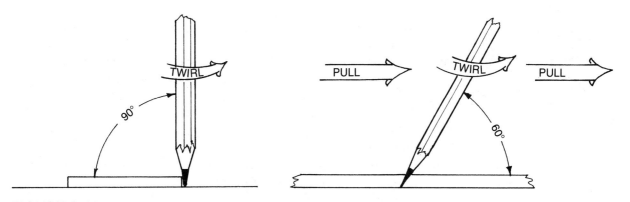

FIGURE 1–21
Guiding the pencil. The pencil is held perpendicular to the top of the T-square or triangle and leans at an angle of approximately 60° in the direction that the pencil moves. The pencil must be twirled as the line is drawn. The lead is guided by the top edge of the drawing guide.

19

as a horse draws a carriage. *The pencil must always be pulled, never pushed.* Pushing the pencil will dent or cut the paper and break the lead. The lead is slowly twirled between the fingers as the pencil is pulled across the page. Vertical lines are drawn from the bottom to the top; horizontals are drawn from the head of the T-square toward the drawing hand. Right-handed diagonals are drawn from bottom to top, and left-handed diagonals are drawn from top to bottom. The direction for drawing diagonals by left-handed drafters is reversed. Properly drawn lines begin and end with a crisp sharp edge and are of a consistent width and darkness throughout their length. They must not dent the paper.

A compass is used to draw arcs and circles. Facility with this instrument is also developed with practice. The compass uses an unclad lead sharpened on a sanding block to a chiseled point (Figure 1–22). The longer the bevel of the lead the longer the point will last; however, as with any other pencil, too long a point will break easily. The long edge of the chisel point is placed on the side toward the center of the compass. Be sure that the needle point and lead point are approximately the same length. All good compasses are designed to facilitate this adjustment by means of a thumbscrew or knurled ring that permits adjustment of both points. Mark the center of the arc or circle to be drawn with a +. Adjust the distance between the points of the compass to the desired radius by turning the knurled adjustment knob on the bow (horizontal rod at the center of the compass). Holding the centering pin firmly in position, lean the compass in the direction it will turn and rotate the lead around the circle or arc. Always pull the lead, never push it. Arcs and circles must be consistent in width and darkness with the rest of the drawing. Junctions with straight lines or other arcs must blend with no apparent break or overlap.

If a setting or building were drawn its actual size, it would be impossible to comprehend the design, and it would be impractical to use the drawing as a reference. Normally, buildings, settings, and individual scenic units are drawn in reduced scale. On the other hand, miniature forms such as jewelry may be drawn in an enlarged scale. The term **scale** means a proportional reduction or enlargement in a drawing of some actual object in life. The term also refers to the instrument used to determine proportional measurements drawn in-scale. An architect's scale bears the proportional scales most frequently used for drafting in the performing arts. The most common scales in which these drawings are made are ¼″ = 1′-0″ and ½″ = 1′-0″. In other words, when drawing in the scale of ¼″ = 1′-0″, a quarter-inch on the paper represents one foot in actuality; everything drawn in this scale is shown in that proportional relationship to life size. If a form is 4′-0″ long in actuality, it would be drawn four quarter-inches long in scale. This translation to scale can be made fairly easily using a standard desk ruler, but when a line 4′-7¼″ long must be drawn in scale, the translation becomes complicated. Architect's scales allow the drafter to translate any foot or inch dimension quickly and easily to correct proportional size.

Each edge of a triangular architect's scale has two interrelated scales engraved on it. The name of the scale is engraved at the end of the measuring section. The first "foot" of each scale is subdivided

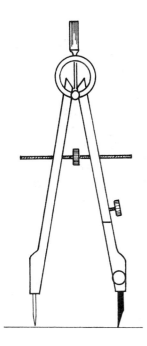

FIGURE 1–22

Sharpening the compass. The compass lead is sharpened to a chisel point on a sanding block. The bevel points away from the center of the compass when the lead is in place. The lead and the centering pin should be the same length.

20

into inches. Figure 1–23 shows a portion of a ¼″ scale. A series of large numerals is associated with long tick marks on the edge of the scale; they progress in two's from 0 to 46. Each tick mark of the same length represents one foot in the scale of ¼″ = 1′-0″. Thus, if a line is two feet long it would be measured from 2 to 0; a line twenty-four feet long would be measured from 24 to 0. If a line were three feet and nine inches long, the nearest whole dimension, in this case 3, would be put on one end of the line and then the distance in inches beyond 0 would be measured in the subdivided section of the scale. On each edge of the instrument the smaller scale is a 50 percent reduction of the larger scale. Thus, the ¼ scale shares the same edge as the ⅛ scale. The two scales count from opposite ends. Also, the foot marks of the smaller scale represents half-foot marks of the larger scale. Conversely, the foot marks of the larger scale represent two-foot marks of the smaller scale. The section of the scale representing inches is divided variously. On the smallest scales each increment in the subdivided section represents 2″, in the middle scales each increment represents 1″, and in the larger scales a foot is divided into ¼″ subdivisions.

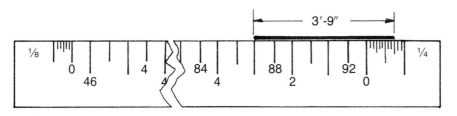

A scale may also be used to draw an enlarged view; thus one half-inch in scale may represent one-sixteenth of an inch in actuality, and sixteen half-inches in scale would represent one inch in actuality. Because a scale may be used to reduce or enlarge views proportionately, it is designated on the instrument simply as ¼ or ½. The drafter determines and identifies what this dimension represents.

The most effective communication is achieved with drawings that are clear, complete, and accurate. Competent use of drafting equipment will ease the drawing task and accelerate the drawing process. Several commonsense rules about the work area and equipment should be observed to reduce errors and accidents.

FIGURE 1–23

Using the scale. Two scales appear on each edge of a standard architect's scale. The long tick marks represent one-foot increments of the larger scale; the short tick marks represent one-foot increments on the smaller scale. Each scale has one section subdivided. A line is measured by placing the nearest whole-foot dimension at one end of the line and measuring back to the subdivided portion of the scale to determine inches.

Rules for Mechanical Drawing

1. Do not eat or drink at the drawing board.
2. Dust the drawing board and wipe off all instruments before beginning work.
3. Keep equipment or books not in immediate use off the drawing board.
4. Do not use edges of the T-square or triangles as guides for cutting paper with a knife.
5. Use only the upper edge of the T-square as a drawing guide or base to support triangles.

6. Always keep the head of the T-square on the same side of the board.
7. Do not use the scale as a straight edge.
8. Use only properly pointed pencils.
9. Do not sharpen pencils over the drawing board.
10. Do not fold drawings.

BASIC GEOMETRY

Once an understanding of drafting equipment and materials is achieved, the novice drafter must learn to use that equipment in an efficient manner. Although the drafter need not be a mathematician, it is important to understand the basic language, constructions, and formulae of geometry. This knowledge can enhance the accuracy of drawings and speed the drawing process.

Figures 1–24 through 1–26 contain descriptions and examples of some of the basic geometric forms with which the drafter should be familiar.

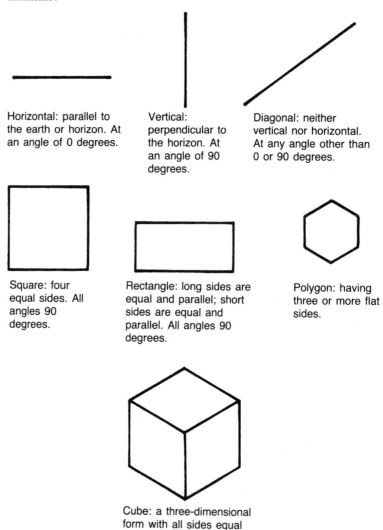

FIGURE 1–24
Basic geometric forms.

Horizontal: parallel to the earth or horizon. At an angle of 0 degrees.

Vertical: perpendicular to the horizon. At an angle of 90 degrees.

Diagonal: neither vertical nor horizontal. At any angle other than 0 or 90 degrees.

Square: four equal sides. All angles 90 degrees.

Rectangle: long sides are equal and parallel; short sides are equal and parallel. All angles 90 degrees.

Polygon: having three or more flat sides.

Cube: a three-dimensional form with all sides equal and parallel. All angles at 90 degrees.

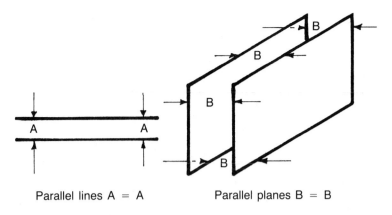

Parallel lines A = A   Parallel planes B = B

Parallel — All portions of two or more lines or planes are located equidistant.

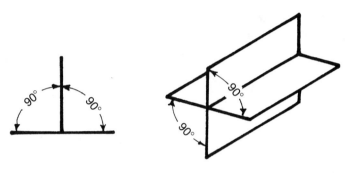

FIGURE 1–25
Basic angles.

Perpendicular — Two lines or planes intersect at an angle of 90 degrees.

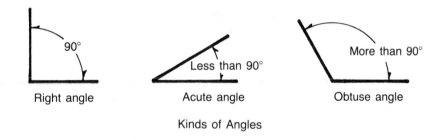

Right angle   Acute angle   Obtuse angle

Kinds of Angles

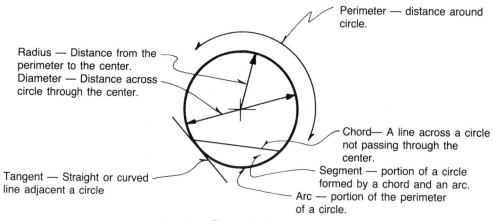

Perimeter — distance around circle.

Radius — Distance from the perimeter to the center.
Diameter — Distance across circle through the center.

Chord— A line across a circle not passing through the center.

Segment — portion of a circle formed by a chord and an arc.

Tangent — Straight or curved line adjacent a circle

Arc — portion of the perimeter of a circle.

a. Parts of a Circle

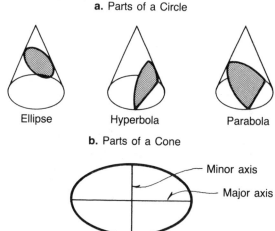

Ellipse   Hyperbola   Parabola

b. Parts of a Cone

FIGURE 1–26

a) Parts of a circle, b) Parts of a cone, c) Parts of an ellipse.

Minor axis

Major axis

c. Parts of an Ellipse Figure

BASIC GEOMETRIC CONSTRUCTIONS

1. To Draw Parallel Lines.

a. *With the T-square and triangle.* If vertical, horizontal, or at an angle of a drafting triangle, parallel lines may be drawn by measuring the distance between the lines with a scale or stepping that distance off with a divider and drawing the lines with a T-square and triangle.

b. *With two 30-60 triangles.* **(Figure 1–27a)**

1) Form a rectangle by placing the hypotenuse of the two triangles against each other. Place one edge of the rectangle on the existing line.

2) Slide the second triangle up or down the hypotenuse of the first triangle until the opposite edge of the rectangle comes to the location desired for the parallel line. Draw the new line against the edge of the guide.

c. *With a compass.* **(Figure 1–27b)**

1) Set the radius of the compass at the desired distance to the new line (R).

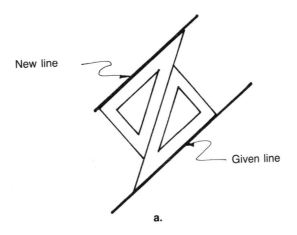

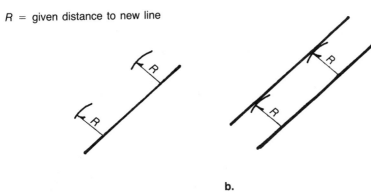

a.   **FIGURE 1–27**

R = given distance to new line

b.

2) Place the pin of the compass on the existing line at a random location and draw an arc. Repeat at a second random location.
3) Using a straightedge aligned at the apex of each arc, draw the new line.

2. To Draw Perpendiculars.

a. *With the T-square and triangle.* Align the base of a 30-60 triangle with the base line. The vertical leg of the triangle should be placed at the location desired for the perpendicular. Draw the perpendicular guided by the triangle. If the perpendicular is a true vertical the T-square may be used as the baseline.

b. *With a compass.* **(Figure 1–28)**
   1) Label the point at which the perpendicular is to be constructed as A. Use A as a centering point. Draw an arc of any convenient radius (R-1) across the baseline on both sides of A. Label these arcs B and C.

R1 = any convenient radius
R2 = any convenient radius greater than R1

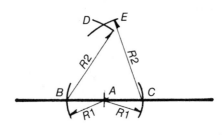

FIGURE 1–28

a.

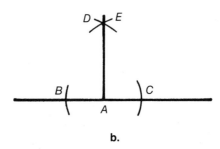

b.

2) Adjust the compass to R-2, which is any convenient radius greater than R-1. Place the pin of the compass on the intersection of arc B and the baseline, and draw a new arc D above the baseline. Repeat this procedure on arc C to form arc E.

3) Draw a line from A through the intersection of arcs D and E.

3. To Bisect (Divide in Half) a Line.

a. *With a triangle.* **(Figure 1–29a and b)**

1) Draw a 30°, 45°, or 60° diagonal from one end of the line to be divided toward the center of the line. Repeat at the opposite end of the line, using the same angle and baseline.

2) The point at which the diagonals cross is the center of the baseline. Using a T-square and triangle, drop a vertical to the baseline.

b. *With a compass.* **(Figure 1–29c and d)**

1) Adjust the compass to a radius greater than one-half the length of the line.

2) Place the compass at the end of the line, and draw an arc across the line. Repeat at the opposite end of the line.

3) Connect the intersection of the two arcs.

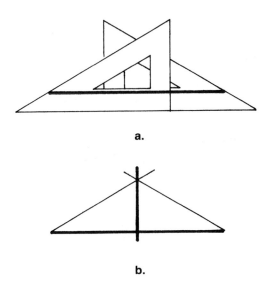

a.

b.

FIGURE 1–29

R = Radius greater than one-half the length of the line.

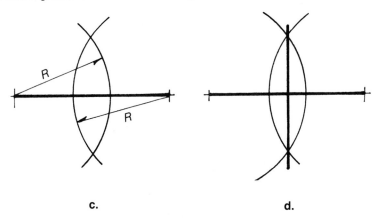

c.   **d.**

4. To Divide a Line into Equal Parts—Method 1. (Figure 1–30)

a. Given line AB, draw line AC at any convenient angle.

b. Beginning at point A, divide the new line into as many equal parts as desired, using any convenient division (such as one inch). This may be accomplished by measuring the divisions with a scale or by stepping the line off into equal parts with a divider.

c. With a straightedge, connect the open end (B) of line AB with the last division of the new line (D).

d. Attach each additional division of AC to line AB by drawing lines parallel to BD.

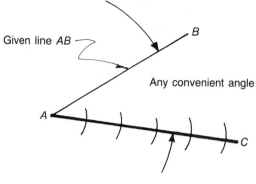

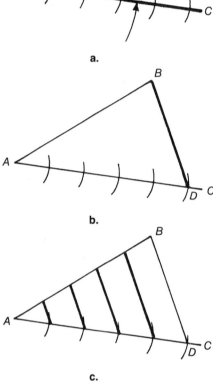

FIGURE 1–30

5. **To Divide a Line into Equal Parts—Method 2. (Figure 1–31)**
   a. Given line AB, using a T-square and triangle draw a vertical (BC) at one end of the given line.
   b. Using any convenient scale, place the zero mark of the scale at point A. Adjust the opposite end of the scale up or down until the desired number of divisions falls precisely on the vertical line. Mark each increment of the scale.
   c. Using a T-square and triangle, draw a vertical line from each increment mark to the given line.

Given line *AB*

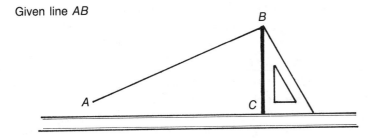

a.

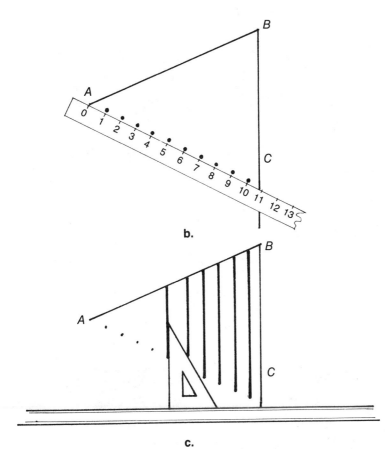

b.

FIGURE 1–31

c.

6. **To Find the Center of Most Polygons with an Even Number of Sides. (Figure 1–32a, b, and c)**
   Connect the corners of the form with diagonal lines. The intersection of the diagonals will be the center of the form.

7. **To Find the Center of a Polygon with an Odd Number of Sides. (Figure 1–32d and e)**
   a. Find the center of each side of the polygon by bisecting each side with a compass (number 4, above) or by measuring.
   b. Draw a line from each corner of the form to the centerline of each opposite side. The intersection of the lines identifies the center of the form. Usually no more than three diagonals are necessary to find the center of a form.

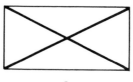

a.

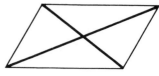

b.

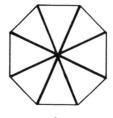

c.

FIGURE 1–32

d.

e.

8. **To Transfer an Angle. (Figure 1–33)**
   a. Given angle ABC and line A′B′, place the compass point on A and strike an arc at any convenient radius. Label the intersections of the angle and the arc D and E.
   b. Strike an arc with this same radius on line A′B′.
   c. On the given angle, place the compass at D. Adjust the compass so the radius is equal to the distance to point E.
   d. Locate the compass at D′ on the new angle and draw the arc to establish point E′ on the new construction.
   e. On the new construction, draw a line from A′ through E′ to create the new angle.

f. Should it be necessary to locate the baseline of the new angle, its position may be found in relationship to a horizontal or vertical line drawn with a T-square or triangle. Steps 8a through e should then be performed to determine the position of the new baseline in relation to the horizontal or the vertical.

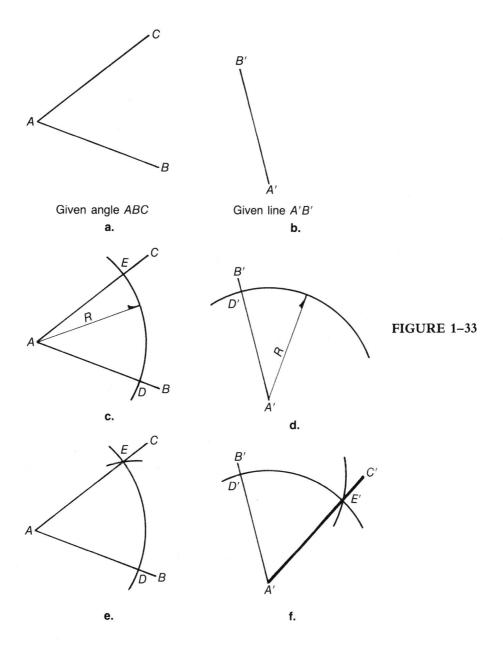

Given angle *ABC*
a.

Given line *A'B'*
b.

c.

d.

FIGURE 1–33

e.

f.

9. To Bisect an Angle. (Figure 1–34)

a. Given angle ABC, locate a compass at A and strike an arc at any convenient radius. Label the intersections of the arc and the legs of the angle D and E.

b. Adjust the compass to any convenient radius greater than one-half the distance between D and E.

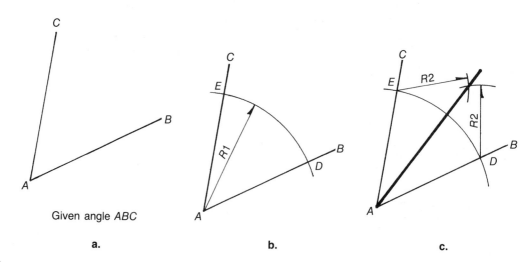

R1 = any convenient radius
R2 = any radius greater than one-half the distance between D and E

Given angle *ABC*

a.

b.

c.

FIGURE 1–34

    c. Locate the compass on point D and strike an arc. Repeat on point E.

    d. Join the intersection of the two final arcs with point A.

10. To Draw a Polygon to a Given Dimension Using a Protractor. (Figure 1–35)

    a. Draw a circle equal in diameter to the distance between opposite corners of the polygon. Mark the vertical and horizontal centerlines of the circle.

    b. Determine the number of sides the polygon is to have. Divide that number into 360°. The result of this equation will be the number of degrees between each side of the polygon.

    c. Align the protractor on the centerlines of the circle by placing 0° on the horizontal axis and 90° on the vertical axis. Measure the degrees necessary to the first side of the polygon and mark this point. Draw a line from the center of the circle to the perimeter of the circle through this new mark.

    d. With a compass or dividers adjusted to the distance between the horizontal centerline and the new line, step off the necessary number of spacings around the circle.

    e. Connect the points around the perimeter of the circle.

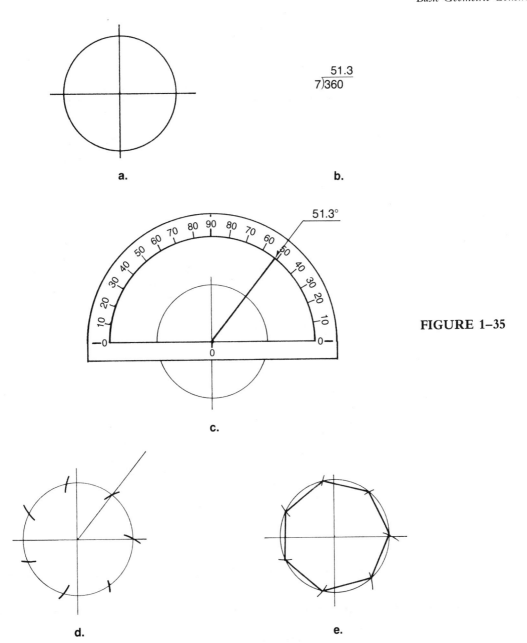

FIGURE 1–35

11. To Draw a Hexagon When the Distance between the Corners Is Known. (Figure 1–36a)

a. Draw a circle equal in diameter to the distance between the opposite corners of the hexagon. Draw the vertical centerline of the circle.

b. Maintaining the same radius that was used to draw the circle, place the point of the compass at the intersection of the centerline and the perimeter of the circle. Draw an arc. Repeat on the opposite side of the circle.

c. Connect the points on the perimeter of the circle.

FIGURE 1–36

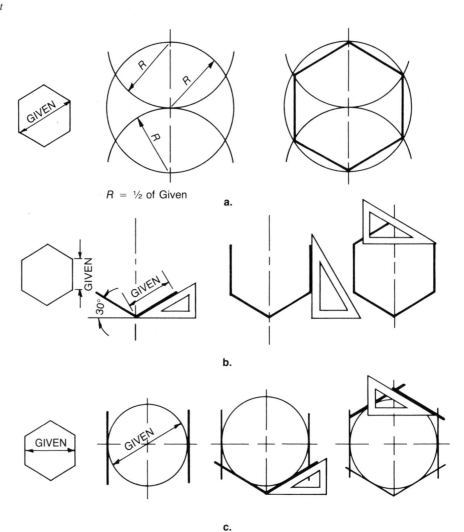

R = ½ of Given

a.

b.

c.

12. **To Draw a Hexagon When the Length of Each Side Is Known. (Figure 1–36b)**
   a. Draw the vertical centerline of the hexagon.
   b. Using a 30° triangle, draw a line the correct length to the right and left of the vertical centerline.
   c. Attach a vertical of the proper length to each 30° diagonal.
   d. Using proper-length lines, connect the end of each vertical with a 30° line to the top of the centerline.

13. **To Draw a Hexagon When the Distance between Parallel Sides Is Known. (Figure 1–36c)**
   a. Draw a circle equal in diameter to the distance between the parallel sides. Draw the horizontal and vertical centerline of the circle to extend beyond the circle.
   b. Draw a vertical line outside the circle and tangent to it at the horizontal centerline.
   c. Draw 30° lines to the right and left of the vertical centerline outside the circle and tangent to it at the center of each line. The new angled lines should cross the two verticals.
   d. Repeat at the top of the form.

14. **To Draw an Octagon When the Distance between Parallel Sides Is Known. (Figure 1–37)**

   a. Draw a square equal to the distance between the parallel sides. Find the center of the square as directed in number 6, above.

   b. Set a compass at a radius equal to the distance from one corner to the center of the square.

   c. Draw an arc with this radius, using each corner of the square as a centering point.

   d. The point at which each end of each arc intersects the square is a corner of the octagon. Connect the points around the square.

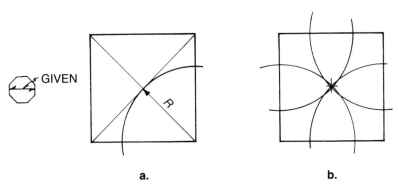

a.   **b.**

FIGURE 1–37

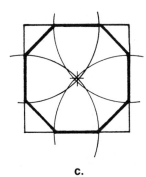

c.

15. **To Draw an Arc Tangent to the Lines of a Right Angle. (Figure 1–38)**

   a. Using the intersection of the two lines forming the angle as the centering point (A), draw an arc between the points where the lines of the angle will intersect the tangent arc. Label the points where the arc intersects the lines of the angle B and C.

   b. Using B and C as centering points and maintaining the initial radius on the compass, bisect the angle as directed in number 9, above. Label these arcs D and E.

   c. The intersection of D and E will be the center of the tangent arc. Maintaining the same radius, draw the tangent arc between B and C.

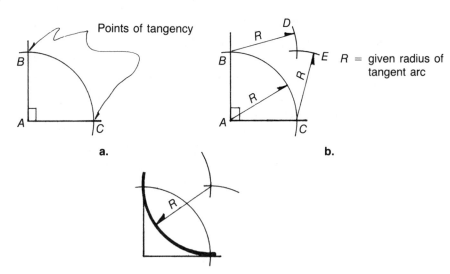

FIGURE 1–38

a.

b.   R = given radius of
     tangent arc

c.

16. **To Draw an Arc of a Given Radius Tangent to Two Lines at any Angle. (Figure 1–39)**
    a. Using one of the procedures described in number 1 above, draw a line parallel to each given line the same distance toward each other as the given radius.
    b. Using the intersection of the new lines as the centering point, draw the arc of the given radius between the original lines and tangent to them.

17. **To Draw a Circle with a Given Radius Tangent to a Line at a Given Point. (Figure 1–40)**
    a. Construct a perpendicular at the point of tangency (A).
    b. Set the compass to the given radius of the circle. Place the needle of the compass at A, and strike an arc on the perpendicular. Label the new arc B.
    c. Using the intersection of the perpendicular and arc B as the centering point, draw the circle.

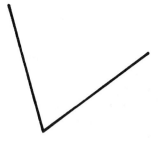

Given angle

a.

Given radius of tangent arc

b.

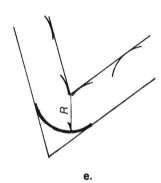

c.

d.

FIGURE 1–39

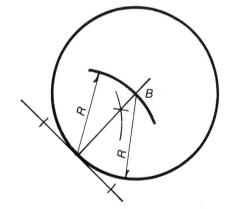

e.

R = given radius of tangent circle

a.

b.

FIGURE 1–40

37

18. Common Geometric Formulae. (Figure 1–41)

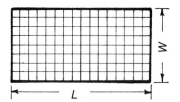

Area of a rectangle:
Length × width = area

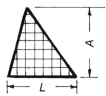

Area of a triangle:
Length of base × altitude = area

FIGURE 1–41
Geometric formulae to determine area, volume, and circumference of common forms.

Area of a circle:
πR^2 = area
π = 3.14
R = radius

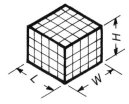

Volume of a cube:
Length × width × height = volume

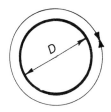

Circumference of a circle:
πD = circumference
π = 3.14
D = diameter

Exercises

Prepare the work area and the drafting equipment. Remember that the instruments should be located on the drawing-hand side of the board. Sharpen a 2H pencil. Do not point the lead over the drawing board, and be sure to wipe off the lead after sharpening. Tape a sheet of vellum onto the drawing board.

1. Locate the T-square one inch below the top edge of the paper. Holding the pencil properly and guiding it against the top edge of the T-square, draw five lines all the way across the paper. Remember to twirl the pencil and to maintain the proper orientation of the pencil to the guide and the paper. Inspect each line. It should be consistently dark, wide, and straight.

2. Using a drafting eraser, remove a portion of each line and dust the sheet. A properly drawn line should be dark enough to see easily but should not dent the paper. If the paper has been dented, a ghost of the line will appear under the erasure.

3. Place a 30-60 triangle on the top edge of the T-square so that the narrowest angle is toward the top and the shortest side is resting against the blade of the T-square. The body of the triangle should be under your drawing hand. Draw three vertical lines then three diagonal lines at 60° to the left. Now reverse the triangle and draw three 60° lines to the right. Rotate the triangle and draw three 30° lines to the left. Inspect the lines for legibility and consistency. Erase a portion of each line to see if the paper has been dented.

4. Replace the 30-60 triangle with the 45 triangle. Draw three vertical lines and three 45° lines to both the right and left. Inspect these lines.

5. Using the T-square, 45, and 30-60 triangles reproduce the design in Figure 1–42 as follows:
  a. Draw a rectangle 3″ × 5″.
  b. Locate and draw the horizontal and vertical centerlines.
  c. Using the three guides, draw each line within the pattern. Each diagonal line may be obtained with one or both triangles.

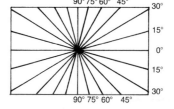

FIGURE 1–42

6. Mark a center point with a small +. With your compass draw a circle with a 1½″ *radius*. Using the same centering point, draw a second circle with a 1½″ *diameter* inside the first circle. Inspect the lines. They should be of consistent darkness and width. The center hole should be only a small pin prick.

7. Reproduce Figure 1–43.
  a. Mark a center point with a small +.
  b. Place the T-square across the circle at the + and draw a horizontal line across the circle. Place the T-square below the circle, with the 30-60 triangle resting on its top edge. Draw a vertical through the + across the circle.
  c. Place the pin point of the compass on each intersection of the vertical and horizontal lines and draw four more circles.

8. Reproduce Figure 1–44.
  a. Mark the center point with a + and draw a circle with a 1½″ radius.
  b. Draw the horizontal and vertical centerlines of the circle as described in Exercise 7b.
  c. Add two 45° diagonals crossing the center + of the circle.

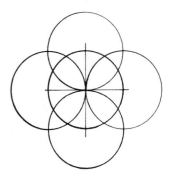

FIGURE 1–43

FIGURE 1–44

d. Place the pin point of the compass at the intersection of the horizontal centerline and the outer edge of the circle. Adjust the compass so that the lead touches the intersection of the vertical centerline and the circle. Draw an arc from one side of the circle to the other. Without adjusting the compass, repeat this arc at each end of each straight line.

9. Using each of the ten scales on a triangular architect's scale, measure and draw each of the following:

    a. On each scale, a line 3'-0" long.

    b. On each scale, a rectangle 6" wide and 2'-6" long.

    c. On each scale smaller than ½, draw a rectangle 5'-2" wide and 24'-8" long.

    d. On each scale larger than ½, draw a 30-60-90 triangle with a base measuring 3'-9½" long. The 30° angle should be at the top.

10. Turn to the section entitled "Geometric Constructions." Following the stated procedures, draw each one of the constructions.

CHAPTER 2

Mechanical Drawing Conventions

INTRODUCTION

Designer's elevations, plans, and working drawings are the primary means of graphic communication between the planners of a production and the artisans who create the setting. Each of these drawings communicates specific information about the layout, construction, and finishing details of the production. While an architectural style of drawing is used for television and film, the system of symbols and lines and the style of presentation used for drawings of settings in the theatre have evolved from architectural graphics. The differences between drawings for the theatre and drawing for television or film are primarily differences of content rather than distinctive uses of line, symbols, or scale. The characteristics that define good architectural drafting—clarity, consistency, accuracy—also define good mechanical drawing for the performing arts. Although both architecture and the performing arts employ a similar graphic vocabulary—including the types of views, the language of lines, and the general drawing layout—there are some differences in the types of scale, lines, and symbols that are specifically found in the theatre.

THE LANGUAGE OF LINES

The primary element of drafting is the language of lines; this is the drafter's alphabet. A variety of styles of line are used to distinguish particular information on drawings. This convention is especially necessary when the drawings are to be duplicated as monochromatic prints. Lines may be thick, thin, straight, curved, solid, or dashed in various patterns. Each type of line has a specific meaning which, once understood, simplifies communication. No matter what their form, all lines must be equally black. However, differences in the relative width of a line, called **lineweight,** have specific meanings. Two lineweights are used: thick or heavyweight lines for the most important information on a drawing and thin, lightweight lines for information that is present to clarify the content of the drawing. The types of line used for theatre drafting are shown in Figure 2–1. As indicated by its name, each type of line fulfills a specific function.

The dimensions identified in the descriptions below refer to the usual size of lines and spaces for drawings in a scale of $\frac{1}{2}'' = 1'-0''$. An increase or decrease in scale may require a proportional increase or decrease in the actual length of dashes and spaces; however, the proportional relationships must be maintained.

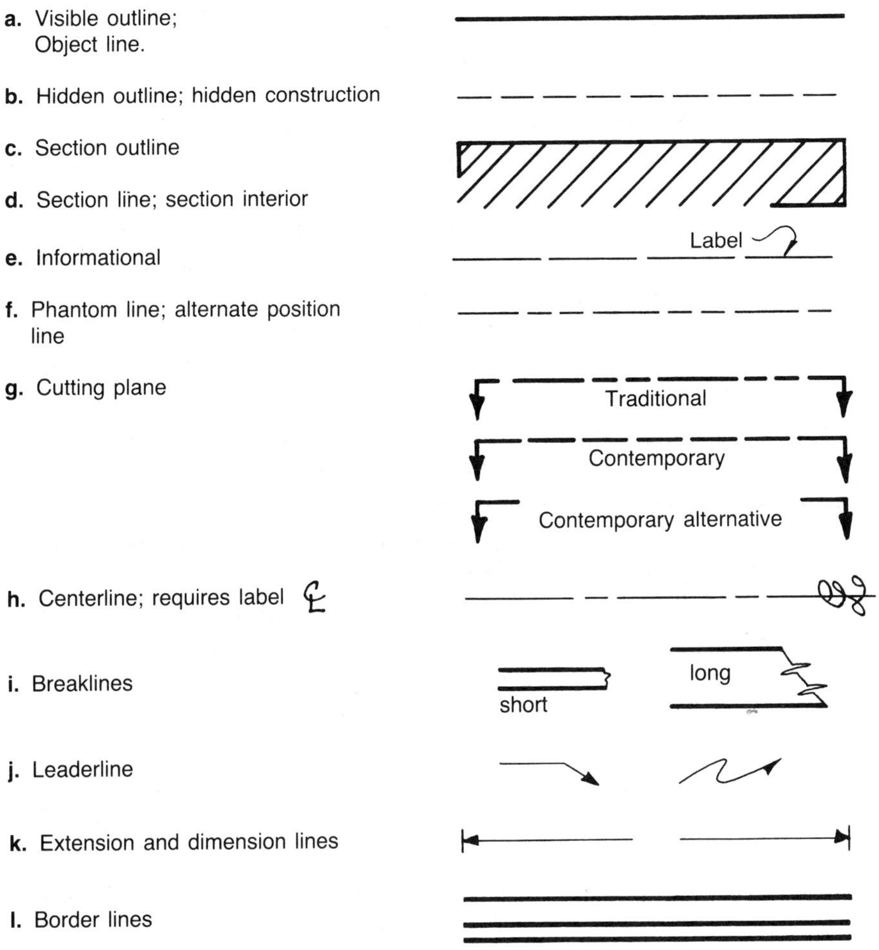

a. Visible outline;
Object line.

b. Hidden outline; hidden construction

c. Section outline

d. Section line; section interior

Label

e. Informational

f. Phantom line; alternate position line

g. Cutting plane

Traditional

Contemporary

Contemporary alternative

h. Centerline; requires label ℄

i. Breaklines

long

short

j. Leaderline

k. Extension and dimension lines

l. Border lines

FIGURE 2–1

Standard use of lines for theatre drafting. (From "Graphic Standards Board Recommendations for Standard Graphic Language in Scenic Design and Technical Production," reprinted by permission of the United States Institute for Theatre Technology Graphic Standards Board, Education Commission, and Board of Directors.)

1. **Visible Outline or Object Line.**

   A thick, solid line that is drafted to the precise shape of an object, showing all edges and planes visible in the view drawn.

2. **Hidden Outline or Hidden Construction.**

   A thick, dashed line, with each dash ¼″ long and separated by ⅛″ spaces. This line is drawn to the precise shape of an edge or plane that is not visible in the view from which the drawing is made, but whose presence is important to understand the drawing. A typical application of this line would be to show the structure of a platform frame that was hidden underneath its top.

3. **Section Outline.**

   A thin, solid line outlining the actual shape of a surface that has been cut through to expose the interior structure.

4. **Section Line or Section Interior.**

   A series of thin, solid lines drawn between section outlines at an angle less than 90° to the edge of the paper. These lines indicate the presence of mass that has been cut through in the sectional view. A variety of angles and patterns may be used to distinguish different materials shown in the view.

5. **Informational Lines.**

   A thin line composed of long dashes separated by short

spaces; the usual rhythm of this line is ½″ line, ⅛″ space. This line has a variety of applications, each requiring a label.

a. *Plaster line.* Drawn at the upstage side of the proscenium from the stage right to the stage left edge of the opening. The line is labeled "Plaster Line."

b. *Set line.* Drawn at the extreme downstage edge of a proscenium setting or at the perimeter of a thrust, arena, or nontraditional set to indicate the edge of the acting area. The line is labeled "Set Line."

c. *Curtain line.* Drawn at the upstage edge of the plane on which the act curtain travels or falls. The line is labeled "Curtain Line."

d. *Ceiling line.* Drawn at the perimeter of the ceiling over a set. The line is labeled "Ceiling" or "Ceiling Line."

6. **Phantom Line or Alternate Position Line.**

A thin, dashed line composed of a long dash and two short dashes; the usual rhythm of this line is 1″ line, ⅛″ space, ¼″ line, ⅛″ space, ¼″ line, ⅛″ space. This line is used to show that an object or elements of an object repeat between two points, but the repeating portions are not drawn; for instance, the spindels in a railing. The line may also be used to indicate that an object will move or will be used in more than one position. The primary position of the object is drawn as a visible outline, and the alternate position of the object is drawn as a phantom line. The phantom line may also be used as a secondary centerline; for instance, to locate a transverse axis for use as a centerline on an arena stage.

7. **Cutting Plane.**

A thick line that may be drawn in one of three styles. The traditional cutting-plane line is composed of a long dash and two short dashes separated by shorter spaces. The usual rhythm for this line is ½″ line, ⅛″ space, ¼″ line, ⅛″ space, ¼″ line, ⅛″ space. The line terminates with a 90° angle and solid arrowhead. The arrowhead is three times as long as its width. The arrow points toward the portion shown in the sectional view. The name of the section (for instance, A-A) is placed at the point of the arrowheads, with the letter oriented toward the bottom of the page. An alternative to this style of line uses thick dashes of equal length; the line terminates as described above. A third style of cutting-plane line uses only a pair of thick 90° angles, arrowheads, and labels placed at either end of the cutting plane with no connecting lines between the arrowheads. This approach identifies the cutting plane without interrupting the content of the drawing. There are some limitations to the use of this style of line, especially for showing off-set sections.

8. **Centerline.**

A thin line composed of a long and short dash separated by shorter spaces. The usual rhythm for this line is 1″ line, ⅛″ space, ¼″ line, ⅛″ space. The line is labeled ℒ or ℄ near its lowest end on the page. The centerline is used to indicate the primary center of an object or a space.

9. **Breaklines.**

   A thin, serpentine line that indicates a portion of an object is removed from the drawing. Note the difference between long and short breaklines.

10. **Leaderline.**

   A thin, serpentine or angled line terminating in a half-arrowhead or a dot. The half-arrowhead is six times as long as its width. This line leads the eye of the reader from printed information located outside the drawing to the object or location described. The arrowhead or dot is placed at the object or space described—not at the note. A half-arrowhead is normally used; however, a dot is occasionally used to refer to an entire surface. Drafting for television and film requires the use of only straight leaderlines.

11. **Extension and Dimension Lines.**

   These thin, solid, straight lines are used in combination to identify the size of an object or space.

   a. *Extension lines* are drawn perpendicular to the point or plane at which a measurement is taken. The line never touches the surface measured; $\frac{1}{16}''$ clearance is maintained between the line and the point it identifies. Each extension line is of sufficient length to extend at least $\frac{1}{8}''$ beyond the dimension lines it encloses.

   b. *Dimension lines* are drawn parallel to the surface they measure. They terminate in a whole arrowhead at the extension lines or the surface from which a measurement is taken. The arrowhead is drawn three times as long as its width. Dimensions are placed in a break near the center of the line.

   c. *Dimension lines used in television and film drafting* are solid, unbroken lines that terminate in an arrowhead, a dot, or a diagonal slash. Dimensions are placed above the line in horizontal planes and outside the line in vertical planes.

12. **Border Lines.**

   A thick, solid line or a pair of thick, solid lines spaced $\frac{1}{8}''$ apart and located $\frac{1}{2}''$ in from the edge of the paper. These lines enclose all the information on the drawing with a squared frame.

LETTERING

The majority of information communicated on a drawing is pictorial; however, it is necessary to include dimensions, notations, and titles in written form. This information is lettered on a drawing in a clear and uniform style. The quality of lettering on a drawing affects its overall appearance and frequently affects the quality of work produced from the drawing in the shop.

The standard lettering style for most drafting is upper-case **single-stroke Gothic.** These letters are all capitals. Every element of every letter is drawn with consistent line widths. The letters are formed without embellishments of any kind. There are two acceptable styles of single-stroke Gothic: **vertical** (Figure 2–2a), with every vertical stroke of the letters perpendicular to the bottom of the drawing, and **slant** (Figure 2–2b), which places the vertical strokes of the letters at an angle of 68° to the bottom of the drawing.

a.

b.

FIGURE 2–2

a) Single-stroke vertical gothic alphabet, b) Single-stroke slant gothic alphabet.

Guidelines are necessary to attain attractive, readable lettering. These are very lightweight lines placed at the top, bottom, and horizontal center of each line of lettering. Guidelines are usually drawn with a 4H lead, visible to the drafter while lettering but otherwise barely apparent when the drawing is complete. Lettering aids are available to assist with the placement of guidelines. Among the most popular aids are the Braddock-Rowe lettering triangle and the Ames lettering guide, both designed for use in conjunction with a T-square to locate three to five guidelines for most lettering heights.

Purpose determines the vertical size of letters. Most lettering on a drawing, including notes and dimensions, is ⅛" high; titles are ³⁄₁₆" high, and large-scale titles may be lettered as tall as ¼". Special applications make the use of taller letters occasionally necessary; however, larger letters are more difficult to form neatly.

The space between the lines of lettering is related to the height of the letters. In general, at least one-half the height of the letters should be left between lines of lettering. This requires that a space of at least ¹⁄₁₆" exist between lines of ⅛"-high letters, ³⁄₃₂" between lines of ³⁄₁₆" lettering, and ⅛" between lines of ¼" letters. Horizontal spacing of letters is a visual rather than a mechanical task. Although the majority of letters and numerals in the single-stroke Gothic alphabet are similar in width, a few letters are exceptionally wide (M and W, for instance) and others are exceptionally narrow (I, for instance), or appear to be narrower because of an open side (F and J). Adjustment must be made in the horizontal spacing of letters to accommodate these actual and perceived differences (Figure 2–3). The spaces between words are relative to the size of the lettering also. Normally, the width of one average-size letter is left between words. The space is doubled between sentences on the same line.

FIGURE 2–3
Horizontal spacing of letters is a visual rather than a mechanical task. a) Visual spacing, b) The space between letters is equal, c) The space allowed for each letter is equal.

A soft lead (H or HB) sharpened to a slightly rounded conical point eases the lettering task. It is important to sharpen the lead often and continually rotate the pencil between strokes to achieve even wear on the lead and prevent the point from flattening. Every stroke of every letter should be drawn with equal pressure to achieve lines of equal width and blackness.

Large-scale freehand lettering can be a difficult task. A few aids exist to help the drafter. Lettering templates allow the formation of consistently shaped attractive letters, although these are generally designed for use with inking tools and are not especially convenient for lettering with a pencil. Freehand and template lettering may be replaced with dry-transfer letters, which are especially useful for very large-scale letters. **Dry-transfer letters** are available in a variety of styles and sizes. The drafter simply locates the selected letter over the drawing and rubs the plastic medium to transfer the letter to the vellum. Alignment and spacing of the letters are still the responsibility of the drafter. Template lettering and dry-transfer letters should be reserved for special applications.

GENERAL SYMBOLS

In addition to a systematic use of lines and lettering, standard drafting symbols exist for information that is frequently repeated on drawings. Although they are available, these symbols are not requisite. They are presented in Figure 2–4 as a convenient shorthand.

Location from which a sightline is determined.

North. Used on plans where a directional orientation is necessary, such as the plan of an arena stage.

N B   *Note bene*, or note well. An abbreviation for the word "note" used to attract the reader's attention to important information lettered on the drawing.

O.C.   On center. Used in dimensioning to indicate repeated spacings or dimensions from the center of one object to the center of another when a dimension is consistently repeated.

R&R   Reverse and repeat. The symbol indicates that only one-half of a view is drawn and that the opposite half is a mirror image of the portion shown.

X   Open. A lightweight freehand X, meaning that the portion outlined and containing the X is cut away.

FIGURE 2–4

General architectural drafting symbols.

SCALE

It is both impractical and impossible to make meaningful life-size drawings of scenery or props. To enable the viewer to comprehend a setting or scenic unit in its entirety, it is usually necessary to draw a miniaturized view. When all the life-sized dimensions of a form are reduced in proportion to each other and a fixed unit of measurement is used as the basis of the proportional reduction, the drawing has been done to scale. It is possible to draw an object in enlarged scale by proportionately increasing each dimension or in reduced scale by proportionately decreasing dimensions. The scales usually used in theatre drafting are charted below. The first dimension identifies the proportional reduction of the second dimension; thus, in the first entry ⅛″ on the drawing represents one foot of the actual object or space.

Scale	Use
⅛″ = 1′-0″	Designer's thumbnail sketches and preliminary plans. Plans for extremely large settings.
¼″ = 1′-0″	Some design drawings, renderings, design elevations, plans, and lighting plots for large sets or large theatres. Plans and elevations for film.
½″ = 1′-0″	Most plans, design drawings, elevations, and working drawings for scenery and props.
¾″ = 1′-0″	Detail construction drawings for film.
1″ = 1′-0″	Detail construction drawings and painter's elevations.
1½″ and 3″ = 1′-0″	Construction and design details.

½″ = 1″	Construction and design details of miniature parts.
Full scale	Construction and design details as necessary.
No scale	Frequently used for sketches not drawn to scale but dimensioned to indicate the sizes desired.

Enlarging scales, such as 1″ = ¼″, may be used by costume and properties designers to explain the construction of jewelry or trim pieces.

A single scale is normally used for an entire page of drawing. However, it is not uncommon to add detailed views in an enlarged scale. When this is done, the detail drawing must be clearly distinguished from the other views which are drawn in the predominant scale. The enlarged scale must be identified with the label "Scale: x = y′-z″" located near the lower-right corner of the detail view.

DIMENSIONING

In addition to knowing the placement, shape, and materials of construction, the drafter must also know the dimensions of each element composing a unit. Dimensions complete the information on the drawing and compensate for any minor drafting errors or distortion that may occur when the drawing is printed.

Dimensions are placed on a drawing by using extension and dimension lines so that both the object being measured and the dimensions are clear and easy to read. Extension lines are used to identify the points at which measurements are taken; dimension lines indicate the length and direction of measurements. Normally all dimensions are placed outside of a unit; however, for clarity, it is sometimes necessary to locate a dimension within the drawing.

Few rules for dimensioning are absolute. Although the rules below usually apply, the drafter must choose to adhere or not adhere to them judiciously.

1. Dimensions are located on a drawing to be read from the bottom or right edge of the paper only (Figure 2–5a, b, c, d).
2. Dimensions are lettered with ⅛″-tall numerals in a break near the center of the dimension line.
3. Dimensions less than one foot are given only in inches: ½″, 6″, 9¼″.
4. Dimensions of one foot or greater are always given in both feet and inches, separated by a dash. The inch dimension is given even when it is zero: 1′-9″, 9′-3″, 42′-6¼″.
5. In contrast to rule 4, platforms, stair-tread heights, and the height of any walking surface are dimensioned in inches only, even when the dimension is one foot or greater. The dimension

FIGURE 2–5

Dimensioning. Dimensions are placed near the center of the dimension line. a–d) Dimensions are read from the bottom or from the right edge of the drawing. e–j) When less space than needed is available for a dimension, dimenson lines can be placed outside of extension lines, or dimensions can be placed outside of extension lines with a leader line running to the area between the extension lines.

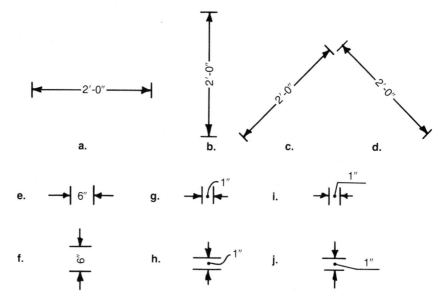

of walking surfaces is placed in a circle near the center of the walking surface.

6. Dimension lines with complete arrowheads must always be present. When possible, the dimension lines should be placed between extension lines. When the area measured is too small to allow placement of both dimension lines and the dimension between the extension lines, shorter dimension lines are placed outside the extension lines with their arrowheads pointing toward the area measured. Only the dimension is placed between the extension lines (Figure 2–5e and f).

7. Dimensions requiring more space than is available between extension lines are located near the area measured. A leaderline is drawn from the dimension to the area between the extension lines. An arrowhead or dot terminates the leaderline. All these dimensions are oriented to be read from the bottom of the page (Figure 2–5g, h, i, j).

8. Extension lines may cross each other and may cross object lines, although the practice should be minimized whenever possible.

9. Dimension lines should cross no other line unless absolutely necessary.

10. The first row of dimensions adjacent to a form should be placed at least ¼″ from the surface; successive rows of dimensions should be spaced at least ¼″ apart.

11. Angles may be dimensioned in degrees, using extension and dimension lines to identify the angle (Figure 2–6a), or they may be dimensioned by locating the ends (coordinates) of sloping planes (Figure 2–6b). The latter method is preferred for working drawings. The methods of dimensioning should not be mixed on a drawing.

12. The dimension of a hole is given as a diameter (Figure 2–

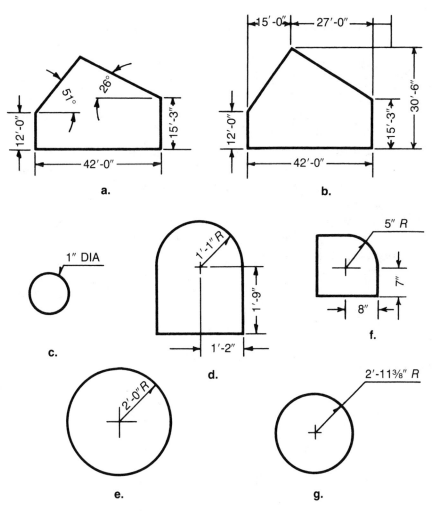

FIGURE 2–6
Angles can be measured. a) In degrees from a vertical or horizontal axis, or b) By locating the coordinate positions of corners. c) The size of a hole is given as a diameter on a leader line pointing to the perimeter of the hole. d–g) A circle or arc is dimensioned as a radius. The location of the center of the circle must be identified by a + and dimensions given to locate that point.

6c). The information is placed on a leaderline directed to the perimeter of the hole. The dimension is labeled "DIA."

13. The dimension of a circle or arc is given as a radius on an extension line from the center of the arc (indicated by a lightweight +) to the perimeter of the circle or arc (Figure 2–6d and e). The radius is identified by the letter "R" following the dimension. When there is too little space to allow placement of the radius dimension within the drawing of an arc or circle, the dimension is placed outside the arc on a leaderline extending to the center of the arc (Figure 2–6f and g). The position of the center of the arc must be identified by a +, and dimensions must be given to locate that point.

14. Dimensions should be repeated on a drawing only when necessary for clarity or when the first notation is greatly separated from a later reference.

The choice of placement and the quantity of dimensions on a drawing should be based on clarity of communication. The guiding principle must always be: *what does the craftsperson who will use the drawing need to know?* Three styles for placing dimensions are in common use: baseline dimensions, continuous-line dimensions, and parallel dimensions.

51

1. **Baseline dimensions** are the most meaningful to the shop carpenter. In this style, all measurements are made from a baseline such as the floor or an edge of the object, or from a reference line, such as the centerline of the object or space. This style of dimensioning requires the most space around the drawing, but it provides the most meaningful information for construction (Figure 2–7a).

2. **Continuous-line dimensions** are convenient for layouts where spacing between parts is important; for example, the placement of rails on a flat. The continuous-line dimensions are usually accompanied by a dimension indicating the overall length of a side (Figure 2–7b). The dimensions may be placed in a continuous line or off-set for reading clarity.

3. **Parallel dimensions** are least often used for scenic construction. They provide overall dimensions from a centerline or point and indicate spacing (Figure 2–7c). Either baseline or continuous-line dimensions will usually provide more valuable information to the craftsperson.

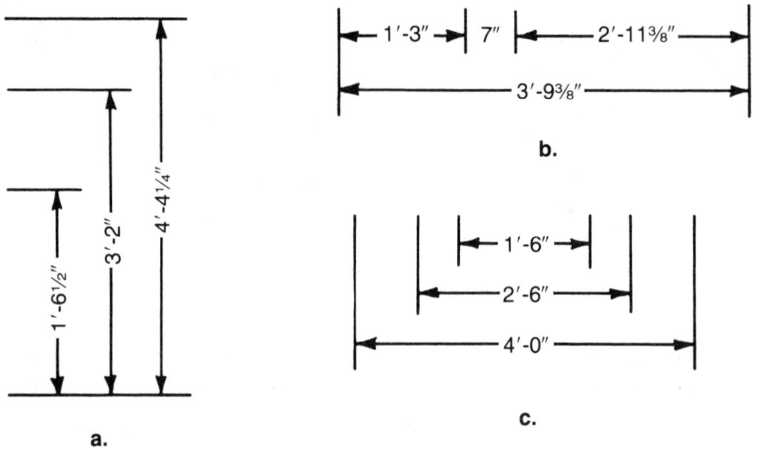

FIGURE 2–7

Styles of dimensions. a) Baseline dimensions, b) Continuous dimensions, c) Parallel dimensions.

TITLE BLOCKS AND TITLE STRIPS

A drawing is complete only when all the reference and explanatory information necessary to interpret it is present. Such data might include one or several views of the object, dimensions, notes, and specifications regarding the materials and methods of construction. Titles and general reference information must be present to identify the drawing. This information is placed in a title block or title strip. A **title block** is located in the lower right-hand corner of the drawing, near the border but not touching it. The title block is outlined with a borderline and is designed in a pattern similar to Figure 2–8a. **Title strips** are located along and adjacent to the bottom borderline in a pattern similar to Figure 2–8b. The same information is contained in either style of title:

Title of the drawing
Title of the production, act, scene—as appropriate
Name of the producing organization or theatre

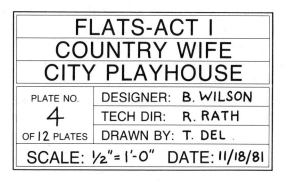

a.

b.

FIGURE 2–8
Titling drawings. a) Title block, b) Title strip.

Drawing or sheet number
Name of the designer
Name of the drafter
Predominant scale of the drawing
Date of the drawing

Other information may be included in the title block or strip if applicable: name of the director, name of the technical director, name of the lighting designer, space for approvals, space for revision dates, space for a union stamp. The designation "Plate x of y plates" may be used instead of simply "sheet number."

Work begins on a drawing by determining the quanity of information to be included, the appropriate scale for the drawing, and the placement of all the information on the page. In general, each drawing should fulfill a single purpose such as the plan of a setting or the construction of a unit or similar types of units. It is usual for a drawing to include multiple views of an object or of several units of a setting; for example, working drawings for all the flats or platforms used in a single setting or for an entire show. All of this information must be clearly labeled.

Each page of drawings must be not only clear and accurate but also attractive. It must be possible to discern information easily, and movement from view to view must be clear and orderly. Sufficient "white space" free of drawings, notes, and dimensions must be left on each sheet to allow information to be read clearly. Each view of an object or space must be clearly labeled. The label is visually centered beneath the view. Any general information which refers to that specific view is located in proximity to the label. Finally, the overall drawing must be visually balanced, with consideration for all the information associated with the drawing, including dimensions, notes, titles, title block or strip, and the presence of borderlines surrounding the page (Figure 2–9).

FIGURE 2–9
Plate layout. 1) Drafting view(s), 2) Title of view(s), 3) Title block or strip, 4) Borderline, 5) Notes.

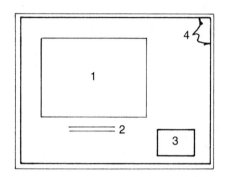 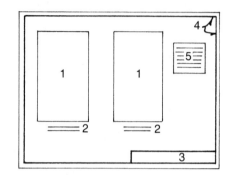

Accuracy, clarity, and consistency are the guiding principles of effective drawing. The primary goal of production drawings is effective communication. The drafter must not only be skillful at the drawing task but also have a solid understanding of construction practices. The artisans who build the scenery and properties, directors, choreographers, and other designers who use the drawings must be able to interpret their contents. Communication can occur only when both the "writer" and the "reader" understand the language being used.

1. Using a 2H lead pencil for the thin lines and an H lead for the thicklines, reproduce all the sample lines shown in Figure 2–1.

2. Using an H pencil for both the thick and thin lines, reproduce all the sample lines shown in Figure 2–1.

3. Using a 4H lead, draw a rectangle measuring 9″ wide and 4½″ high. Divide the form into six equal rectangles, each measuring 3″ wide by 2¼″ high. Use a 2H lead for thin lines and an H lead for thick lines. Complete the drawing as follows:

   a. In the top-left rectangle, draw a series of thin horizontal lines spaced ⅛″ apart. Also draw a series of thin vertical lines spaced ⅛″ apart.

   b. In the top-center section, draw a series of thick horizontal lines spaced ³⁄₁₆″ apart. Draw a series of thick vertical lines spaced ³⁄₁₆″ apart.

   c. In the top-right rectangle, draw a series of thin diagonal lines at an angle of 30°. Draw a series of thick diagonal lines to cross the first series at an angle of 60°.

   d. In the bottom-left square, draw a series of horizontal lines, spaced ³⁄₁₆″ apart, composed of long, thin dashes. Each dash should measure approximately ½″ in length and the dashes should be spaced ³⁄₁₆″ apart. Draw a series of vertical lines, spaced ¼″ apart, composed of short, thin dashes. Each dash should measure ¼″ long and the dashes should be spaced ⅛″ apart.

   e. In the bottom-center section, draw a series of horizontal lines, spaced ¼″ apart, composed of short, thick dashes. Draw a series of vertical lines, spaced ¼″ apart, composed of long, thick dashes.

   f. In the bottom-right rectangle, draw a series of lines spaced ⅛″ apart on a 45° diagonal composed of thick, short dashes. On the opposite 45° diagonal, draw a series of lines, spaced ⅛″ apart, composed of long, thin dashes.

   g. Draw a double borderline around the 4½″ × 9″ rectangle and a thick borderline between each section of the rectangle.

4. Mark a centering point with a + for making a large circle. Set the radius of a 6″ or 8″ bow compass to 4″. Draw a thick circle. Reduce the radius ¼″ and draw a thin circle on the same center. Reduce the radius another ¼″ and draw a thick circle on the same center. Reducing the radius ¼″ at a time, continue to draw circles on the same center, alternating thick and thin lines between each circle. The smallest circle should have a ½″ diameter. Remember to keep the lead sharpened.

5. Repeat Exercise 4, using dashed lines rather than solid lines.

6. Refer to Figure 2–2. Letter the single-stroke Gothic vertical or slant alphabet and numerals with letters ⅛″ high, ³⁄₁₆″ high, and ¼″ high.

7. Establishing proper spacing as you work, letter your name, complete address, and phone number on separate lines underneath each other in each of the following heights: ⅛″, ³⁄₁₆″, ¼″, and ⅜″.

8. Letter the following sentence with letters ⅛″ high, using each of the following leads: 2H, H, and HB. COSTUME DESIGN, SCENE DESIGN, AND STAGECRAFT USE GRAPHIC TECHNIQUES THAT ARE IN-HERENT TO THE PERFORMING ARTS.

9. Using your choice of leads and working on a clean sheet of paper, reproduce Figure 2–10 as a complete and properly laid-out plate. Include the drawing, dimensions, notes, titles, title block or strip, and border.

FIGURE 2–10

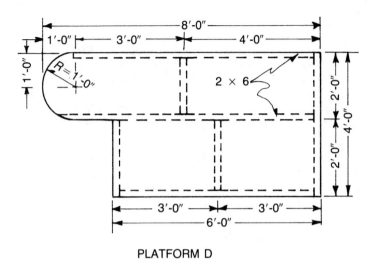

PLATFORM D

CHAPTER 3

Drafting Views

INTRODUCTION

Graphic communications among members of the production staff utilize standard drafting views applied to the specific needs of the performing arts. These drawings fall within four categories: ground plans that show the horizontal layout of objects comprising a space, orthographic projections that show each surface of an object individually for the purpose of construction or painting, pictorial drawings that show several planes of an object simultaneously, and sections that reveal the internal structure of objects. All these drawings serve a common purpose: to explain the materials and processes of construction which will result in the finished product desired.

GROUND PLANS

Ground plans (or floor plans; the terms are used interchangeably) are drawings that show the horizontal shape, position, size, and relationship of the objects comprising a setting. Whether they are developed as the initial step in the design process or evolve during that process, these drawings are used by all members of the production staff to determine such things as actor movement, lighting design, or the construction and handling of scenery. Ground plans are one of the primary sources of information for most additional construction drawings.

A **ground plan** is a view of the setting from above, with a portion of the top of the scenery removed to reveal the most characteristic view of the way the parts are arranged. The line that cuts across the set to reveal the plan is placed at an average height of four feet above the floor but may be staggered up or down in a pattern providing the greatest amount of information with the least number of hidden lines (Figure 3–1).

The resulting drawing shows the shape, size, and position of each element that comprises the setting. Because they are frequently repeated, some scenic elements such as doors and windows are represented in plans by symbols. The symbols are drawn true-to-size but do not

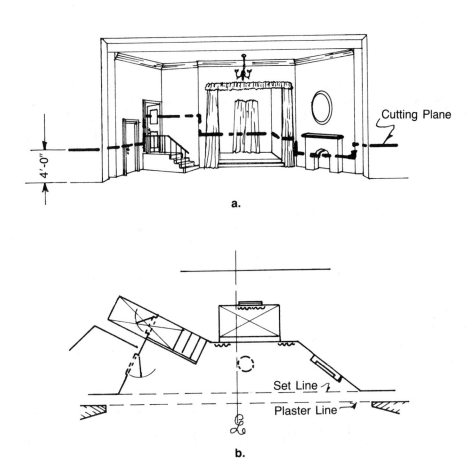

a.

b.

FIGURE 3–1

The ground plan is determined by a line that cuts across the set at an approximate height of 4'-0" but staggers up or down to reveal the most characteristic view of the setting from above. a) Shows the line cutting across this set to reveal the plan shown in b).

require labels, due to a common understanding of their meaning. The symbols used in ground plans for the theatre are shown in Figure 3–2. These symbols have been adopted in the United States by the professional organization of designers and technicians, the United States Institute for Theatre Technology (USITT). Any scenic unit or set dressing not represented by a symbol is drawn to the outline of its actual shape and size and is then labeled. All visible objects are drawn with thick, solid lines. Anything occurring above the line cutting across the set—for example, a ceiling or chandelier—is drawn with an alternate position line; any important objects that lie beneath the visible surface are drawn with hidden lines.

In addition to showing the set and its contents, the ground plan must include lines that will provide spatial references similar in purpose to the longitude and latitude lines on a globe. For a proscenium theatre, the ground plan includes a centerline on an axis that runs up- and downstage at the middle of the proscenium opening. The proper line-type and centerline label are always included. One of two lines may be used as a transverse axis—either the plaster line or the set line. The **plaster line** crosses the stage from right to left at the upstage side of the proscenium arch; its label reads "Plaster Line." The **set line** also crosses the stage from right to left but is located at the furthest downstage position of the setting, such as the tormentors; its label reads "Set Line." Either line is drawn as a thin, consistent, long dash. The centerline and the set or plaster line provide fixed axes from which all measurements to locate the proscenium setting may be made. Thrust, arena, and

59

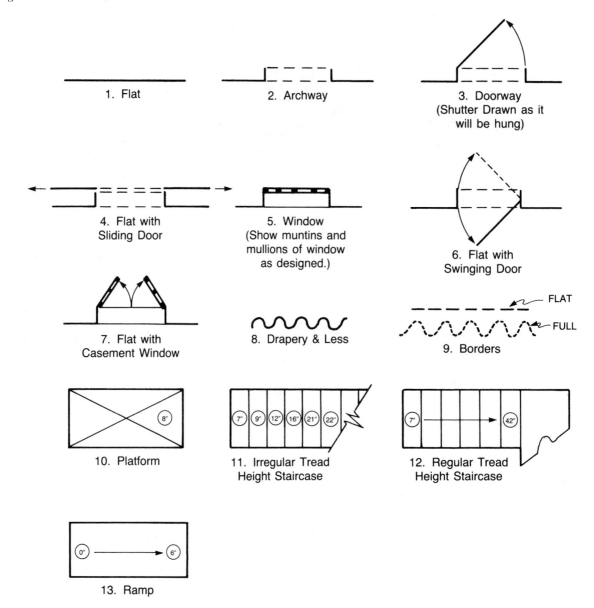

FIGURE 3–2

Standard symbols for ground plans. (From "Graphic Standards Board Recommendations for Standard Graphic Language in Scenic Design and Technical Production," reprinted by permission of the United States Institute for Theatre Technology Graphic Standards Board, Education Commission, and Board of Directors.)

other nonproscenium settings also require a pair of transverse axes from which locating measurements can be made. Normally a centerline represented by the standard symbol and label is used in one direction, and another line placed in an arbitrary location perpendicular to the centerline is drawn as a transverse axis. Since its position is arbitrary, dimensions must be given to locate the secondary axis, usually as measurements from fixed architectural features such as the walls of the room (Figure 3–3).

Most ground plans are drawn in the scale of ½″ = 1′-0″. Plans of excessively large spaces or plans requiring only limited detail may be drawn in reduced scale, usually ¼″ = 1′-0″. Drawings in smaller scales increase the possibility of error during construction; however, smaller-scale plans are satisfactory for drawings that are primarily informational in purpose.

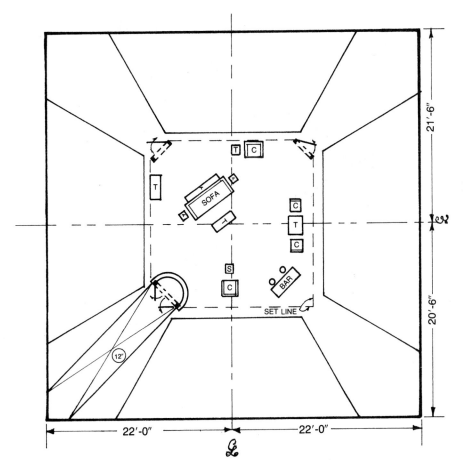

FIGURE 3–3
Ground plan for an arena theatre production. Note that two centerlines have been used and their positions identified in relation to the walls of the room.

PROJECTION DRAWINGS

Plans show the size and shape of the setting as a whole. However, they provide little information about the vertical appearance of the scenery or the construction of individual units. Additional detailed drawings are necessary to communicate this information clearly and efficiently. These drawings may include elevations, orthographic projections, pictorial drawings, and sections.

Elevations

An **elevation** is a drawing of an object seen as if the drafter were standing squarely in front of it with the observed surface projected onto a sheet of glass held between the drafter and the object (Figure 3–4). The drawing consists of what is seen on the glass surface. All visible features of the object, from this viewing position, are drawn as visible lines. Any important details concealed in this view are drawn as hidden lines.

FIGURE 3–4
The drafter's view to draw an elevation. The drafter stands squarely in front of the plane to be drawn and includes all features on the drawing seen from this position as if those features were projected onto a sheet of glass between the drafter and the surface shown.

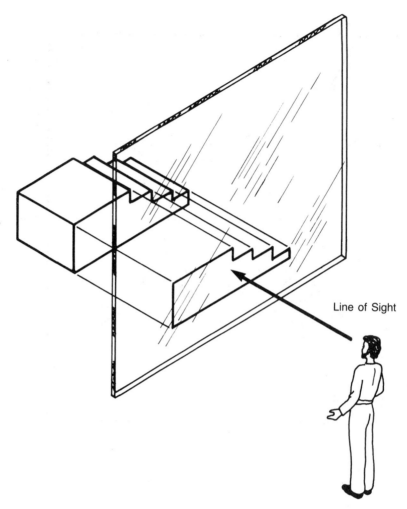

Line of Sight

Orthographic Projections

Orthograpic projections are multiple-view drawings that show each side of a three-dimensional object as an individual elevation. The drafter views an object as if it were placed squarely inside a glass box with the shape of the object, as seen on each side, projected onto the glass surfaces. The drafter moves around the box to view each of the six sides as an elevation (Figure 3–5). Every surface of the object parallel to a glass side will be a **true view** of that side of the object. On the drawing, the glass box is mentally unfolded and then placed in a pattern that logically relates the position of each side of the viewing box (Figure 3–6). The top, front, and bottom views fall on a common centerline. Views of the front, rear, and sides occur on the same baseline. The reader of the drawing must mentally reassemble the box to envision the object three-dimensionally.

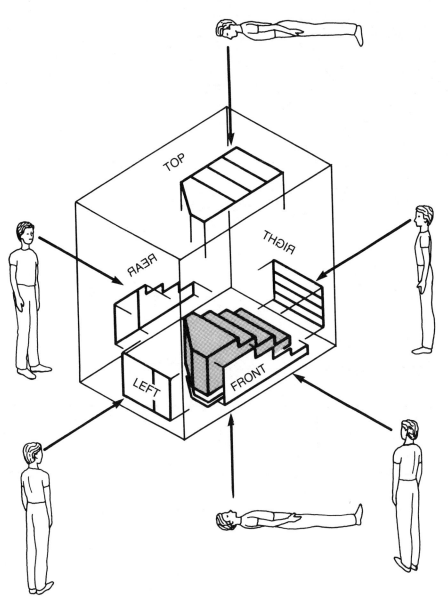

FIGURE 3–5
An orthograpic projection consists of six elevations. The drafter moves around the object to view each plane independently as if the object were placed in a glass box.

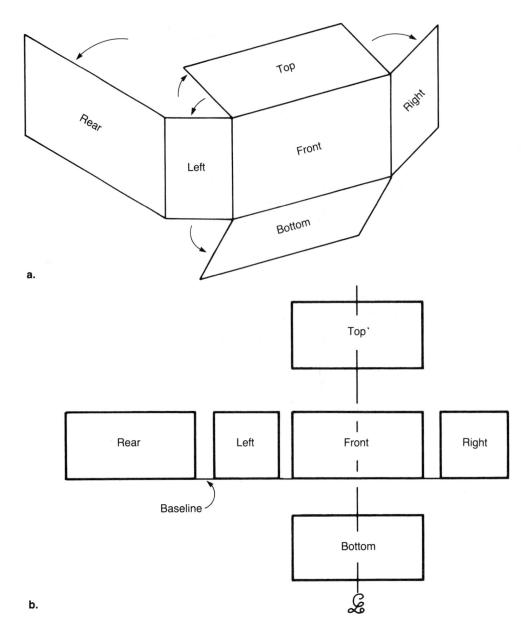

a.

b.

FIGURE 3–6

a) The glass box is unfolded and each plane of the object is drawn in the logical pattern shown in b). A common centerline is used for the top, front, and bottom views. A common baseline is used for the rear, left, front, and right views.

It is seldom necessary to draw all six sides of an object as "seen" in the glass box. Symmetrical objects usually can be described in only three views—the top, front, and right side, since the remaining sides would simply duplicate the information given in these views. A cylinder requires only two views, top and front. Only one view is needed for profile pieces cut from a piece of plywood or for a piece of hardware cut out of steel plate, since there is no variation in thickness. There are some occasions when four, five, or all six elevations must be shown for adequate communication. In addition, **auxiliary views** may be necessary to show the true shape of surfaces located on a plane not parallel with any surface of the enclosing glass box, such as the left end of the cabinet in Figure 3–7. Because this end of the cabinet is at

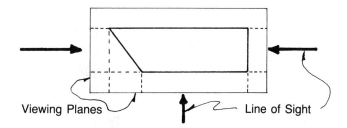

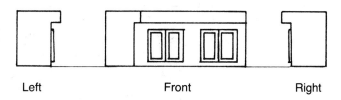

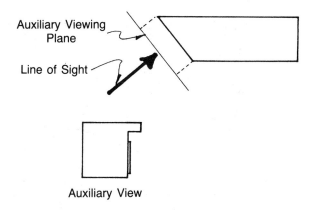

Viewing Planes — Line of Sight

Left   Front   Right

FIGURE 3–7
An auxiliary viewing plane is necessary to establish a true view of a surface not parallel to a plane of the glass box.

Auxiliary Viewing Plane

Line of Sight

Auxiliary View

an oblique angle to both the front and the left side of the glass box, the drawing of this side of the cabinet is foreshortened—that is, distorted—in all views. A true-shape drawing may be made by establishing an auxiliary viewing plane on the glass box that is parallel to the left side of the cabinet. The inclined surface is projected onto the new plane, as shown in Figure 3–7. Were the inclined plane on the top or the bottom of the cabinet, the true-shape auxiliary view would be located on the drawing in a way similar to that shown in Figure 3–8, so that one edge of the auxiliary view is parallel to the inclined plane on the elevation.

FIGURE 3–8

A top view of an inclined plane does not provide a true view. An auxiliary view will provide an accurate description of the inclined plane. The auxiliary view is located on an axis parallel to the surface drawn.

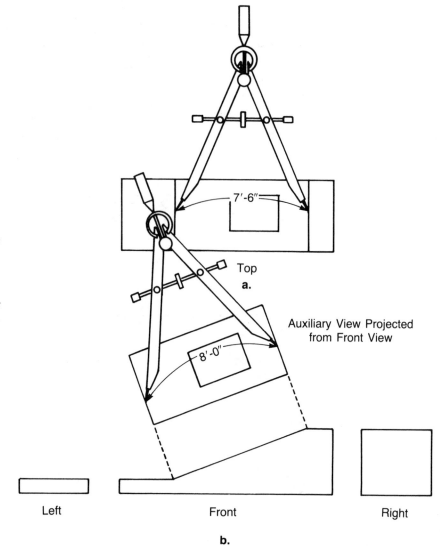

Top
a.

Auxiliary View Projected from Front View

Left   Front   Right

b.

Procedure for Drawing an Orthographic Projection

The work begins with a picture of the object to be drawn. This may be a mental picture in the mind of the designer or a sketch provided to the drafter.

1. **Determine the Drawing Scale.**

   Although most working drawings for the theatre are prepared in a scale of ½″ = 1′-0″, a diminished or enlarged scale may be more appropriate, depending upon the size, complexity, and amount of detail to be included in the drawing.

2. **Determine the Front of the Object.**

   The drafter selects one side of the object as the front view. This decision is based on three characteristics: a) the most representative view of the object, b) the view that will require the least amount of hidden lines, and c) the most efficient use of the drawing space.

3. Figure 3–9.

Determine the location and space required for each view to be included on the drawing. A common centerline is used for the top, front, and bottom views, and a common baseline is used for the front, rear, and side views. The drafter should plan sufficient space for dimensions and notes. In the example, only three views will be needed.

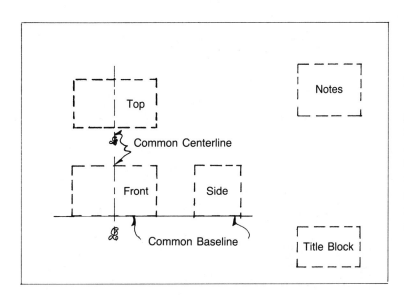

FIGURE 3–9

To begin drawing an orthographic projection, determine the number of views required as well as the quantity of space necessary for each view, including dimensions, notes, and titles. Block out these areas on the drawing with very lightweight lines.

4. Figure 3–10.

Begin with the top view. Draw the overall outline of the object as seen from above. In the example, the outline of the platform top is drawn as visible lines and the indented base as a hidden outline.

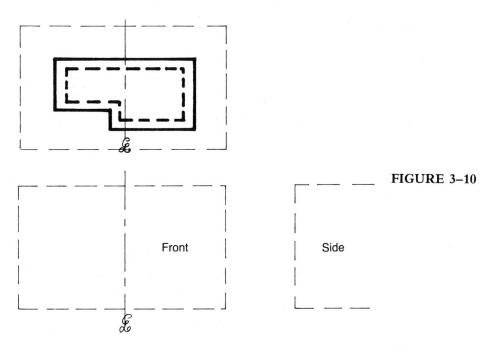

FIGURE 3–10

5. Figure 3–11.

Transfer the dimensions of the top view to the front view (and bottom view, if used) by drawing lightweight projectors down to the spaces assigned to the front and bottom views. Use a T-square and triangle to draw these projectors.

FIGURE 3–11

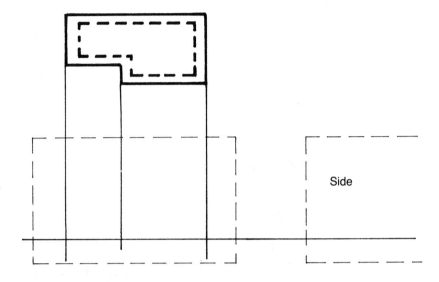

6. Figure 3–12.

Measure the height of the platform on the front view, and then transfer that dimension horizontally to the side view(s), using the T-square.

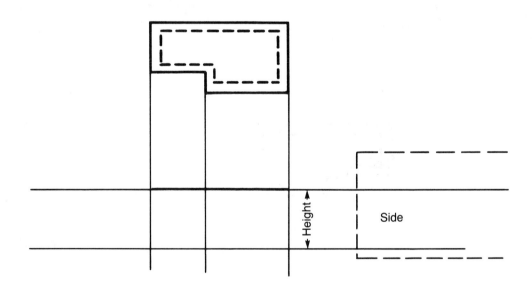

FIGURE 3–12

7. Figure 3–13.

Measure the width of the platform top in the side view. This dimension may be transferred from the top to the side view with drafting instruments or by means of Transfer Procedure A, B or C following.

68

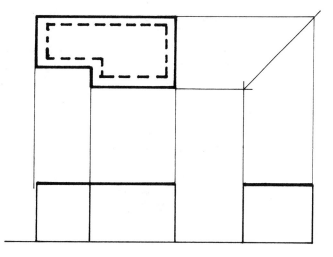

FIGURE 3–13

a. *Transfer Procedure A.* **(Figure 3–14)**
   1) **Figure 3–14a.** Draw a lightweight horizontal line across the page at the lowest edge of the top view of the form.

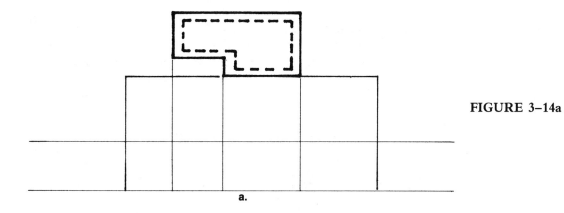

FIGURE 3–14a

   2) Draw a lightweight vertical line up the page until it crosses the first line.
   3) **Figure 3–14b.** Using a 45 triangle, draw a diagonal starting from the intersection of these two lightweight lines and heading toward the upper corner of the paper.

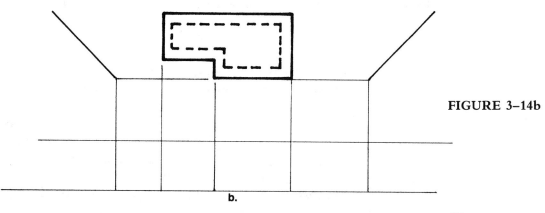

FIGURE 3–14b

4) **Figure 3–14c.** At the top edge of the top view, draw a second horizontal across the page until it intersects with the diagonal line. At this point, drop a perpendicular line down to the base of the side view. The rectangle in the side view accurately forms the outline of the top of the object in this view.

FIGURE 3–14c

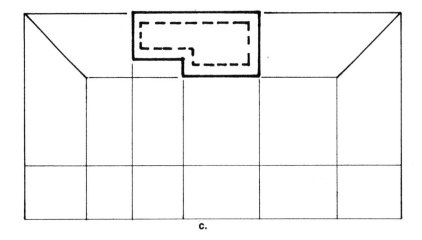

c.

5) **Figure 3–14d.** Repeat the procedure for every detail in every side view. The same diagonal may be used to transfer any detail contained in a view. Information may be transferred up, from the side view to the top view, and also down to a bottom view, if desired.

FIGURE 3–14d

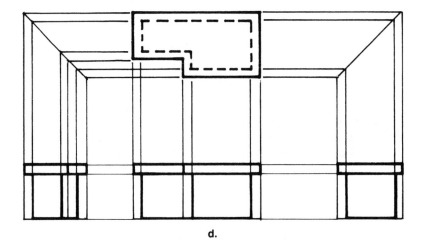

d.

b. *Transfer Procedure B.* **(Figure 3–15)**
1) **Figure 3–15a.** Perform steps 1 and 2 of Transfer Procedure A.
2) **Figure 3–15b.** Adjust a compass to a radius equal to the width of the top of the object. At the intersection of the lightweight horizontal and vertical lines, draw an arc forming a 90° segment of a circle.
3) **Figure 3–15c.** From the bottom of the arc, drop a

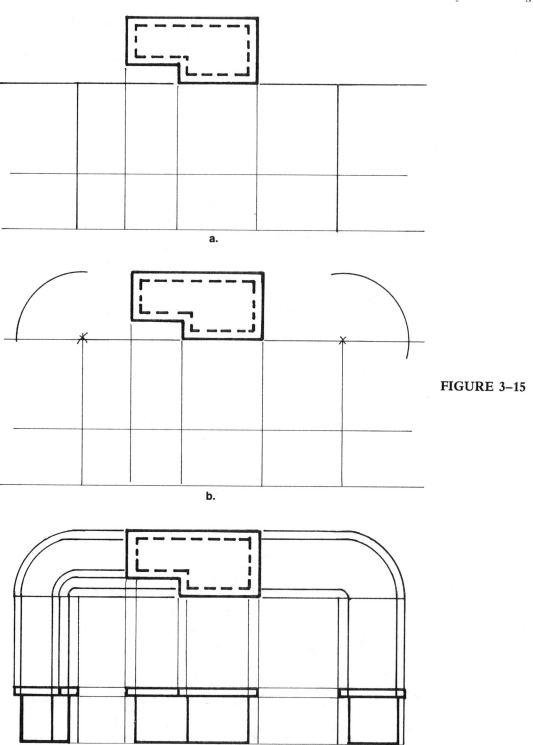

FIGURE 3–15

vertical line to the base of the side view. This forms
the outline of the object in the side view. Repeat the
procedure for every detail to be transferred from the
top to the side view. The procedure may also be used
to transfer information from the side view to the top
or bottom views, as needed.

71

c. *Transfer Procedure C.* **(Figure 3–16)**
Transfer Procedures A and B are most useful for developing multiple views of irregular forms. In addition to transferring the corner of the shape, specific locations can be identified on an irregular form in the most characteristic view; these points are individually transferred to adjacent views using either Procedure A or B. In the example, the side view was drawn first, and then information was transferred to the top view.

FIGURE 3–16

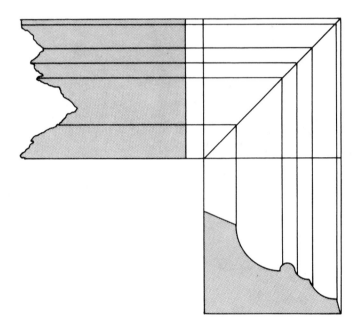

8. Figure 3–17.
Working on the front elevation, draw the outline of the platform as seen from the front. On a side view, draw the base as seen from the side. Using Transfer Procedure A, B, or C, transfer these details to adjacent views, as appropriate. These may be visible or hidden construction lines. Continue the process until the drawing is completed.

FIGURE 3–17

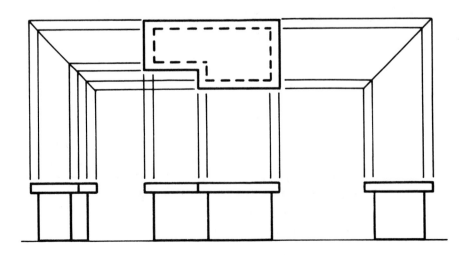

9. **Darken all object lines for printing, and erase all unnecessary lines.**

10. **Figure 3–18.**

    Dimensions are placed on these views where they will have the most meaning to the reader. The outline of the platform top would be dimensioned in the top view, and the outline and details of the front and sides would be most clearly explained on those views.

11. **Add notes and titles as appropriate, including titles of each view.**

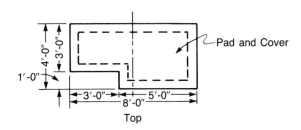

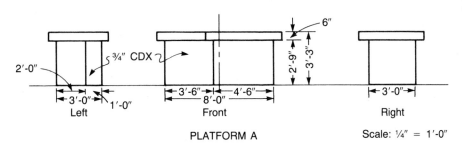

FIGURE 3–18

In drawings of more complex units such as a cabinet, it may be more valuable to draw the top view with the **top removed.** Although it is not a standard practice, this method can give a clearer picture of interior construction, as in the cabinet shown in Figure 3–19. Here the outline of the cabinet top would be drawn using alternate position lines, and the internal detail would be drawn using visible outlines.

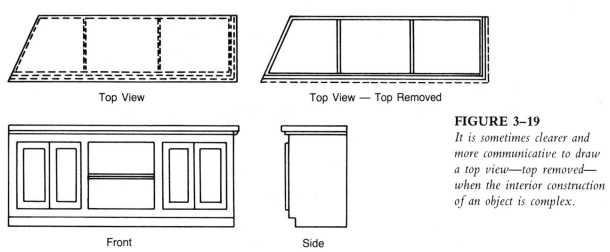

FIGURE 3–19
It is sometimes clearer and more communicative to draw a top view—top removed— when the interior construction of an object is complex.

PICTORIAL DRAWINGS

Some objects can be shown in a single view that reveals height, width, and depth concurrently to provide sufficient information for construction purposes; a three-dimensional representation is necessary for other objects to be comprehended. There are three types of drawing that show all three dimensions simultaneously: isometric projections, oblique projections, and perspective drawings. These views are called **pictorial drawings.** Perspective drawings result in the most realistic appearance of objects and spaces. They are used extensively by designers to create an overall impression of a single unit or an entire set, but they cannot be expressed in real measurements and thus provide little usable information for construction. Isometric projections are frequently used to describe three-dimensional objects for construction purposes. They are relatively easy to draw and interpret. Oblique drawings are used for special applications.

Isometric Projection

Isometric projection bears some similarities to orthographic projection. When drawing an **isometric projection,** the drafter views an object as if it were placed within a glass box. In this case, rather than looking at each plane of the box individually, as in orthographic projection, the viewer can see three planes of the glass box at the same time (Figure 3–20). The drafter stands in line with a corner of the box rather than in front of any one surface. Each side of the box is equally foreshortened in this view.

FIGURE 3–20

An isometric projection is drawn as if the drafter were viewing the object in a glass box from a location that allows vision of three planes of the box at the same time.

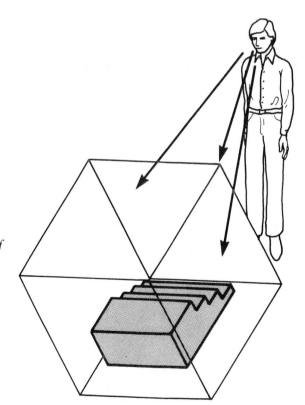

Rules for Isometric Projection

1. The object drawn is mentally placed within a glass box and viewed from a corner of the box.
2. In Figure 3–21, each plane of the box is on an **isometric axis.** There are three isometric axes spaced 60° apart. The orientation of the axes may be in any position, but the spacing between the axes must be maintained.

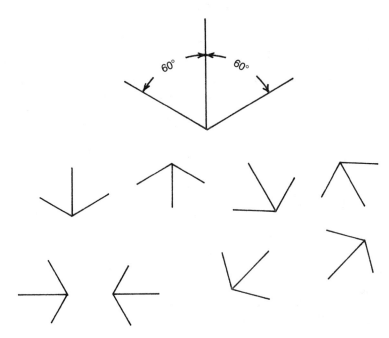

FIGURE 3–21
Isometric axes may be rotated to any convenient position for viewing or drawing, so long as the relationship between the axes remains constant.

3. All lines on or parallel to isometric axes are measurable; lines and planes not on or parallel to an isometric axis are foreshortened.
4. Verticals are true verticals.

Typical Procedure for Drawing an Isometric Projection

1. **Figure 3–22.** Establish the isometric axes. a) Construct a vertical at the center of the form to be drawn. b) Using a 30-60 triangle, draw a baseline to the right and left of the vertical at an angle of 30°. This construction provides the three isometric axes spaced 60° apart. In Figure 3–22 the axes are labeled AB, AC, and AD.

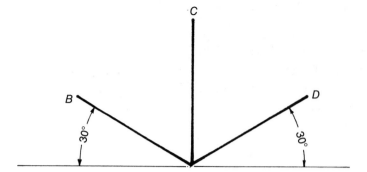

FIGURE 3-22

2. **Figure 3-23.** Using the isometric axes as baselines for the drawing, measure the length of the staircase on axis AB. Construct a vertical at this point.

FIGURE 3-23

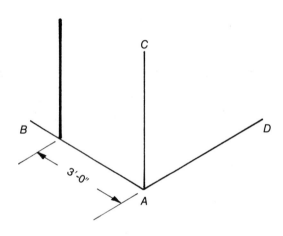

3. **Figure 3-24.** Measure the height of each tread on line AC. Draw a diagonal parallel to isometric axis AB from each of these points toward the vertical at the back of the stair.

FIGURE 3-24

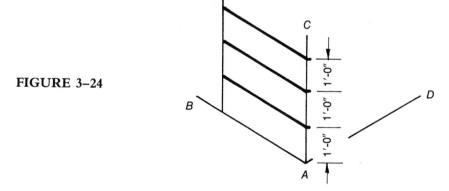

4. **Figure 3–25.** Working on axis AB, measure the depth of each tread. Construct a vertical at each mark.

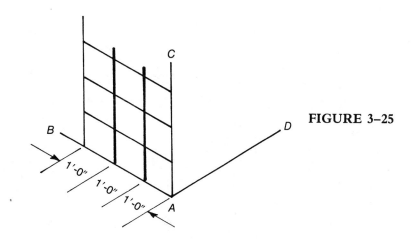

FIGURE 3–25

5. **Figure 3–26.** At each appropriate intersection of lines, draw a digagonal parallel to axis AD.

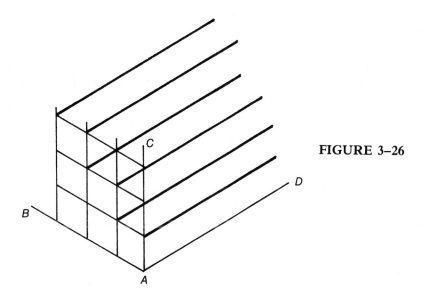

FIGURE 3–26

6. **Figure 3–27.** Measure the width of the staircase on axis AD. At this new point construct a vertical to the height of the first rise.

FIGURE 3–27

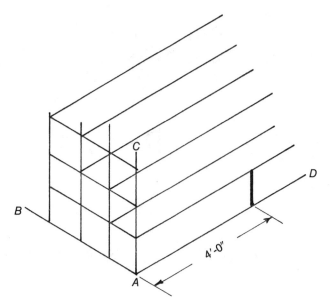

7. **Figure 3–28.** At the top of the newly formed first rise, draw a diagonal parallel to axis AB. Continue drawing verticals and diagonals until the far end of the staircase is completed (Figure 3–29).

FIGURE 3–28

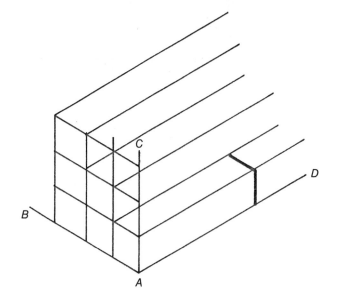

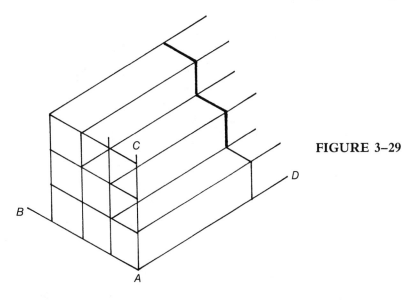

FIGURE 3-29

8. **Figure 3–30.** Erase all extraneous lines, and add any necessary details, dimensions, and notes.

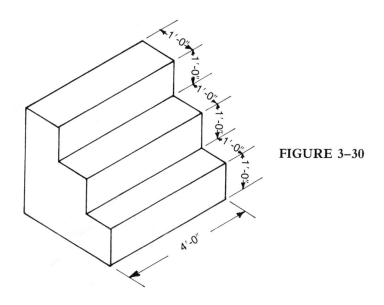

FIGURE 3–30

Planes and Forms Not on an Isometric Axis

As the planes of objects become less parallel to isometric axes, the drawing task increases in complexity. If the form to be drawn as an isometric projection has an inclined surface such as a ramp, the slope cannot be drawn directly, since it will not occur on or parallel to an isometric axis. Instead, the beginning and end of the slope, its coordinates, are measured on the isometric axes, and those points are connected as in Figure 3–31.

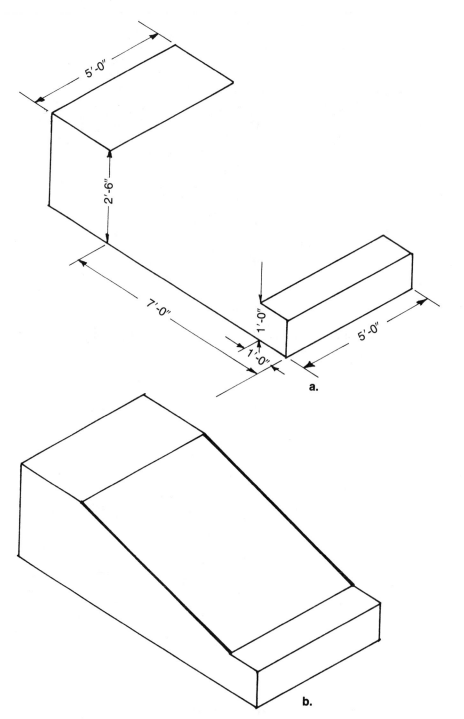

FIGURE 3–31
An inclined plane in an iso-metric projection is drawn by determining the coordinates of the edges of the plane.

A pyramid has only one plane parallel to an isometric axis: its base. It may be drawn with relative ease.

1. Figure 3–32a. Draw the base of the pyramid to the proper dimensions. This will form an isometric square. Draw a pair of diagonals connecting the corners of the square.

2. Figure 3–32b. The intersection of the diagonals identifies the center of the pyramid base. Draw a vertical at the intersections of the diagonals. The apex of the pyramid will occur on this

line. Measure the height of the pyramid on the vertical from the intersection of the diagonals.

3. Figure 3–32c. Connect the point marking the height of the pyramid with each of the visible corners of the base of the pyramid. Erase all extraneous lines.

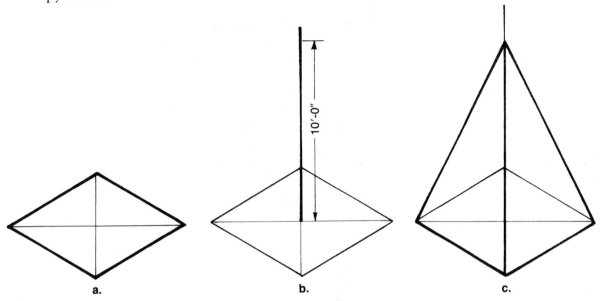

a.   b.   c.

FIGURE 3–32
To draw a pyramid as an isometric projection.

Circles in Isometric Views

Circles and arcs are distorted in isometric views. Circles become ellipses, and arcs become portions of an ellipse. One of three methods may be used to draw circles and arcs on isometric planes.

Point Plotting (Figure 3–33)

1. Figure 3–33a. Draw an elevation of the desired circle on scratch paper. Draw a box around the circle, with the sides of the box tangent to the circle at the two centerlines.

2. Lay out a grid on the box in some reasonable scale, such as a grid line every ¼". The greater the frequency of grid lines, the more accurate the finished drawing.

3. Figure 3–33b. On the isometric view, draw an isometric square with the same dimensions as the square on the scratch paper. Locate the square where the circle is to be placed on the isometric view. Draw the centerlines of the isometric square. Complete the grid on the isometric view, measuring the same increments between lines as on the elevation.

4. On the elevation, measure the points of tangency of the circle with the grid lines. Transfer these points to the same positions on the isometric grid.

5. Drawing free-handed, with a French curve, or with a spline, connect the dots to form the isometric circle.

Four-Center Ellipse (Figure 3–34)

1. Figure 3–34a. On the isometric view, construct an isometric square equal to the diameter of the circle.

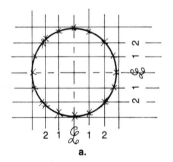

a.

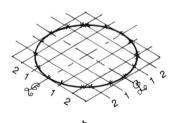

b.

FIGURE 3–33
Using point-plotting to draw an isometric circle.

81

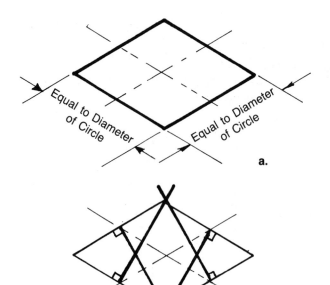

FIGURE 3–34
Using the four-center ellipse to drawn an isometric circle.

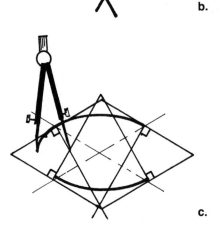

2. Figure 3–34b. Construct a perpendicular at the centerline of each side of the isometric square.

3. Figure 3–34c. Using the intersection of these perpendiculars as centering points, with a compass draw an arc between the pair of centerlines. Each arc should extend from centerline to centerline at the point of tangency with the square. Repeat for each side. The result will be an approximate ellipse.

Ellipse Template   (Figure 3–35)

Special templates are available with 35° ellipses, the correct shape for drawing a circle on an isometric plane. The marks around the openings in the template identify the centerline of the circle when it is drawn in the isometric view. The dimensions given on the template identify the size of the circle rather than the major dimensions of the ellipse.

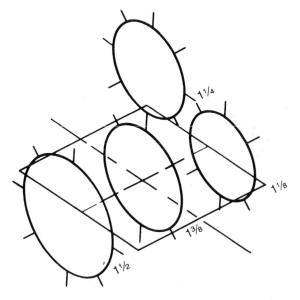

FIGURE 3–35
Using an ellipse template to draw an isometric circle.

1. Determine the center of the circle to be drawn on the isometric view by drawing an isometric square and measuring to the center of each side. Draw each centerline on the isometric axis across the square.
2. Align the ellipse template on the centerlines and draw the ellipse.

Cylinders

Once an isometric circle is drawn, a cylinder can be formed on the drawing with relative ease. Using the point-plotting method, the opposite end of the cylinder can be found by projecting on the appropriate isometric axis each plotted point on the grid to the desired depth for the cylinder. Each line of projection will be equal in length (Figure 3–36). An arc is sketched in to form the opposite end of the cylinder.

An ellipse template may also be used to construct an isometric cylinder as shown in Figure 3–37.

1. Figure 3–37a. Draw the longitudinal centerline of the cylinder on an isometric plane. At each end of the cylinder, construct a line across the centerline that is perpendicular to it.
2. Figure 3–37b. Place the ellipse template on the crossmember of the near line, and align the major axis of the ellipse with it. Inscribe the ellipse.
3. Figure 3–37c. Repeat the alignment procedure at the far end of the cylinder and draw a second ellipse.
4. Figure 3–37d. Connect the intersections of the crossmembers of the front and rear ellipses. Erase all extraneous lines.

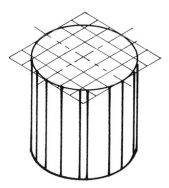

FIGURE 3–36
Using point-plotting to draw an isometric cylinder.

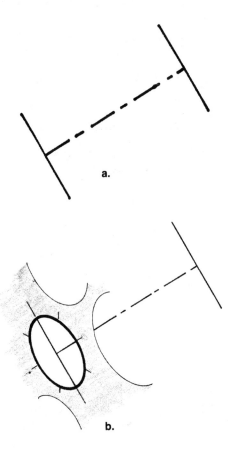

a.

b.

FIGURE 3–37
*Using an ellipse template to
draw an isometric cylinder.*

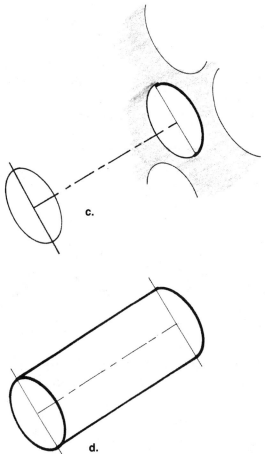

c.

d.

Irregular shapes and details may be transferred to isometric drawings by means of point-plotting or a combination of point-plotting, the four-center technique, and use of an isometric template. Templates, French curves, and splines are especially convenient for this work.

Oblique Drawings

Oblique drawings combine features of both orthographic and isometric views. An **oblique drawing** has one face of an object parallel to the drawing surface and is drawn true to size as in orthographic projection. The adjacent side and the top or bottom of the object are shown on receding planes, as in an isometric projection. Any angle may be used between the horizontal baseline and the receding plane for the side of the object. There are three types of oblique drawings:

Cavalier—in which depth is drawn to true shape and size. The drawing results in a distorted appearance. The depth of the form seems to be drawn at an enlarged scale.

Cabinet—in which the depth is drawn half-size and results in the most natural appearance.

General oblique—in which depth may be drawn to any proportion between one-half and full size.

The boxes shown in Figure 3–38 represent the differences in appearance among the various types of oblique drawings for an object of consistent size.

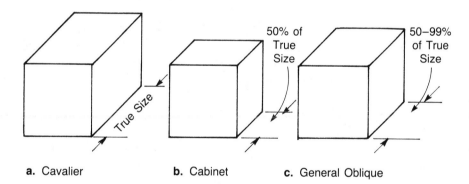

a. Cavalier b. Cabinet c. General Oblique

FIGURE 3–38
Oblique drawings: a) Cavalier—depth drawn true to size, b) Cabinet—depth reduced 50 percent, c) General oblique—depth drawn 50 to 99 percent of true size.

Oblique drawings are commonly used when a three-dimensional view is necessary for adequate communication but the form and/or details of one of the planes of the object are too complicated to be drawn in isometric view.

Procedure for Making an Oblique Drawing

1. Draw an elevation of the most complex surface of the object.
2. Determine and draw the angle between the horizontal baseline of the elevation and the receding plane. Any angle between 0° and 90° may be used.
3. Determine whether a cavalier, cabinet, or general oblique drawing will be made.

4. Project the appropriate details through the depth of the drawing.

5. As in isometric drawings, inclined planes, angles, arcs, and circles will be distorted on the receding surfaces. The procedures used to draw these features on the receding planes are the same as those used for isometric projection.

   a. To draw inclined planes and obtuse angles, measurements from known locations (coordinates) must be made on established axes.

   b. Curves, arcs, and irregular details are transferred to the views by either point-plotting or four-point plotting techniques (pages 81–82).

6. Complete the drawing. Darken all appropriate lines, and insert dimensions as necessary.

Examples of good and poor use of oblique drawing are shown in Figure 3–39. These figures also exemplify the type of object that might best be described by means of oblique drawing techniques.

FIGURE 3–39

Proper use of oblique drawings. The most complex plane of an oblique drawing should be turned toward the observer and the least complicated surface turned away from the observer.

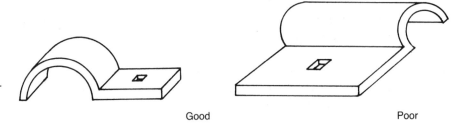

Good   Poor

These views may be used alone or in combination with plans, orthographic views, or isometric views to communicate the appearance of an object fully. This approach to drawing may also be combined with or developed as a sectional view.

Sectional Views

All of the approaches to communication thus far have dealt with the external appearance of units. Frequently it is necessary to know the internal structure of a prop or set piece in order to understand its construction. Sectional drawings provide this information. These views cut through an object on a selected plane, revealing the internal structure of the object on that plane. There are various kinds of sections that the drafter may use: full, half, off-set, revolved, removed, broken out, and exploded.

It is necessary to know the plane on which a sectional view is taken to comprehend the information communicated in the drawing. The location of a section is identified on a primary view, usually a plan, elevation, or pictorial drawing, by one of the three types of cutting plane lines shown in Figure 2–1. A fourth alternative is to identify a cutting plane on a pre-established axis, such as the centerline. The latter approach eliminates the need for additional lines yet clearly identifies the plane on which the sectional view is taken.

Conventions and Rules for Sectional Views

1. The arrowheads on the cutting plane lines that pass through the section point toward the surface that is seen in the sectional view.

2. The section is identified at each end of the cutting plane line with an alphabetic label. The same label is placed beneath the sectional view as a title for the drawing.

3. Sections are located as close as possible to the primary drawing of a unit. Occasionally it is necessary to locate sections on separate sheets; this is a common practice in architectural drawing. In that event, the section cutting plane is identified by the section name, placed on the top half of a circle, with a reference to the sheet containing the section drawing placed in the lower half of the circle.

4. In the section drawing, solid mass is identified by means of thin, evenly spaced, diagonal lines drawn at any convenient angle less than 90°. It is helpful to use a variety of angles for section lines, to distinguish separate parts or materials.

5. Standard parts that occur on the cutting plane but have no consequential internal structure, such as screws, bolts, nails, or rivets, are drawn as solid forms without section lines. Thin ribs, spokes, and other thin metal parts are also drawn solid, even though the cutting plane may pass through them.

6. Visible lines behind the cutting plane are shown in the sectional view.

7. Hidden lines are not shown in the sectional view.

A **full section** (Figure 3–40) is a drawing of the entire length or width of the plane on which the section cutting line is shown. Units with symmetrical parts can be described by combining an elevation with a section view. This may be achieved by drawing a **half-section** (Figure 3–41). These drawings remove a quarter of the object, revealing the interior on one side of the centerline and revealing the exterior as an elevation on the other side of the centerline. Some objects have features at various planes of depth which could be included in a single sectional view if the cutting plane were bent as it passed through the object. These drawings are called **off-set sections** (Figure 3–42). The cutting plane is drawn through the object on the planes of depth

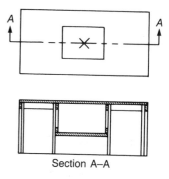

Section A–A

FIGURE 3–40

Full section.

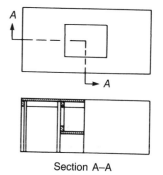

Section A–A

FIGURE 3–41

Half-section. One half of the object is drawn as a section, and the other half is drawn as an elevation.

FIGURE 3–42

Offset section. The section cutting plane is bent at a 90° angle as necessary to show the most representative interior view of the object. The sectional view does not indicate where the cutting plane is bent.

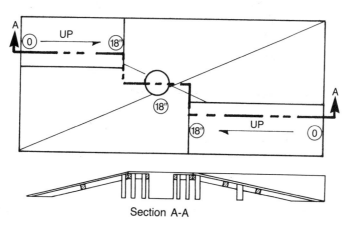

Section A-A

necessary to reveal salient internal construction. Each off-set is at 90°; the planes are drawn in the sectional view as if they were parallel to each other. The vertical line where an off-set occurs is not shown in the sectional view.

It is often necessary to show a cross-section of a molding or other complex detail on a set. **Revolved sections** are a means to communicate this information as part of an elevation. There are two approaches that may be used for revolved sections. In the first approach, the section may be drawn directly on the elevation, as in Figure 3–43a. The section is outlined with thick lines, and all interior mass is cross-hatched with thin diagonal lines. The section is drawn to its true shape at the point at which the section is taken. This point is the centerline of the sectional view. Object lines are not continued through the section view; however, the object lines do abut the view. The second approach to revolved sections, shown in Figure 3–43b, is similar; however, the elevation is broken away on either side of the revolved section. The resultant sectional drawing stands clear of all other lines.

FIGURE 3–43
Revolved sections. In a) elevation lines attach to the sectional view, but in b) the elevation lines are cutaway from the sectional view.

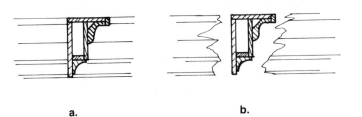

a.   b.

Sometimes it is necessary only to show a portion of internal construction to communicate sufficiently how a unit is constructed. In this case a **broken-out section** may be used. In the example (Figure 3–44), a breakline is drawn through the platform facing to reveal a portion of the leg assembly. Conventional practice assumes that the facing will be completed in construction. Half-sections, revolved sections, and broken-out sections may eliminate the necessity for additional views in a set of drawings. They save space and drawing time, and for certain applications they can communicate a great deal of information more clearly than a separate drawing.

FIGURE 3–44
Broken-out section. Completion of the broken-out area is assumed in construction.

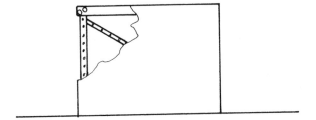

Removed sections (Figure 3–45) are especially useful to describe the profile of objects with varying contours. This approach shows the overall elevation of the object, as well as the specific profile and structure at significant locations. These sections are similar to revolved sections; however, the sectional views are located outside the object. An alternate

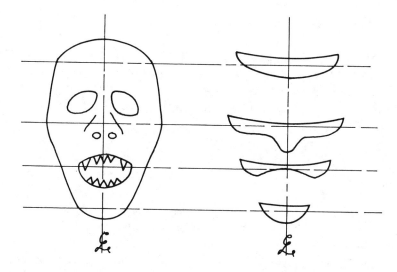

FIGURE 3–45
Removed sections.

position line connects the center of the removed section to the plane on which the section line is taken.

Thus far, sections have been treated as orthographic drawings with the drawing plane and sectional view parallel to each other. Any type of section can be drawn as a pictorial view or combined with pictorial drawings for clarity.

Exploded sections (Figure 3–46) are isometric or oblique sectional drawings of an object taken apart. An isometric or oblique axis is selected as a general plane for the object-as-a-whole. Each part of the object is drawn as a separate pictorial representation on the plane of the object-as-a-whole. Alternate position lines may connect the parts in their normal relationship if this is not apparent in the drawing. Although seldom used by theatre drafters, these views are frequently used as assembly instructions for commercial equipment.

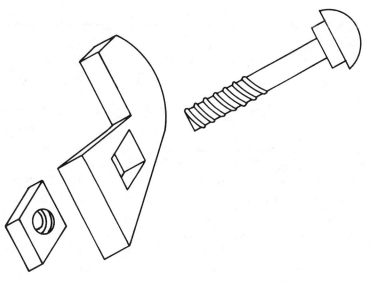

FIGURE 3–46
Exploded section.

STANDARD DRAWINGS USED IN THE THEATRE

Orthographic, isometric, oblique, and sectional drawings provide the drafter with a broad graphic vocabulary to explain the construction and finishing of a set. These views are incorporated in both design and working drawings. Design drawings explain specific details about the appearance of a setting. This group of drawings may include a ground plan and centerline section of each set, a hanging section, composite plan or shift plan for multiset shows, front elevations of each element of the setting, and detail drawings of individual set pieces. A designer working alone may develop these graphics, or they may be drawn by a group of assistants. Practice varies from designer to designer and from shop to shop. Although some shops build solely from designer's models or design drawings, many shops develop complete working drawings based on the information contained in the design drawings. **Working drawings** are used in the shop to guide actual construction.

Plans

The **ground plan** is the single most important drawing made by the designer. It identifies entrances, exits, levels, and the location of all actor-islands and obstacles on the set. This drawing is used by the director, choreographer, lighting designer, properties master, and the carpenters. The information necessary to deal with blocking, however, is different from that needed for construction. Those staff members dealing with actor movement must know the location, size, and shape of all obstacles in the acting area; the carpenters are concerned with the placement, size, and fitting of each element of the setting. The designer prepares separate plans for each group of workers.

Furniture plot or **director's floor plan** (Figure 3–47). Usually drawn in ¼" scale, this plan is used by the director and stage manager to tape out rehearsal space and record blocking in the prompt book. The plan is also used by the properties master to determine the general size, shape, and placement of set dressings. This drawing is most convenient when reproduced on a ¼" grid. The plan is drawn in scale and includes the centerline and set or plaster line. Neither dimensions nor technical notations are included in this drawing.

Designer's ground plan (Figure 3–48). Usually drawn in a scale of ½" = 1'-0", the plan shows the layout and placement of the setting but does not include set dressings. The plan is dimensioned from two reference points. Proscenium settings are dimensioned from the centerline of the proscenium opening and the set or plaster line; nonproscenium settings are dimensioned from transverse axes. Thrust stages may use the centerline and front edge or rear edge of the stage; arena productions may simply use two centerlines of the stage for reference. These dimensions are used to locate the setting on stage. Individual wall units are not dimensioned, since that information is included on elevations. Platform and tread heights are given on this plan.

It is necessary to provide some means to identify the scenery as it progresses through the construction and painting processes. Units for single-set productions may be simply labeled "stage right," "up

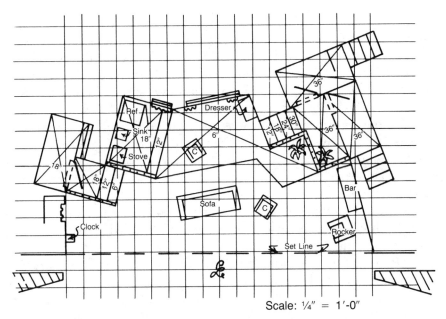

FIGURE 3–47
*Director's floor plan. Shows
the layout of the setting and
the placement of properties.
Usually drawn in the scale of
¼" = 1'-0".*

Scale: ¼" = 1'-0"

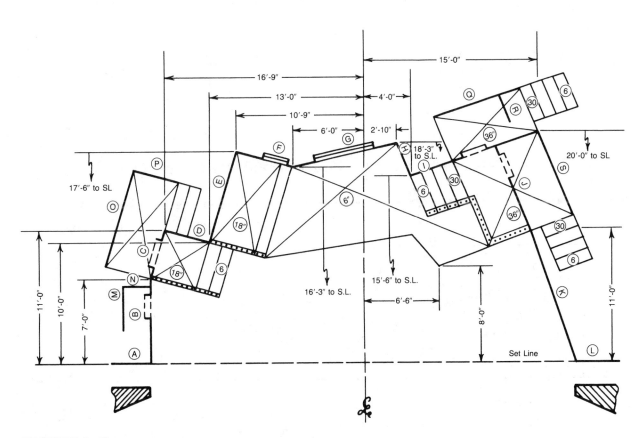

FIGURE 3–48
*Designer's ground plan. Shows the layout and assembly of the setting with as many dimensions as necessary to
locate the scenery on stage and to determine the size of scenic units. Units may be labeled and additional information added as necessary to facilitate construction and assembly. Usually in the scale of ½" = 1'-0" for the theatre
and ¼" = 1'-0" for film.*

91

left," "down center," etc. Since the identity of these units is self-apparent, labels need not be included on the plan. More complex sets require more extensive labeling. The specific style and arrangement of these labels is a matter of shop practice and organization. A common practice is to place labels on the plan in heavy circles located off-stage of the scenery. The labels are made in alphabetical order and placed around the set either from downstage right to downstage left or from down left to down right. Each set of a multiset show may have a prefix numeral or label to identify the scenery belonging to that set. Thus, the scenery from the first set may be labeled I-A or Inn-A, and each additional set will have a different prefix, such as II-A or Boudoir-A. Since the prefix refers to the entire plan, it need not be included with each label on the plan if the prefix is identified clearly elsewhere on the drawing.

Production ground plan (Figure 3–49). This drawing combines the furniture plot (director's floor plan) and the designer's ground plan on a single ½" scale drawing. These plans include not only the furniture but also the reference dimensions to tape out the set for rehearsal and to set up the scenery for production. Designers in busy educational or repertory theatres may use these plans in lieu of drawing a separate plan for the director and another for the shop. In this case the stage manager, assistant director, or a design assistant is responsible for providing the director's floor plan for the prompt book, and the technical

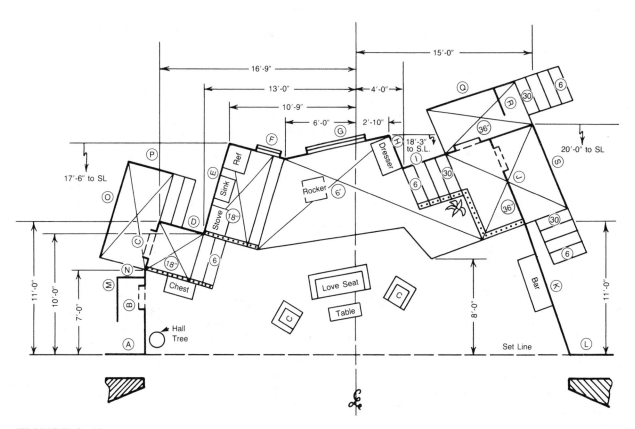

FIGURE 3–49

Production ground plan. Combines the director's ground plan and the designer's ground plan to show the setting with complete technical information, dimensioning, labels, and notes, in addition to set dressings. Usually in the scale of ½" = 1'-0".

director or a design assistant is responsible for providing any necessary revisions for the shop.

Composite ground plan (Figure 3–50). When a production has more than one set, it is necessary to know how and where scenery moves, where it will be stored, and the interrelationship of the settings. A composite plan will provide this information. This is a drawing in any convenient scale that simultaneously shows each of the sets of a multiset show. Each set is represented by a different style line identified in a legend on the drawing. The drawing is only informational; it

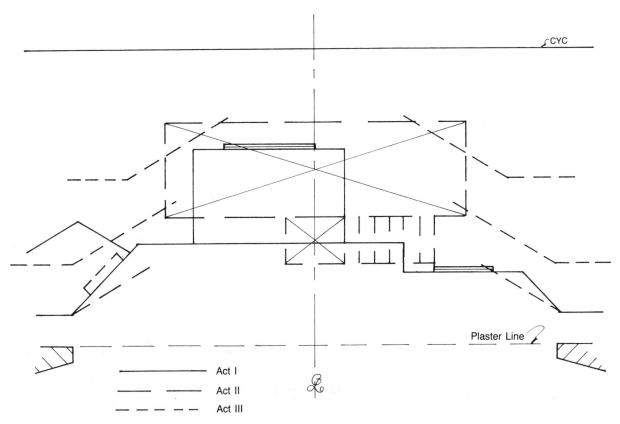

FIGURE 3–50

Composite ground plan shows all of the sets of a multiset show on a single plan. Each set is simplified for clarity and distinguished by its own style of line.

serves no purpose for construction but is used extensively by the scene designer to plan masking, by the carpenter to plan scene shifts, and by the lighting designer to design the lights. It is easiest to make these drawings in ½″ scale as a tracing of the designer's ground plans of the individual sets.

Sections

Ground plans provide only one plane of information: the horizontal layout of the setting. With the exception of platform heights, there is no indication as to the height of scenery, vertical sightlines, trims for flying units, the height of window or door openings, the appearance of dressings and moldings, or the placement of any portion of the setting in the vertical planes of the stage space. A portion of this information will be communicated by means of section drawings. The designer will provide one of two types of sections: a centerline section of the entire theatre or a hanging section of the stage house.

Centerline section (Figure 3–51). These views are usually drawn in either ¼″, ⅜″, or ½″ scale, through a longitudinal section of the entire theatre, they identify sightlines from the most extreme or worst seats in the house; they also show lighting positions, masking, and a simplified sectional drawing of the setting. This drawing is used by the scenic designer to determine sightlines, scenery, and trim heights and, if relatively simple, hanging positions for flown scenery. The section may be made as if looking toward stage right or stage left. If a more representative view can be achieved, the section may be taken on an axis other than the centerline.

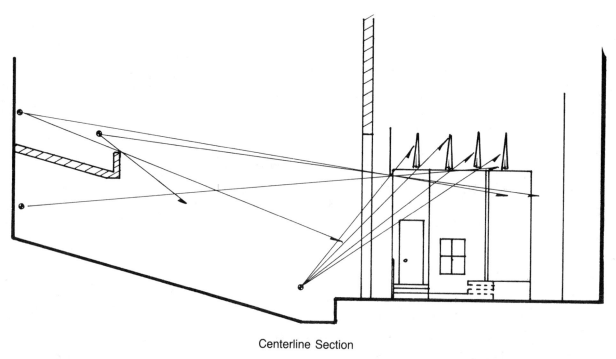

Centerline Section

FIGURE 3–51
Centerline section.

Hanging section (Figure 3–52). A separate hanging plot in either ¼″ scale or ½″ scale is frequently drawn for productions with a large quantity of flown scenery. This is a section view of the stage house in which the use, spacing, and trim of each flown piece of scenery is identified. A sectional view of the set occupying the stage floor is included in the drawing. The amount of detail contained in this view will be dependent upon the needs of the production. Although this drawing is usually a centerline section, it may be drawn from a wing position if this will provide a more representative view. A typed schedule on which batten number, distance from plasterline, function of the batten, and trim height are identified may be substituted for this drawing in less complicated productions or in productions where the graphic illustration is not necessary.

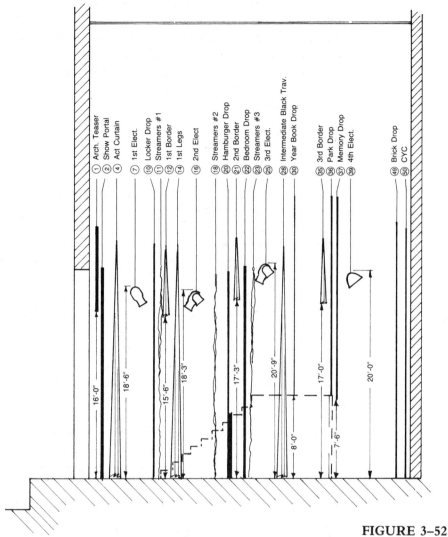

FIGURE 3–52
Hanging section.

Design Drawings

Renderings, plans, and sectional views provide a great deal of information about the placement of the setting on the stage and the relationship of parts; however, such drawings are of limited value to the carpenter, who must know the specific vertical and horizontal dimensions and appearance of the scenery. This information is communicated in design elevations. **Design elevations** are individual views of each unit of the setting, laid out in a logical order to show the true size and shape of each element of the setting. Pictorial drawings and auxiliary views are included as necessary. These drawings are usually drawn in a scale of ½″ = 1′-0″. **Painter's elevations** are essentially design elevations that have been rendered with all of the colors, painting detail, texturing requirements, and notes the scenic artist will need to interpret the elevation. These are usually prepared in ½″ or 1″ scale on illustration board, although some designers paint directly on blueprints of the design elevations.

Models have become an increasingly popular means by which scene designers communicate with their colleagues. Three-dimensional models not only help visualize space (as opposed to the rendering which only implies three-dimensional space), but a fully developed model that can be dismantled eliminates the need for designer's and painter's elevations. In a model, each unit can be dismantled and scaled for construction purposes, and the model provides all information necessary for painting. Models are especially useful to present the scenic design for less traditional proscenium productions and most arena and thrust settings.

Working Drawings

Design elevations and painter's elevations describe the scenery as a finished product: the way it will appear from the front. They are not descriptive of the structure or assembly of the scenery. This information is communicated in working drawings which are prepared by the technical director or studio drafters.

Working drawings are detailed views of the structure of each element of the setting. They frequently contain rear elevations and sectional and pictorial drawings that show all the details the craftspeople will need to know to construct each unit, including the size, shape, grade, and orientation of materials; the placement of hardware; mounting and rigging notes; joining and assembly details; and any handling instructions. Two-dimensional units such as flats are usually drawn as rear elevations; three-dimensional units are drawn as orthographic projections or are presented in pictorial drawings and sectional views. Stock scenery may be drawn as simple outlines to indicate size, placement, and assembly, using inventory reference numbers. Standard hardware symbols approved and adopted by the United States Institute for Theatre Technology (USITT) are used on these drawings as appropriate; the complete catalogue of these symbols is shown in Appendix B. A complete set of design elevations and working drawings is included in Appendix A.

The quantity and type of detail included in working drawings are entirely dependent upon the needs of the production and the knowledge and experience of the technical staff. Few generalizations can be made that apply to all construction situations. Professional shops composed of experienced craftspeople will require less detailed information about basic construction; the greatest concern of these artisans will be the relationship of parts and the finished appearance of the settings. Knowledge of basic construction practice will be assumed, and there will be little need to draw detailed views of standard units. It is not uncommon for professional shops to work primarily or entirely from designer's elevations or demountable models with only a few added notes from the designer or technical director. Some educational and community theatres where the majority of construction is performed directly by the designer may also use this approach. Many community, educational, and regional theatres need the additional information provided in complete, detailed working drawings. Due to the broad range of needs, the specific layout and content of working drawings must be determined individually for each shop and each production.

Exercises

Do each of the following exercises as a properly laid-out drawing. Plan the page carefully, allowing spaces for titles, dimensions, and notes. Be sure to include a title block or strip and a border. Use proper lettering, symbols, and dimensions. Do not be surprised if it is necessary to do a drawing more than once to achieve a proper visual quality and degree of neatness.

1. Review the symbols for plans in Figure 3–2. Draw a sample of each symbol. Assume all door, arch, and window openings in symbols 2 through 7 are 3′-0″ wide.

2. Reproduce the platform shown in Figures 3–10 through 3–18 in a scale of ¼″ = 1′-0″.

3. Reproduce the stairway shown in Figures 3–23 through 3–30 in a scale of ½ = 1′-0″.

4. Reproduce the object shown in Figure 3–31a and b in a scale of 1″ = 1′-0″.

5. In a scale of ½″ = 1′-0″ draw an accurate plan of your bedroom, apartment, or dorm room. Include all walls, windows, doors, stairs, drapes, and furniture.

6. Lay a sheet of tracing paper or drafting vellum over the plan of your room. Working freehand, sketch the room as if it were a proscenium setting for the theatre. Remove one wall of the set and angle (or "rake") the side walls out at an angle. Develop that sketch as follows:
   a. A production ground plan in the scale of ½″ = 1′-0″.
   b. A designer's ground plan in the scale of ½″ = 1′-0″.
   c. A furniture plot in the scale of ¼″ = 1′-0″.

7. Draw a design elevation of each wall of the "set" drawn in Exercises 5a and 5b. Refer to the Appendix for guidance.

8. Find an interesting table that you like.
   a. Draw the table as an orthographic projection in the scale of 1″ = 1′-0″.
   b. Draw at least two different sectional views of the table. They may be included in the orthographic projections or may be separate drawings.
   c. Draw the table as an isometric projection showing the top of the table. Use a scale of 1½″ = 1′-0″.
   d. Draw the table as an isometric projection showing the underside of the table. Use a scale of 1″ = 1′-0″.
   e. Make a cabinet drawing of the table in a scale of ½″ = 1′-0″.

9. Find a photograph of an interesting fireplace. Develop a working drawing of the fireplace as a set piece. Make the drawing in any convenient scale *larger* than ½″ = 1′-0″. Assume you are drawing for a talented but inexperienced carpenter—make all of the decisions the carpenter would ordinarily make. Use as many views as necessary to communicate the means and materials of construction.

10. Return to your drawings for Exercises 6 and 7. Using the designer's ground plan and front elevations as guides, draw a complete set of working drawings for the "set" you have designed. Assume the "set" is to be constructed from flats, platforms, or other standard theatrical elements. Expect the crew working from the drawings to be talented but inexperienced. Include complete details and be sure to use proper hardware symbols as shown in Appendix B.

97

4

Perspective Drawing

INTRODUCTION

Drawing techniques presented in previous chapters provide the production staff with the information necessary to construct scenery and props and to place them on stage. These drawings tell the shop carpenter the size, shape, materials, and techniques of construction; they are used to translate the designer's ideas into actual objects and space. Before decisions can be made about details of construction, the designer must first determine the appearance of the setting. This conception must be expressed in some visual manner. A practical means for this expression is the scenic rendering. A **rendering** is a pencil or ink drawing or a painting of the design idea. Whatever materials and techniques the designer chooses for the rendering, the process usually begins with a perspective drawing of the setting as the designer intends it to appear on stage.

When in daily conversation we use the phrase "to put things into perspective," we are referring to the need to find the proper relationship between objects or ideas. **Perspective drawing** is a method of showing on a two-dimensional surface the proper relationship between three-dimensional objects and space. This process is known as **foreshortening.** The sensation of foreshortening is experienced in daily life. As we observe a bus in the distance moving toward us it appears very small, but as it gets closer it appears to get larger; once the bus has passed it again appears to diminish in size. The bus does not physically change in size. Experience tells us that objects in the distance *appear* smaller than those same objects close to us. We may also notice that neither the color nor the details of the bus are clearly apparent at a distance but that as the bus gets closer, the color becomes more intense and the details of the bus become clearer. If we observe the bus at a distance through a window while standing inside a building, we note that the wall surrounding the window becomes a frame to the scene. Everything within the frame is logically related in size, detail, and color. Now imagine the window as a canvas and the scene through the window painted on the canvas. This street scene then becomes a picture in perspective. The objects in the distance are in *proportionate relationship* to each other and to the objects in the foreground. They are not, however, measurable in the sense of an orthographic or isometric projection. The graphic artist and the scene designer, either by training or perception, learn to create perspective drawings that show proportionate relationships.

Definitions

Perspective drawing is a mathematical system of creating proportional relationships between objects; as a result, specific definitions and rules apply. The perspective scene is viewed from a single, predetermined location called the **observation point (OP)** (Figure 4–1). The picture is viewed on a plane that is analogous to the window in the example above and which becomes equivalent to the surface on which the drawing is to be made. This surface is called the **picture plane (PP).** The line that forms the base of the picture plane is called the **ground line (GL).** Traditionally for the proscenium theatre, the observation

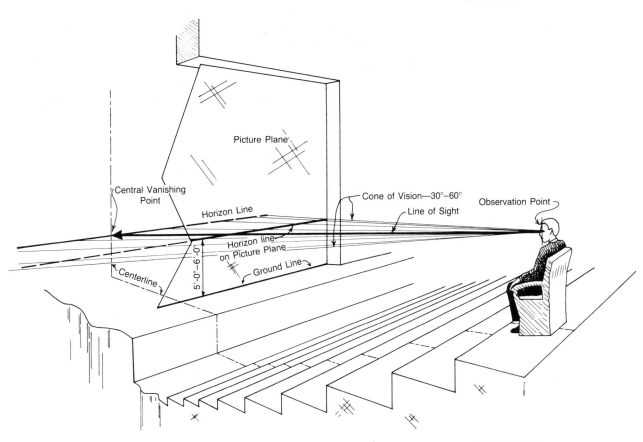

FIGURE 4–1

*The elements of a perspective drawing. The **observation point** is located on the centerline of the drawing and is the position from which the drawing is viewed. It is usually located on the centerline at the same height above the ground line as the **horizon line**. The **picture plane** is the surface on which the scene is projected for drawing and is equivalent to the drawing surface. The base of the picture plane is the **ground line**.*

point is located somewhere near the center of the audience, and the picture plane is located on the plasterline or at the downstage edge of the apron. These locations provide the most representative view of the stage for the majority of proscenium productions. However, a designer may choose a less traditional location for either the observation point or the picture plane in designing for the proscenium theatre and a more arbitrary location in designing for nonproscenium productions. The placement of the observation point and the picture plane are critical to the content of the perspective drawing because they determine the viewing angle of the picture, which is defined as the **cone of vision** from the observation point. A normal cone of vision for theatre application is between 30° and 60° wide. The location of the observation point also determines the height of the **horizon line (HL),** the line on which all horizontal lines not parallel to the picture plane converge. The normal height of the horizon line is between five and six feet above the ground line.

Conventions and Rules

In addition to the definitions above, the following conventions and rules apply:

1. All straight lines remain straight.
2. All vertical lines are perpendicular to the ground line.

3. All horizontal lines and surfaces parallel to the picture plane in the plan remain parallel to the picture plane in the perspective drawing. (Figure 4–2)

4. All horizontal lines at an angle of 90° to the picture plane in the plan recede to the intersection of the horizon line (HL) and the centerline (CL) in the perspective drawing. This point is called the **central vanishing point (CVP).** (Figure 4–2)

FIGURE 4–2

All planes parallel to the picture plane in plan view remain parallel to the picture lane in the drawing. All lines perpendicular to the picture plane recede to the central vanishing point.

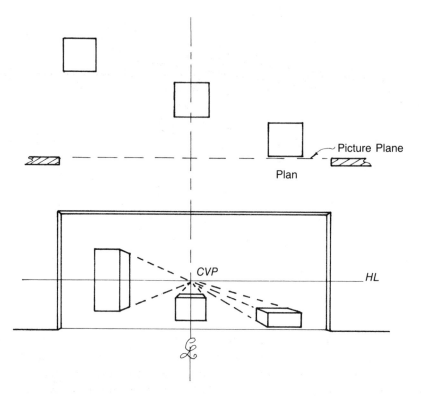

5. All horizontal lines not parallel to the picture plane in the plan incline toward the horizon line; those lines *below* the horizon slant *up* toward the horizon line, those lines *above* the horizon line always slant *down* toward the horizon line. (Figure 4–3)

6. All parallel lines—lines on the same axis—converge to the same point on the horizon line. The location at which the lines converge is called their **vanishing point (VP).** (Figure 4–3)

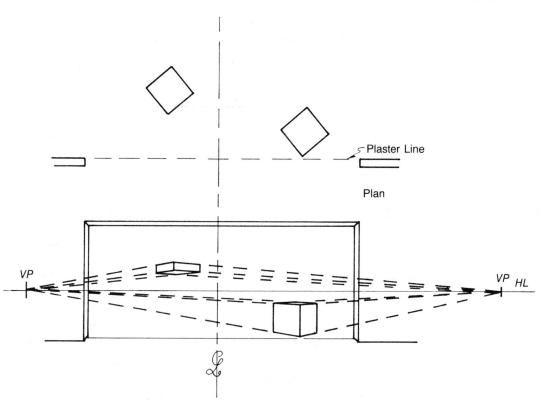

Plaster Line

Plan

VP

VP HL

FIGURE 4–3
All planes neither parallel to nor perpendicular to the picture plane recede to vanishing points located on the horizon line. Parallel planes recede to a common vanishing point.

7. From a normal observation point, the *higher* the horizon line, the *more* floor will be visible; the *lower* the horizon line, the *less* floor will be visible. (Figure 4–4)

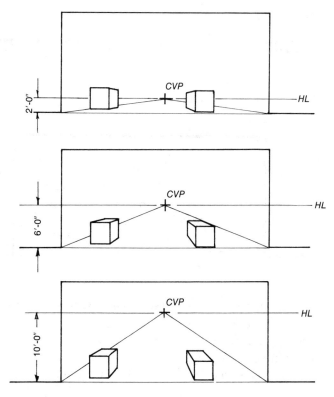

CVP
2'-0"
HL

CVP
6'-0"
HL

CVP
10'-0"
HL

FIGURE 4–4
The higher the horizon line in a perspective sketch, the more floor will be visible.

103

8. The *only* location where a valid measurement may be taken is on the picture plane. All other dimensions are distorted as a result of foreshortening. (Figure 4–5)

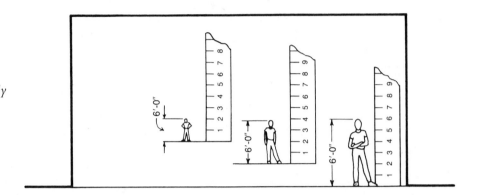

FIGURE 4–5

The picture plane is the only location on the perspective sketch to make accurate measurements.

Perspective drawings may be categorized as either one-point or two-point perspective. These terms refer to the number of vanishing points necessary to draw a form or group of parallel forms. Objects drawn in **one-point perspective** either have no depth or one side of a three-dimensional object is parallel to the picture plane (Figure 4–6). Objects with depth that do not have a surface parallel to the

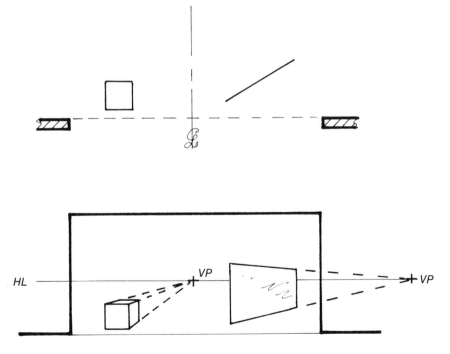

FIGURE 4–6

One-point perspective. a) A three-dimensional object with one plane parallel to the picture plane requires only one vanishing point. b) A two-dimensional object requires only one vanishing point.

picture plane are drawn in **two-point perspective;** that is, two vanishing points are required to draw the form (Figure 4–7). Most settings have scenery and props placed on a variety of axes: each *axis* will have its own vanishing point, and there will be numerous vanishing points for the entire perspective drawing. This method is still two-point perspective

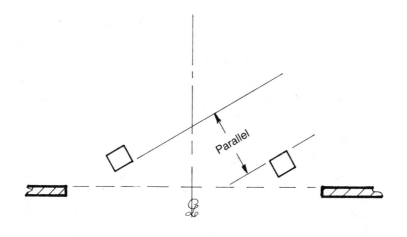

FIGURE 4–7
*Two-point perspective.
Three-dimensional objects not
parallel to the picture plane
requires a vanishing point for
each plane.*

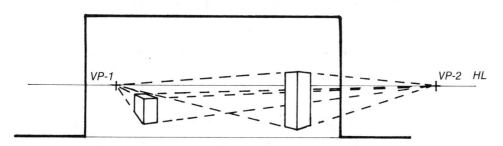

because each object has only two vanishing points. Those vanishing
points may be shared with other objects on the same axis; they may
occur inside or outside the frame of the drawing (Figure 4–7).

Before embarking on the process of drawing in perspective, the
reader may find a summary of the conventions and rules of perspective
drawing to be valuable:

1. The position from which the scene is viewed is called the
   observation point (OP). It is normally located at the most
   representative seat in the theatre and establishes the cone of
   vision for the scene at an angle between 30° and 60°.

2. A location must be selected on which the drawing will be
   based; this surface is called the picture plane and is usually
   set at the plaster line or at the edge of the apron for the
   proscenium stage. The baseline of the picture plane is called
   the ground line (GL).

3. The horizon line (HL) is normally located at a height above
   the ground line that is parallel with the height of the eye at
   the observation point. The normal location of the horizon
   line is five to six feet above the ground line.

4. All parallel horizontal lines converge on the horizon line at
   a common point called the vanishing point (VP), which may
   or may not be within the picture plane.

5. All horizontal lines perpendicular to the picture plane have
   their vanishing point at the intersection of the centerline of

105

the drawing and the horizon line. This point is called the central vanishing point (CVP).

6. All straight lines remain straight.

7. All vertical lines are drawn perpendicular to the ground line.

8. All horizontal surfaces and lines parallel with the picture plane remain parallel with the picture plane.

9. All horizontal lines not parallel with the picture plane incline toward the horizon line.

10. The lower the horizon line, the less floor is visible in the drawing; the higher the horizon line the more floor is visible.

11. Objects in the foreground appear larger than objects in the distance.

12. Objects in the foreground reveal more detail and are more intense in color than objects in the distance.

PROCEDURE FOR MAKING A PERSPECTIVE DRAWING

1. **Figure 4–8.**
   Lay out the ground plan in proper scale on a clean sheet of paper. Beginning at the downstage right edge of the set, label each junction of the walls, as in the example—A, B, C, D, E, F, G, H. Carefully mark and label the centerline (CL) and the plaster line (PL). Tape the ground plan near the top edge of the drawing board. Tape a second sheet of paper to the board directly below the plan.

2. **Figure 4–8.**
   Using the triangle and T-square, extend the centerline of the plan onto the new sheet of paper. Also, drop the lines forming the stage-right and stage-left edges of the proscenium arch to the new sheet of paper. Label these lines PPR and PPL (picture-plane right and picture-plane left). A few inches above the bottom edge of the new sheet of paper, draw a horizontal line between PPR and PPL. Label this line GL (ground line). Measure the height of the proscenium arch on the centerline from the ground line. Draw a horizontal line at this height between PPR and PPL. These four lines create the frame of the picture plane for the perspective drawing. Measure 6'-0" up from the ground line on the centerline, and draw a horizontal line the entire width of the paper at this height. Label this line HL (horizon line).

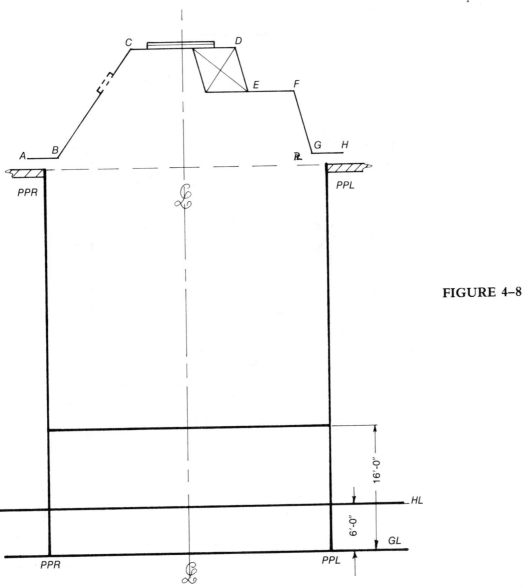

FIGURE 4–8

3. Figure 4–9.

The observation point will be located on the centerline below the plan. In a perspective drawing with a narrow cone of vision, the observation point may occur within or below the picture plane; the wider the cone of vision, the closer the observation point will occur to the plan. In the example, a 60° cone of vision is used. Working on the plan and using a protractor, measure an angle of 30° (one-half the cone of vision) toward the centerline and below the intersection of PPR and the plaster line. Using a lightweight line, connect the intersection of PPR and the plaster line to the centerline below the plan by passing a line through the 30° mark just made. Repeat on the opposite side. Label the point where the three lines cross OP (observation point). Keeping point OP, erase these diagonals PPR and PPL between the plaster line and the picture plane. These lines are no longer needed.

107

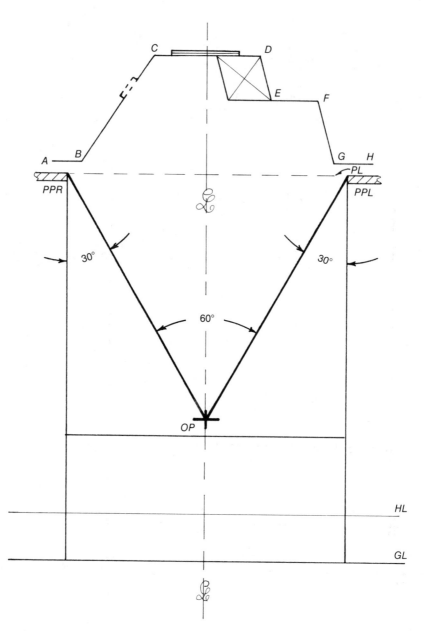

FIGURE 4–9

Note: In the examples throughout this section all *new* lines are drawn with **thick** lines for clarity, although the instructions may call for a lightweight line.

4. **The vanishing points will occur on the horizon line (HL) but are found first on the plasterline (PL).**

   Because lines AB, CD, EF, and GH are parallel to the plasterline and thus to the picture plane, they will have no vanishing points. Also, because lines DE and FG are parallel to each other, they will have the same vanishing points. Thus it will be necessary to find only two vanishing points to draw the major wall elements of this setting, one for wall BC, which will be called Vanishing Point-1 (VP-1), and one for walls DE and FG, which will be called Vanishing Point-2 (VP-2).

a. **Figure 4–10.** Using a lightweight line, construct a perpendicular to wall BC that will extend below the plan; label this line BC'. Construct a perpendicular to BC' that will cross through OP. Extend the perpendicular from OP to the plasterline. It will occur stage left of the plan. Label this point #1. Using the T-square and triangle, drop a vertical from point #1 to HL. Label the intersection of these lines VP-1.

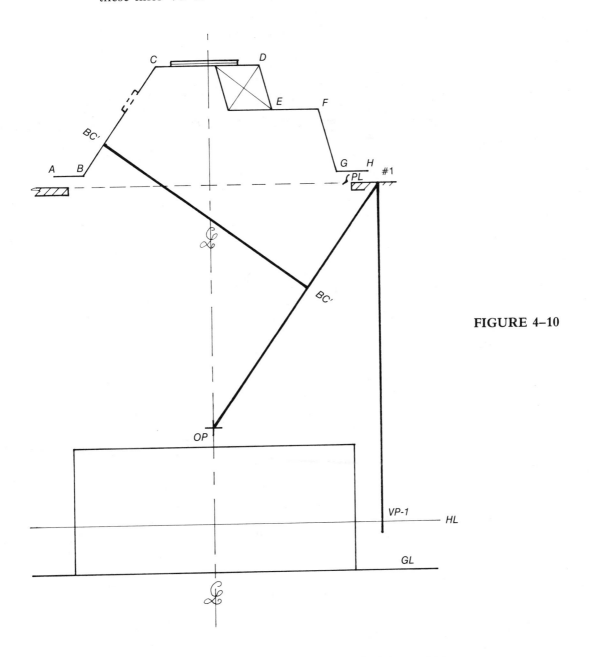

FIGURE 4–10

b. **Figure 4–11.** Repeat the process above to find the vanishing point for wall FG by constructing a lightweight line perpendicular to FG that will extend below the plan. Label this line FG'. Then construct a perpendicular to FG' that crosses through OP. Extend the new line from OP to the

plaster line. It will occur stage right of the centerline.
Label this point #2. Drop a vertical from point #2 to the
HL. Label the intersection of the new vertical and the
horizon line VP-2. Erase the lightweight lines used to find
the vanishing point, since they are no longer needed.

FIGURE 4–11

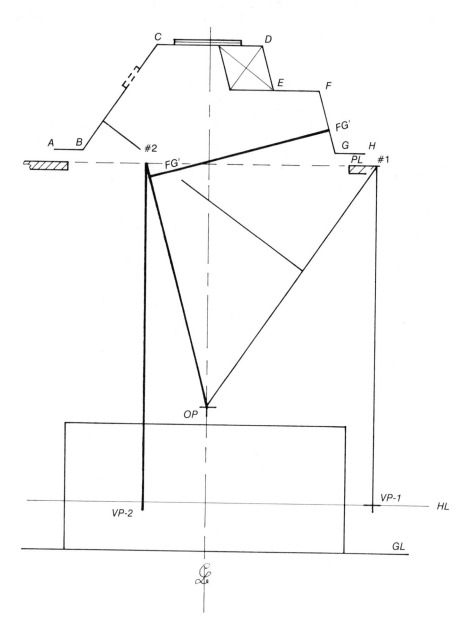

5. Figure 4–12.

On the plan, extend wall BC downstage to the plaster line with a lightweight line. Label this point B″. Drop a vertical from B″ to GL. This vertical will become a measuring line to determine all primary heights in the setting; label the line ML (measuring line).

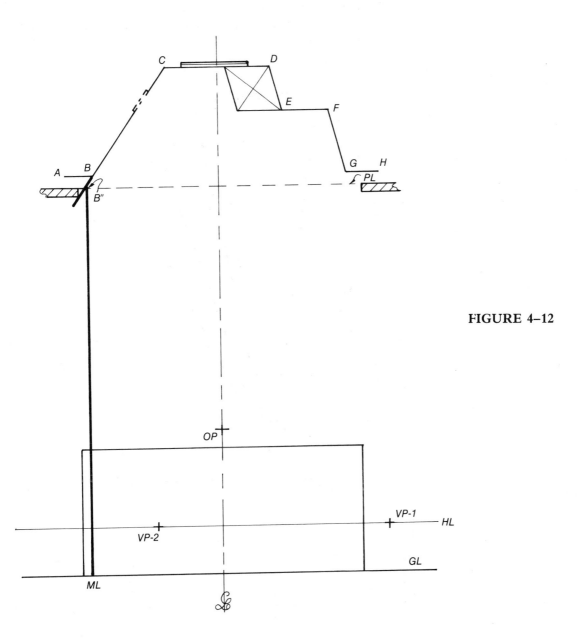

FIGURE 4–12

6. Figure 4–13.

The location of each major corner of the set must be "moved" to the plaster line. Draw a lightweight line from OP to each wall intersection—points B, C, D, E, F, and G. It will not be necessary to locate points A and H, because they fall outside of the picture plane behind the proscenium arch. At the plaster line, label the intersection of each new line to correspond with the point to which it connects—B′, C′, D′, E′, F′, and G′.

FIGURE 4–13

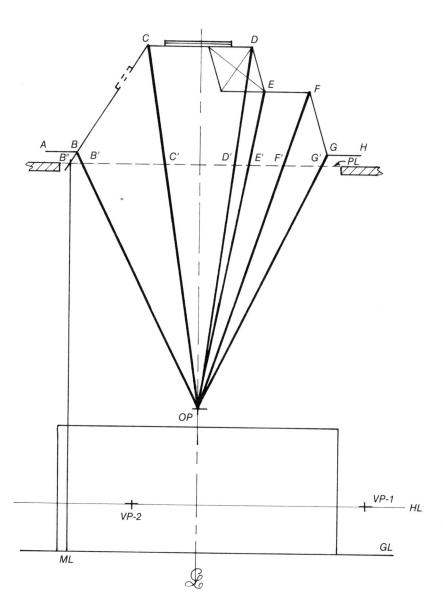

7. Figure 4–14.

Drop a vertical from both B′ and C′ through the picture plane to GL. Draw a lightweight line from the intersection of GL and ML to VP-1.

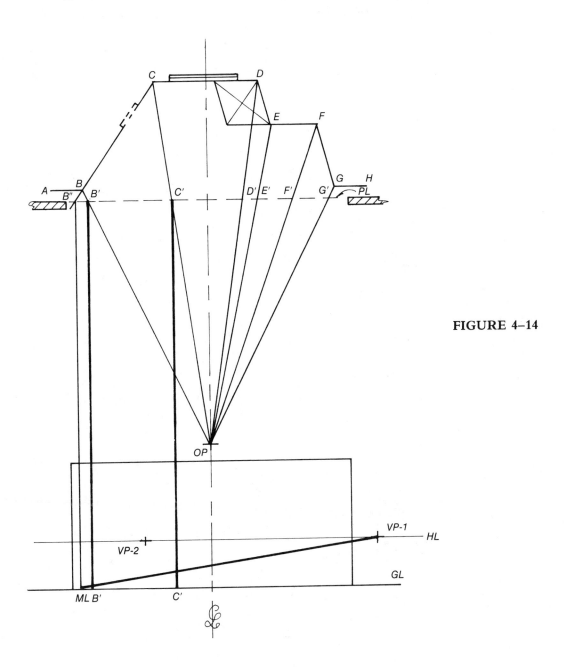

FIGURE 4–14

8. Figure 4–15.

On ML, measure the height of wall BC from GL. In the example the wall is 14′-0″ tall. With a lightweight line, connect the measurement to VP-1. The area defined by the lines drawn from ML to VP-1, and the lines dropped from B′ and C′ outline wall BC. The portion of the lines enclosing this area may be darkened, and all other lines used to draw this area may be erased.

FIGURE 4–15

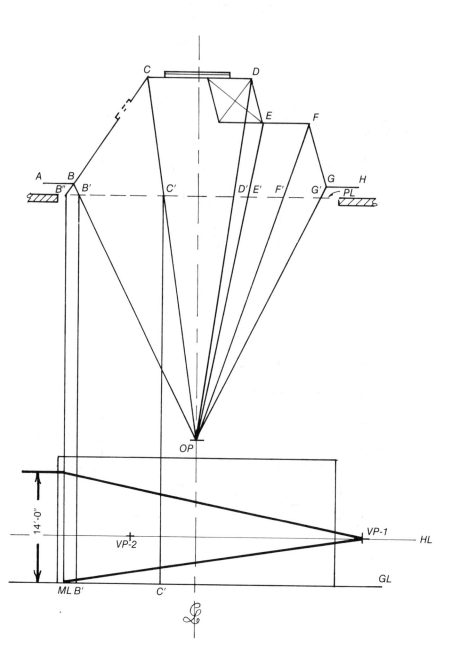

9. Figure 4–16.

Drop a vertical from D′ through the picture plane. Because wall CD is parallel to the picture plane, it will not have a vanishing point. Also because wall CD is the same height as wall BC, it will not be necessary to determine its height; that height is given at the upstage edge of wall BC. To draw wall CD, connect a horizontal line from the bottom upstage corner of wall BC to line D′, and connect the top upstage corner of wall BC to line D′ with another horizontal line. Lines C′, D′, and the two new horizontal lines form the outline of wall CD.

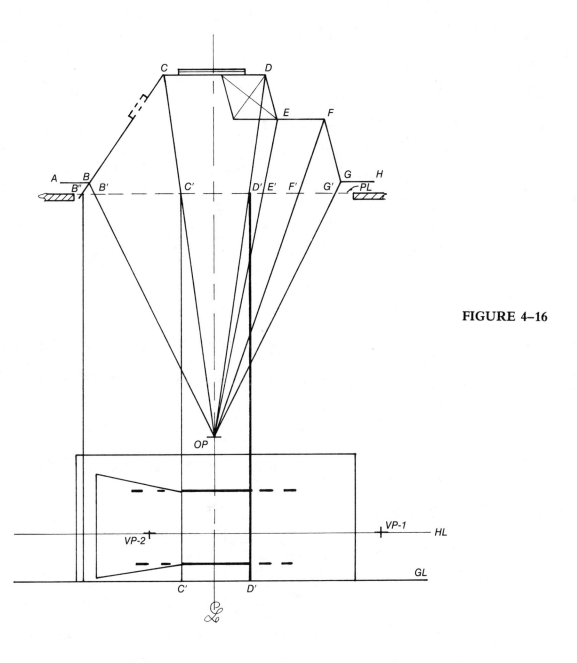

FIGURE 4–16

10. Figure 4–17.

Although wall DE occurs on a platform, it will be easier to draw the wall first and add the platform later. Begin by dropping a vertical from point E′ to GL. Wall DE is the same height as the other walls; however, it has a different vanishing point because it is neither parallel to the picture plane nor parallel to wall BC. Wall DE uses Vanishing Point-2 (VP-2). Using the stage left corner of wall CD as the guide for height, draw a line from VP-2 through the top stage-left corner of wall CD, and continue the line to vertical E′. Draw a second line from VP-2 through the bottom stage-left corner of wall CD, and continue to vertical E′. Wall DE is now defined by the two new diagonal lines and the verticals D′ and E′.

FIGURE 4–17

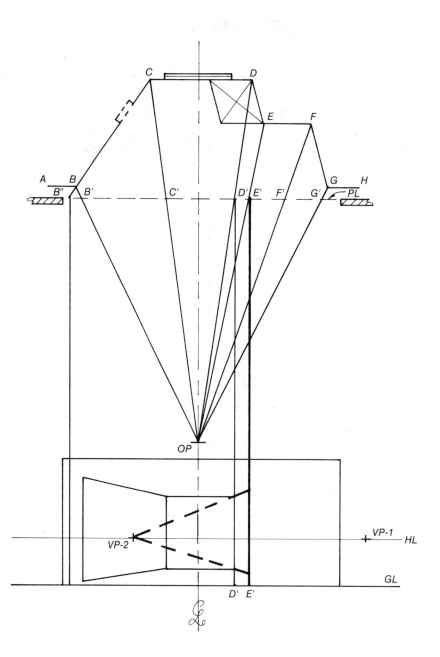

11. Figure 4–18.

Wall EF is parallel to the picture plane and to wall CD; therefore it has no vanishing point and is drawn with horizontal lines. The wall can be drawn by simply dropping a vertical from point F′ and connecting the top and bottom stage-left corners of wall DE to line F′ with a pair of horizontal lines.

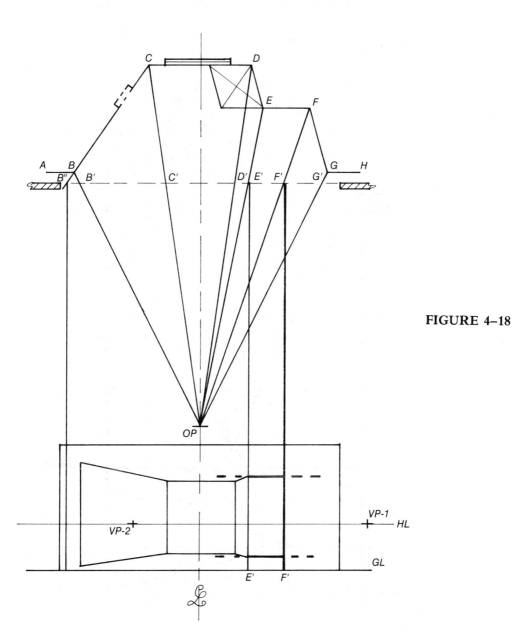

FIGURE 4–18

12. Figure 4–19.

Wall FG is parallel to wall DE and will thus use the same vanishing point. Begin by dropping a vertical from G′. Following the same procedure as described in step 10 above, connect VP-2 with the top stage-left corner of wall EF, and continue the line to G′; then connect VP-2 with the bottom stage-left corner of wall EF, and continue to G′.

FIGURE 4–19

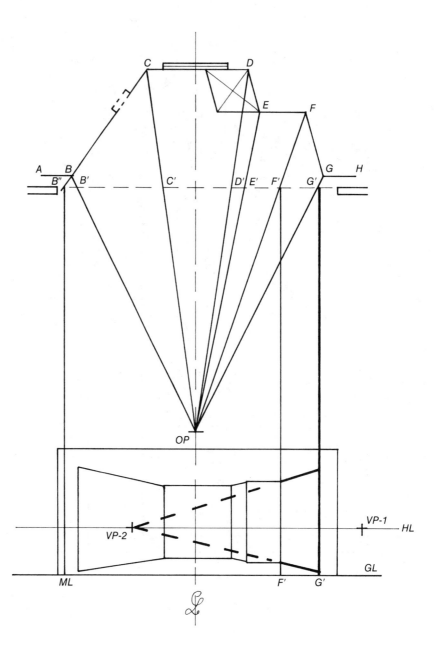

13. Figure 4–20.

Walls AB and GH can now be drawn. Since these walls are also parallel to the picture plane (and to walls CD and EF), they will not have a vanishing point. The visible portion of these walls may be drawn with horizontal lines connecting the top and bottom corners of wall BC to the stage-right edge of the picture plane, and connecting the top and bottom corners of wall FG to the stage-left edge of the picture plane. These steps complete the perspective construction of the basic walls of the setting. At this point, only outlines of the walls appear. The drawing process continues in the following manner.

The next major element of the setting to be drawn is the one-foot-high platform stage left. To simplify the task, all lines that are not part of the drawing within the picture plane should be removed, with the exception of line ML.

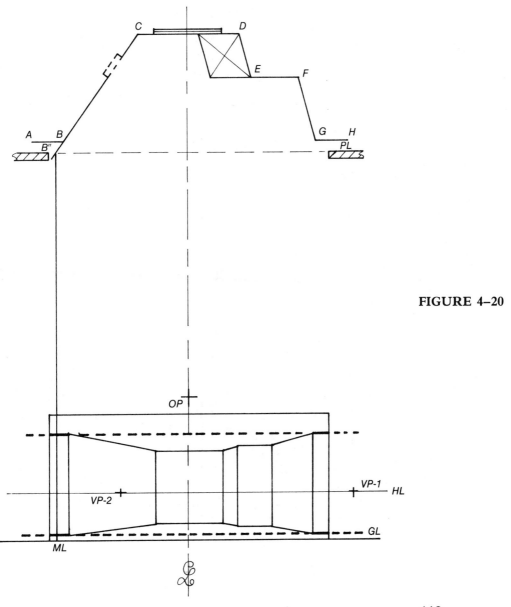

FIGURE 4–20

14. **Figure 4–21.**

    On the plan, label the two on-stage corners of the platform I and J. Draw a line from OP to I and to J and label the points that cross the plaster line I′ and J′, respectively. Drop a vertical from I′ and J′ into the picture plane.

15. **Figure 4–21.**

    Since the platform rests on the floor, the bottom edge may be easily found. The downstage edge of the platform is an extension toward stage right of the bottom of wall EF until that line crosses J′. Since IJ is parallel to DE, the lines forming the stage-right edge of the platform will use VP-2. Draw a line from the on-stage corner of JE to VP-2. It should connect with the intersection of I′ and with the bottom of CD. The outline of the bottom edge of the platform is now complete.

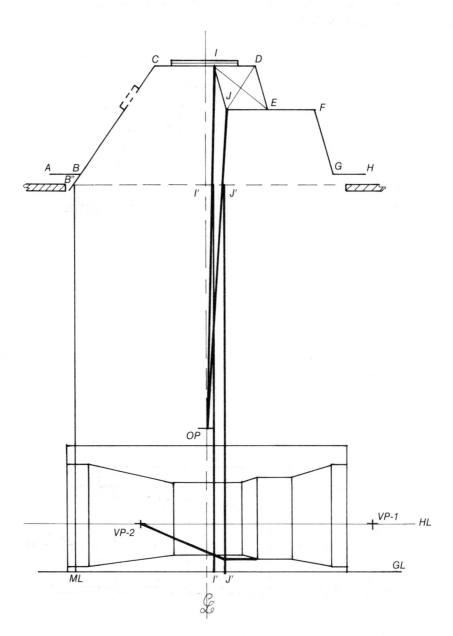

FIGURE 4–21

16. Figure 4–22.

To find the top of the platform, measure a height of 1'-0"
on line ML. Using VP-1 to determine the angle, extend a
line from this one-foot mark to line C'. Now extend the
line as a horizontal across wall CD to D'.

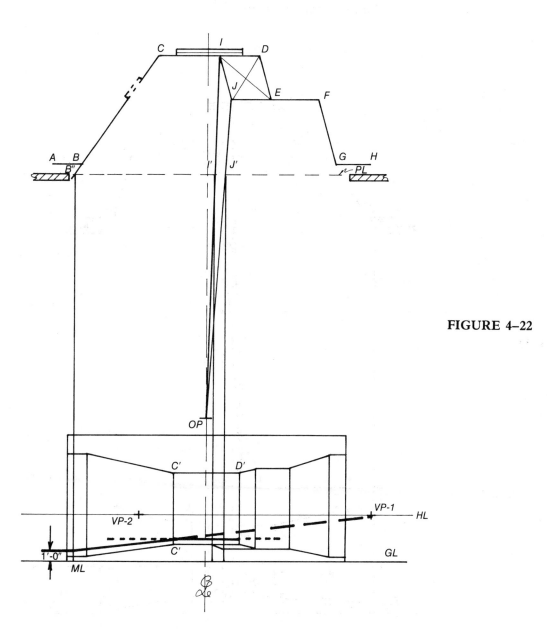

FIGURE 4–22

17. Figure 4–23.

Using VP-2 to determine the angle, extend the one-foot-high line to E′. Draw a horizontal from E′ to J′ at the same height. Finally, connect this one-foot high line to CD, where the extended one-foot-high line crosses I′. Erase the lines "inside" the platform.

FIGURE 4–23

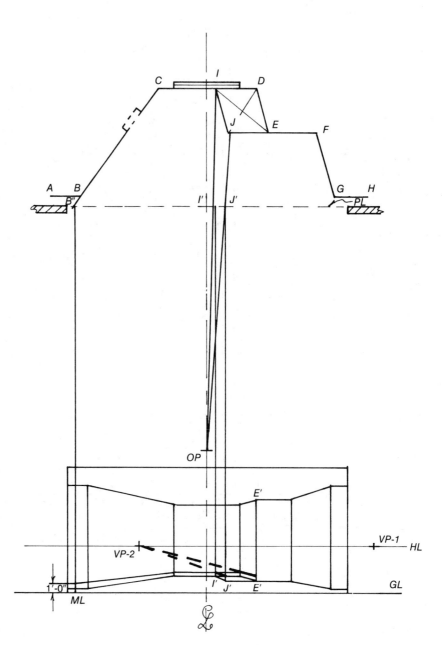

18. Figure 4–24.

The arch may now be constructed. On the plan, label each corner of the arch and the reveal (thickness)—in the example, K, L, M, and N. Starting at OP again, draw a line to each newly labeled point. Where each new line crosses the plaster line, label the lines K′, L′, M′, and N′, respectively. Drop verticals from K′ and L′ into the picture plane. Measure the height of the 7′-0″ door opening on ML, and attach this point to VP-1.

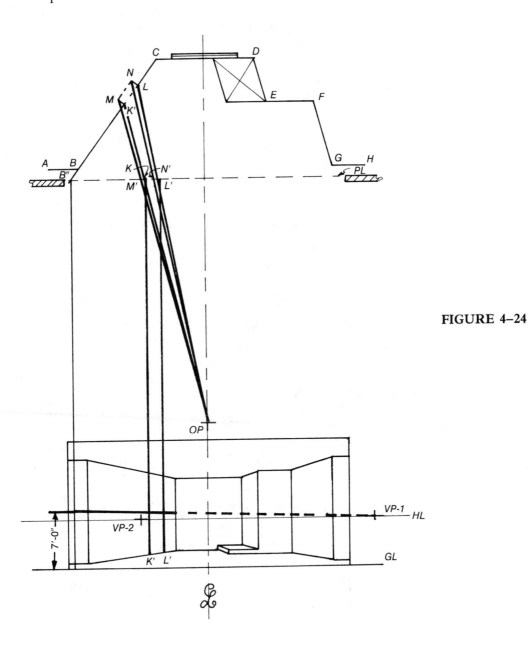

FIGURE 4–24

19. Figure 4–25.

Drop a vertical from N' into the picture plane. Vertical M' will be hidden behind wall BC and will not be necessary for the drawing. The reveal LN is on a different axis from all surfaces drawn thus far. It will be necessary to find the vanishing point for this new axis by returning to step #4 and following the procedure of constructing perpendiculars. There is an alternative method of drawing wall LN if the vanishing point occurs off the paper. In this case, the following procedure can be utilized. On the plan, extend wall CD toward stage right, the same distance as the width of the reveal. Also, measure that same distance on wall AB, from point B toward point A. Install a "phantom wall" on the plane defined by these two points, and extend the wall to the plaster line. The "phantom wall" is parallel to wall BC. Draw a line from OP to each of these new points, and drop

FIGURE 4–25

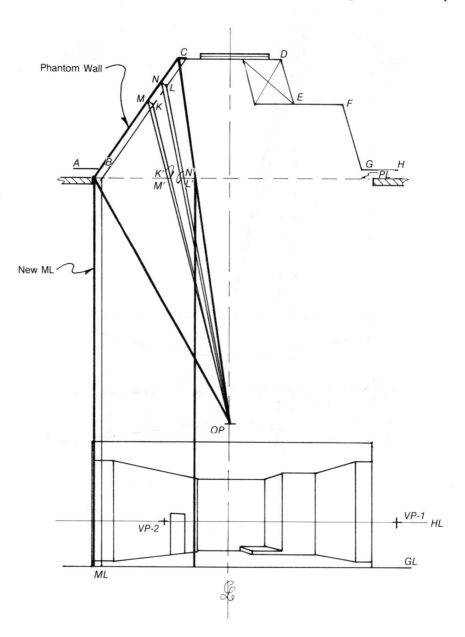

verticals to the picture plane. The furthest downstage line
will be a new measuring line.

20. Figure 4–26.

Attach the intersection of the new measuring line and GL
to VP-1 with a lightweight line. Now mark the height of
the arch (7'-0") on the new measuring line, and attach that
seven-foot mark to VP-1 with a lightweight line. Draw a
line—from the intersection of L' and the top of the arch on
wall BC, to the intersection of N' and the line from the new
ML, to VP-1 on the phantom wall. Also, draw a line at the
bottom of the opening—from the intersection of L' and wall
BC to N' and the line from the intersection of GL and the
new ML that goes to VP-1. Erase the phantom wall and all
lines associated with it, leaving the outline of the arch and
reveal. Also erase the lines crossing the bottom of the arch
opening.

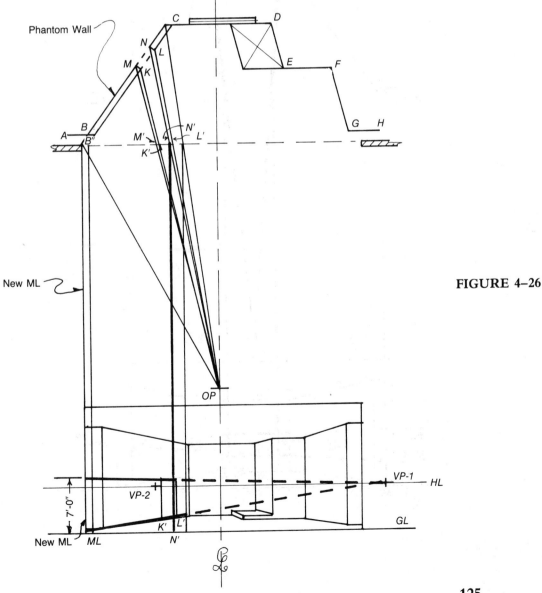

FIGURE 4–26

21. Figure 4–27.

On the plan, label each corner of the window opening O, P, Q, and R. Draw a line from OP to each newly labeled point. Label each line from OP to correspond with the proper point: O′, P′, Q′, and R′. Drop verticals from O′ and P′ into the picture plane. The top of the window is also 7′-0″ high. Since wall CD is parallel to the picture plane, all horizontal lines on that surface will remain horizontal. Returning to the 7′-0″ mark on ML, draw a lightweight line to VP-1. Where that line crosses C′, draw a horizontal line across CD. Measure 3′-4″ on ML from the ground line; connect that point to VP-1. Where this new line crosses C′, draw a horizontal across CD.

FIGURE 4–27

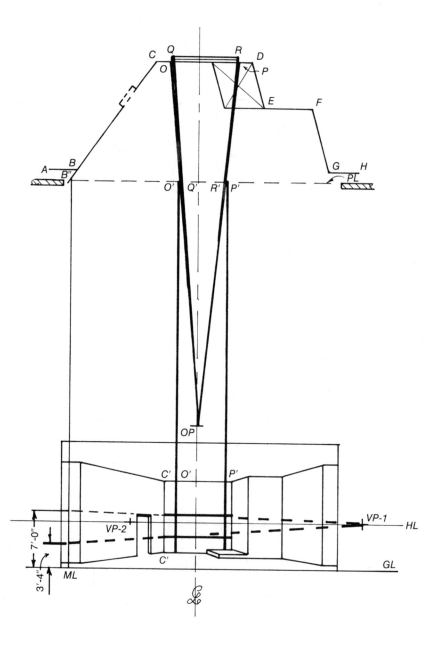

22. Figure 4–28.

Drop verticals from Q′ and R′ into the picture plane. The verticals should appear between lines O′ and P′. The vanishing point for the window reveal will be the central vanishing point (CVP). Attach each corner of the window opening to CVP. Erase all lines between Q′ and R′.

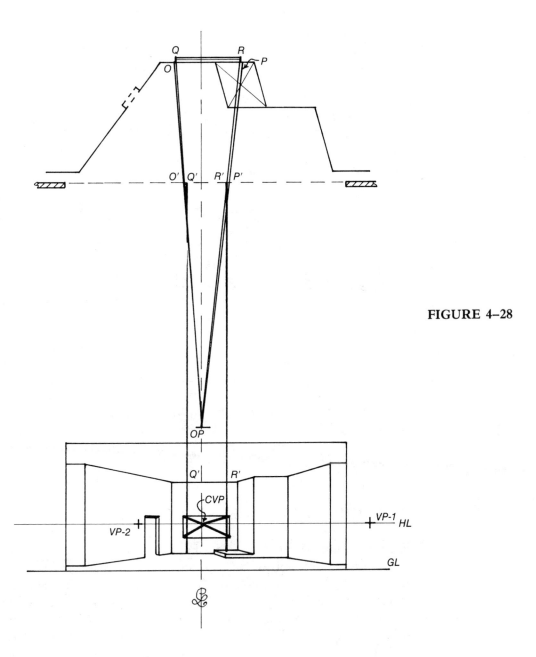

FIGURE 4–28

The perspective sketch of the basic setting is now complete (Figure 4–29). Settings usually have furniture within them. If furniture is placed against a wall, it can be drawn in a manner similar to the platform in this example. If the furniture occurs away from a wall, a phantom wall may be constructed from the furniture to the nearest wall to determine heights in a manner similar to the phantom wall used to construct reveal LN. It may be necessary to establish additional vanishing points if furniture is on a different axis from any of the walls. Or it may be more convenient, depending upon the location of the furniture, to establish a new measuring line for each furniture piece. Furniture offers an additional complication: seldom is it rectangular. The most practical means to draw furniture in perspective is carefully to draw a perspective box with various planes that establish the primary planes of the furniture; the actual shape and details of the furniture can be sketched into the rectilinear perspective frame freehand.

FIGURE 4–29

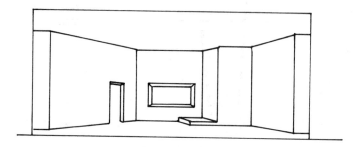

Once the drawing is completed, the details can be sketched to complete the stage picture. It is usually preferable to trace the completed perspective drawing on clean paper, eliminating working lines and erasures. The tracing must be done with extreme care, since errors as small as a pencil point will distort the perspective view. It is also important to know that the smaller the scale of the perspective drawing, the more difficult the drawing task, and the more severe any errors will appear. Most designers prefer to work in ½″ scale.

MEASURING-LINE PERSPECTIVE

The process described above, vanishing-point perspective, provides an accurate representation of the designer's intention for the appearance of the setting. Frequent utilization of this mechanical process can become a tedious task, especially when numerous productions may be designed for the same or similar theatres. An alternative system of perspective drawing, measuring-line perspective, is available to designers working regularly in consistent or similar spaces. This alternative system requires an understanding of the mechanical system described above; it also requires an initial investment of time to develop a permanent layout. The advantage of the measuring-line system is that once the grids have been developed, a perspective drawing of a setting can be made quite rapidly and much less drawing space is required.

Measuring-line perspective consists of two permanent grids that become underlays for all future perspective drawings. To make the underlays permanent, it is recommended that they be inked in their final form on high-quality vellum, bristol board, or hot-press illustration board. Both grids should be drawn in the rendering scale the designer usually uses, normally ¼″ or ½″ = 1′-0″.

Measuring-Line Perspective—Permanent Parts

1. **Figure 4–30.**

   The first step in this method consists of a simple graph of the acting area. An accurate plan of the empty stage is drawn, showing the apron, proscenium arch, and back wall of the theatre. The plan is then divided into a grid with each square two feet wide and two feet deep. (The use of ¼″ scale may necessitate limiting each square to a four-foot-by-four-foot area.) Beginning at the centerline, draw downstage-to-upstage lines that divide the space equally on either side of the centerline. If the acting area is not divisible by two, extend the grid beyond the edge of the proscenium on each side to an even dimension. Label each line at the plasterline or at the apron, whichever will be the usual location of the picture plane. Beginning at the centerline, count each line toward stage right and then toward stage left.

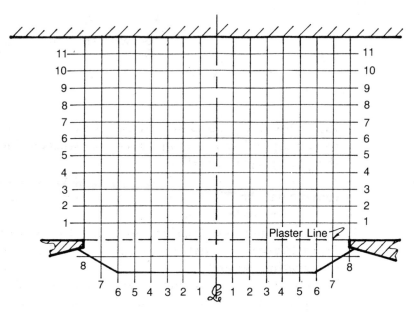

FIGURE 4–30
Measuring-line perspective floor grid.

2. **Beginning at the location of the picture plane (either the plaster line or the edge of the apron), divide the up- and down-stage space into two-foot-wide sections.**

   Label the lines from downstage to upstage by numbering them 1, 2, 3, and so forth. The result should be a graph of the acting area with each square equaling two feet.

3. **Figure 4–31.**

   On a clean sheet of vellum or illustration board, draw the picture plane, inserting the centerline; place the horizon line at 6′-0″. Label the intersection of these two lines CVP.

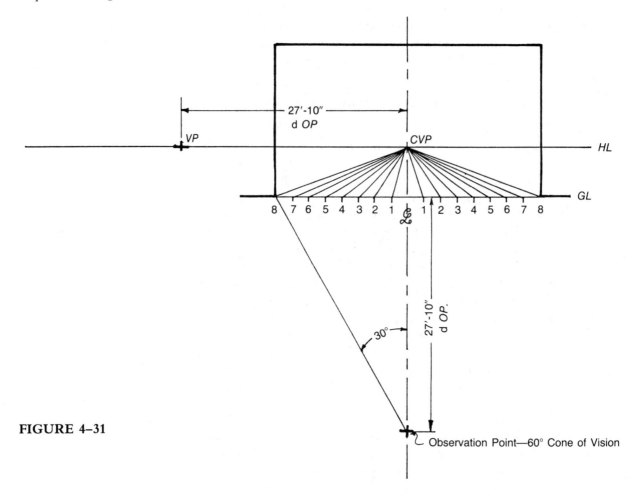

FIGURE 4–31

4. **Just below the ground line, mark off two-foot divisions to correspond with the upstage-to-downstage lines on the plan prepared earlier.**

   Since these lines are at 90° to the picture plane, they will converge at the central vanishing point. Draw a line from each of the labeled marks to the CVP.

5. **Using the process described in step #3 of Vanishing-Point Perspective, determine the distance to a normal observation point.**

   For a 32'-0"-wide proscenium opening, a 60° cone of vision will place the observation point 27'-10" from the picture plane. It is necessary only to find the *distance* to the observation point. That location will serve no other function; label that distance d-OP. Extend the horizon line to *stage* **right** of the picture plane—a sufficient length to measure d-OP in that direction from the centerline. Label this new point VP. (*The distance from the* **plasterline** *to OP should equal the distance from the* **centerline** *to VP.*) Point VP determines the location of the vanishing point for a 45° line within the acting area. Since only the distance to the observation point is needed, the process of finding the vanishing point is simplified. This vanishing point will be used to determine the perspective depth of the stage and each onstage-offstage grid line in the picture plane.

6. **Figure 4–32.**

Determine the depth of the acting area in the plan. Measure that same distance (in the example, 24'-0") from the *stage-right edge of the picture plane* (the same side as point VP) *toward the stage-left edge* of the picture plane. Label that point A. Draw a line from A to VP.

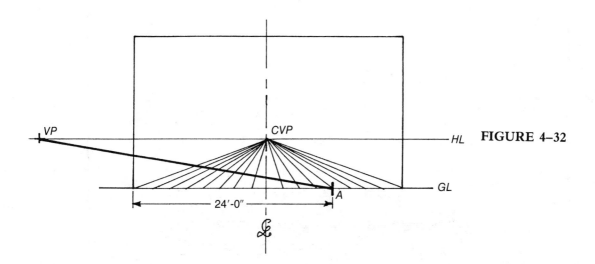

FIGURE 4–32

7. **Figure 4–33.**

Where line A-VP crosses the furthest offstage diagonal line drawn to CVP, draw a horizontal across all of the up- and downstage lines. This line is the upstage edge of the acting area. Label this horizontal to correspond with the furthest upstage horizontal on the plan.

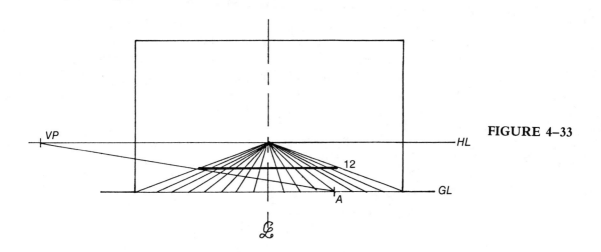

FIGURE 4–33

8. Figure 4–34.

Where line A-VP crosses each of the remaining up- and downstage lines, draw a horizontal across each of the diagonals to CVP. Label each horizontal to correspond with the same lines on the graphed plan. Erase all lines outside of the grid area.

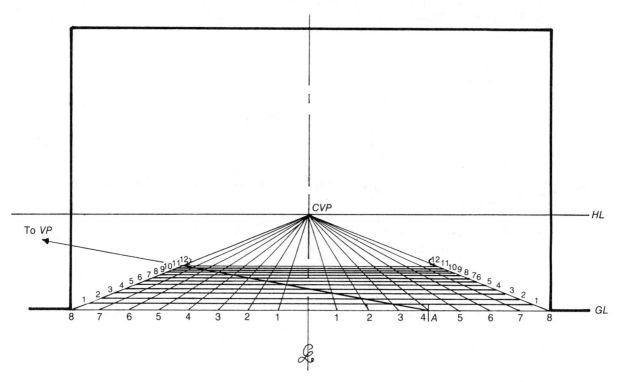

FIGURE 4–34

9. Figure 4–35.

Mark the stage-right and stage-left edges of the picture plane with one-foot increments.

The resulting drawing provides a perspective grid of the acting area floor that corresponds to the grided floor plan. Both grids may now be inked. While working on the perspective drawing, it is helpful to sketch a 6'-0"-tall human figure, just outside the picture plane, to serve as a reference for scale.

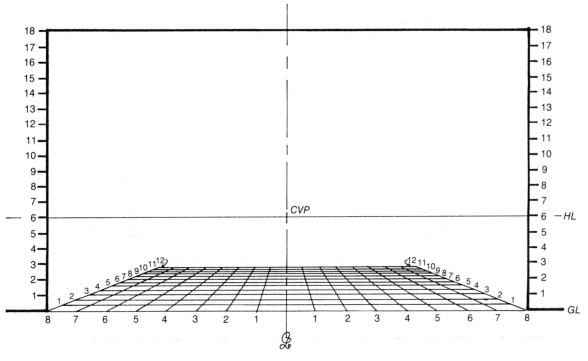

FIGURE 4–35

Use of the Measuring-Line Grids

A perspective drawing on the grid starts with the designer preparing the ground plan of the setting as an overlay on the ground-plan grid. The preferred kind of paper to use is one that allows easy visibility of the graph through the plan. The plaster line and centerline of both drawings must be carefully aligned. The designer then places a clean sheet of tracing paper or vellum over the perspective grid and marks the picture plane, centerline, and horizon line.

1. **Figure 4–36.** Transfer the plan of the setting from the ground plan to the perspective grid, using the coordinates of the two grids to determine locations on the perspective drawing. Install a vertical at each major change of direction.

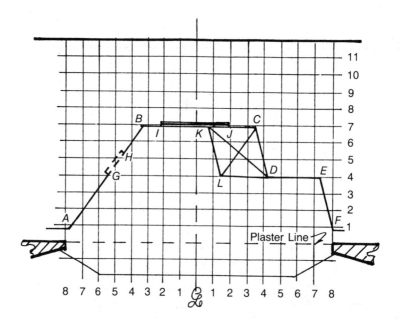

FIGURE 4–36

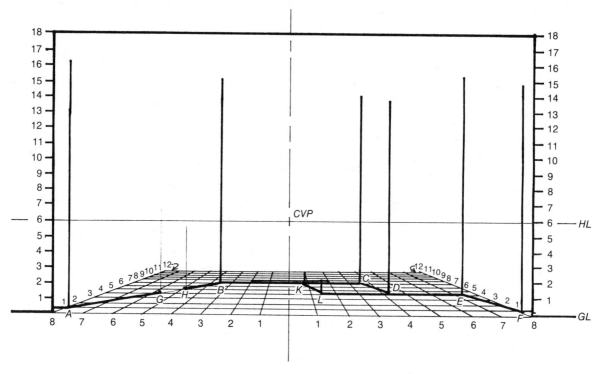

2. **Figure 4–37.** Find the 14'-0" height on the measuring line at stage right. Draw a line from that mark to CVP. Extend a horizontal from the bottom of the furthest downstage right wall to the furthest stage-right grid line. Construct a perpendicular at this point. Where the vertical line crosses the line from ML to CVP, draw a horizontal back to the furthest downstage right vertical. That point is the proper height of the wall.

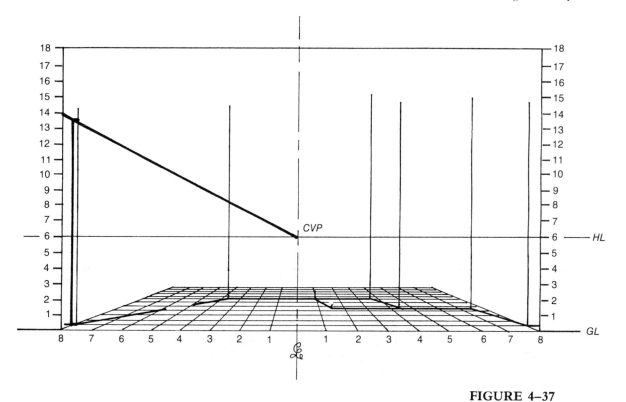

FIGURE 4–37

3. **Figure 4–38.** Repeat this procedure at the upstage corner of the stage-right wall.

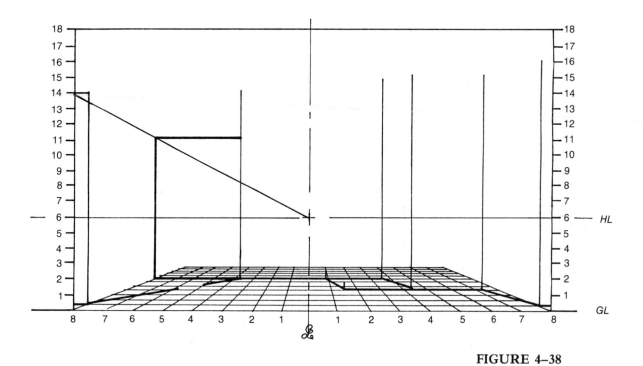

FIGURE 4–38

4. **Figure 4–39.** Connect the two new points. The outline of the stage-right wall has now been drawn.

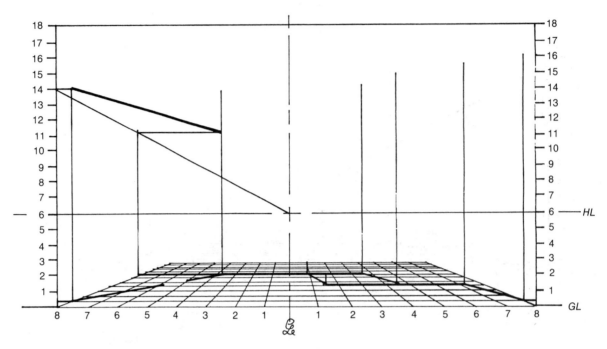

FIGURE 4–39

5. **Figures 4–40 and 4–41.** Repeat this procedure for each element of the setting, using either the stage-right or stage-left measuring line, whichever is more convenient, until all elements of the setting have been outlined (Figure 4–42). Sketch in details to complete the perspective drawing.

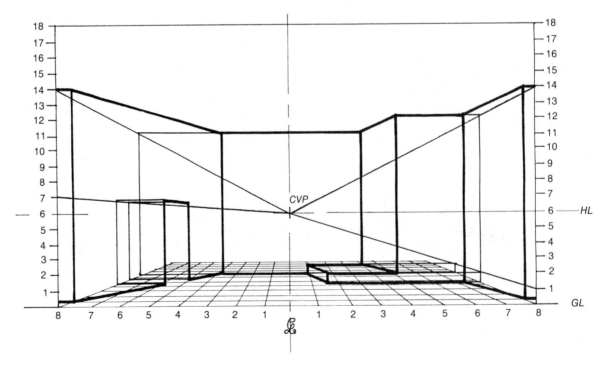

FIGURE 4–40

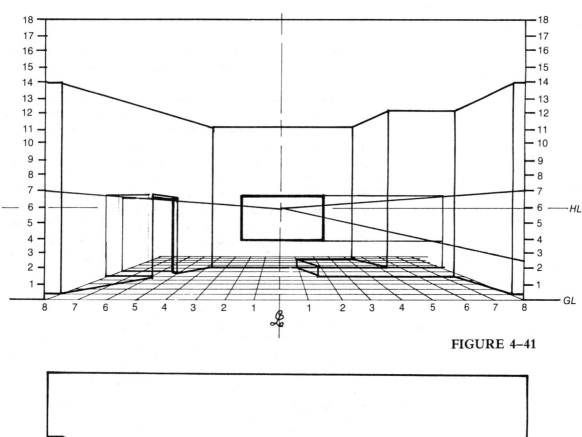

FIGURE 4–41

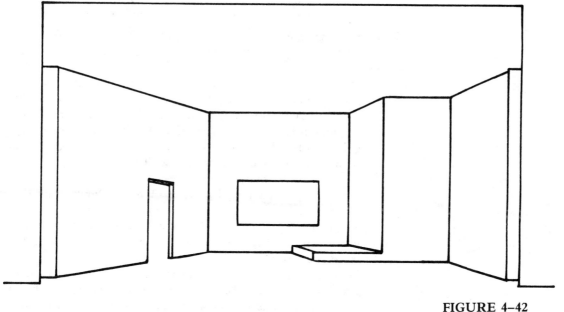

FIGURE 4–42

As the designer becomes increasingly experienced at the techniques of perspective drawing, the procedures will become easier to perform. The designer will also discover that the mechanics of any system eventually become limiting and will find it necessary to expand these mechanical systems with freehand sketching to complete the picture and create the sense of style desired. The mechanical process of perspective drawing, then, becomes a guide for placing and shaping the objects within the space; it should not restrict the designer's work.

The drawings developed thus far have been purely linear, with little consideration given to the treatment of texture, light, shadow, or color. Treatment of these design elements will be discussed in a later chapter.

Exercises

1. A clear perception of perspective in nature—of foreshortening—is helpful to understanding the art of perspective drawing. Some exercises in objective seeing are helpful.

   a. Stand in the middle of a long street lined with trees or telephone poles. Observe the scene carefully for a long time, noting what happens to the trees that are further away from you. Does their size appear to change? Do the colors change? Can you see more details in the nearer trees? If the street is long enough, do the trees or poles seem to converge at a distance? Observe all of this carefully. Try to set aside your customary "knowledge of the world" and really look at what is in front of you.

   b. Stand inside a building and look out of a window. Note the buildings in the distance and all of the natural objects. Consider what happens to color, texture, and degree of visual detail from this point of view. Imagine the scene in front of you painted on the window. Identify the ground line, horizon line, and central vanishing point.

   c. Observe someone walking toward you from a great distance. Notice how the person appears to change in size as he or she gets closer. Notice also that at each step of the way the objects surrounding the person change proportionately. If the person were a child, how would the scene appear differently?

2. Exercises in one-point perspective prepare the mind and hand for more complex work. Applying the rules of perspective, develop one or more of the following sketches.

   a. Draw a picture plane using T-square and triangle. The picture plane should measure twelve inches wide by eight inches high. Draw a horizon line across the picture plane, three inches above the bottom line. Draw the centerline. Identify the central vanishing point. Within this frame, draw an imaginary railroad track lined with telephone poles on either side. The track and poles should diminish to the central vanishing point.

   b. Draw another picture plane as in step 2a. Draw an imaginary street scene with skyscrapers, storefronts, sidewalks, street lights, etc., in one-point perspective. The street should start at the ground line and proceed to the central vanishing point, up the center of the picture plane.

   c. Draw another picture plane as in step 2a. Draw an imaginary street scene as in 2b in one-point perspective. However, this time place the street off-center in the drawing so that two-thirds of the picture plane is covered by the front of one of the buildings. The street will angle to the central vanishing point behind the large building at the front of the picture plane.

3. Although a careful reading of this chapter may be helpful in understanding the procedures of mechanical perspective drawing, the best learning process is performing the task step by step. Reproduce the setting drawn in the vanishing-point-perspective section of this chapter (Figures 4–8 through 4–29).

4. Once you have mastered the technique of vanishing-point perspective following the procedure outlined for the example, develop a perspective sketch for your own ground plan.

5. Develop a measuring-line perspective grid. Draw your own scenic design in perspective on this grid.

CHAPTER 5

Figure Drawing and Costume Rendering

by
Deborah Dryden

INTRODUCTION

Figure drawing is the art of drawing realistic representations of the human form. It is a skill needed by all designers and drafters in the performing arts, especially the costume designer, who is responsible for the creation of all clothing, trimmings, and accessories worn on stage or before the camera. Drafters occasionally have to draw props, scenic units, or accessories that accommodate the human form; they also find that they need to include figures in drawings to establish the scale of an object or space in relation to the body. Scene designers include figures in sketches and renderings not only to establish the proportional relationship of a setting to the actors but also to show ways in which the space may be used.

Makeup and costume designers draw human figures most consistently. Makeup designers must be able to render not only the face but the entire figure in order to coordinate makeup designs with costumes and sometimes to plan makeup for the entire body. Costume designers, of course, must be able to render the figure in a variety of poses and in careful detail to express their design ideas.

Figure drawing is a distinctly different art from mechanical drawing or perspective sketching. In contrast to drafting, figure drawing is a freehand technique that makes little or no use of T-squares, triangles, templates, or the other drawing guides. The subject of figure drawing, the human body, is predetermined for the artist and familiar to all who will view the sketch. In the normal figure, there is a fixed relationship between arms, legs, head, and torso. The placement and general proportion of body parts are predetermined. The artist can select poses, clothing, and gestures but must create a credible sketch of the figure that is reasonably proportioned and balanced. Also, figure drawings are usually three-dimensional. Whether a figure is facing full-front or at an angle to the observer, and whether the figure is standing or seated, there is always some foreshortening of the torso and limbs.

The combination of a generally fixed form and the requirement that it be drawn proportionally correct and in proper perspective creates significant demands on the artist. The work is complicated further because, unlike either of the perspective-drawing methods discussed in the previous chapter, there are few rules or mechanical guides to aid the artist in the development of the basic structure of the human form.

Figure-Drawing Resources

Figure drawing can be learned only by study and practice. Few artists have a natural facility for drawing the human figure. The best way to begin learning is to study the body. Careful observation and analysis of the figure in life and in photographs are essential.

Regular drawing practice is essential for the artist. Whenever possible, drawing should be done from live models, to enhance the knowledge and understanding of the human form and to develop facility at representing the body in sketches. In the absence of live models, a picture source-file can provide the artist with images for study and practice. The **picture source-file** is a collection of photographs and sketches of the figure in various body positions. The file may contain newspaper or magazine photographs; posters; prints of paintings; and detailed illustrations of faces, hands, feet, shoes, and other costume accessories or body details. The picture source-file should provide models for the artist to use in daily drawing practice and references for specific design work. In addition, the illustrations in books on human anatomy can acquaint the artist with the skeletal and muscular structure of the human form. However, neither the source-file nor anatomy books can ever substitute for the experience of drawing from live models.

In addition to a source-file, the artist should keep a **drawing notebook.** This can be a sketch pad or hardbound notebook with blank pages that is a convenient size to carry at all times but not so small as to restrict drawings to a miniature scale. The notebook is used for daily drawing practice and for exercises and drawing experiments. It allows the designer to work out specific drawing problems before tackling the designs for a production; it also provides a constantly available practice pad for the exercises recommended at the end of this chapter.

Drawing Equipment and Materials

The art of figure drawing requires only a minimal investment in tools and equipment. A basic set of equipment for costume and figure drawing should include:

1. A large pad of newsprint for drawing practice. Newsprint is one of the most economical forms of drawing paper; its disposability makes it ideal for practice drawings and rough sketches.

2. A pad of drawing paper, tracing paper, or drafting vellum for rough costume sketches.

3. A variety of art papers for costume renderings, including charcoal and watercolor paper and illustration board. Through experience, the artist will come to prefer different types of papers and boards for various design and drawing styles as dictated by the production and by the artist's own technique.

4. A few graphite pencils in varying degress of softness, a stick of charcoal, a charcoal pencil and a Conté crayon. Charcoal comes in pencil form, as vine charcoal which is somewhat

fragile, very messy but also very dark, and as compressed charcoal which is sturdier and broader than vine charcoal. Conté crayons are small, waxy sticks that can be used broadside for large sweeping strokes or whose tip can be used for more detailed drawing. Mechanical and automatic drafting pencils are not recommended for use in figure drawing, since the widths of line they produce are too limiting for depicting costumes and the human figure.

5. It is useful to have at least one fresh kneaded rubber eraser and an artgum eraser on hand. The stronger erasers found on the end of pencils or electric drafting erasers are not recommended.

6. Workable spray fixative should be used upon completion of a sketch to prevent smudging.

DRAWING THE FIGURE

Proportions

Human body proportions are related to the size of the head. Thus, when drawing the figure, establish the head size first. The head is an oval that is pointed at the chin and broader above the ears. This oval can be divided into quadrants to establish the eye and nose lines (Figure 5–1). Standard body proportions are geared to number of head lengths; an average body is 7½ human heads high. Fashion drawing elongates the body for a special purpose; however in costume design, which is more closely related to the proportions of the "real" figure, it is practical to use eight heads as the standard vertical proportion.

After establishing the head size, lightly sketch eight heads down the page. This may be done with a ruler at first and by eye as experience increases. Draw a horizontal line between each head length, and label each line from top to bottom 1, 2, 3, and so forth. Line #1 corresponds to the length of the head; #2 the chest; #3 the waist; #4 the crotch; #5 the lower thigh; #6 the area below the knee; #7 the lower calf; and #8 the ground line. (Figure 5–2). It is important eventually to develop the ability to sense these proportions by eye.

The ground line in a costume sketch serves to prevent the figure from appearing to float in space. When drawing the clothed figure, it is helpful to use the ground line for establishing the approximate heel height, hem, and train lengths.

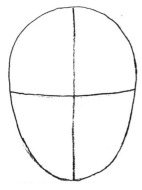

FIGURE 5–1

The head oval divided into quadrants to establish the eye and nose lines.

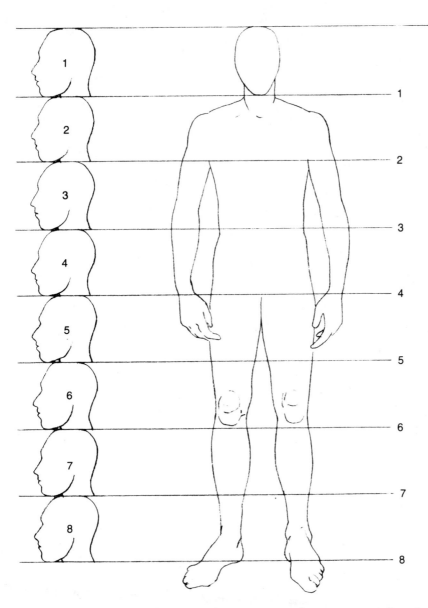

FIGURE 5–2
The eight-head proportion system.

The rudimentary horizontal proportions for a costume sketch are the shoulder and waistlines (Figure 5–3). The shoulder line varies in width: on the male, the line can be up to two head lengths wide; on the female, it can be one and one-half head lengths wide. These proportions can be varied relative to character, just as the waist, normally no more than two head *widths* wide, is a natural point of adjustment for character work.

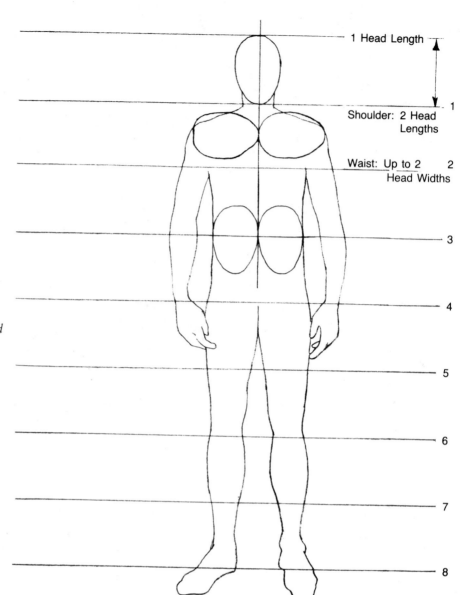

1 Head Length

Shoulder: 2 Head Lengths

Waist: Up to 2 Head Widths   2

1

3

4

5

6

7

8

FIGURE 5–3

Horizontal proportions for the male figure based on head lengths.

Notice that when people stand, their weight is rarely shared equally by both legs. In a relaxed pose, a person often stands with one leg "engaged," or supporting the majority of the weight, while the other leg is relaxed. Costume designers frequently show the figure in this relaxed posture.

When the weight of the figure is shared unequally between the legs, the torso shifts direction slightly to accommodate the weight shift and to preserve the center of gravity. This is particularly noticeable in the angle of the shoulder line and the lower hip line. When the weight of the figure is distributed unevenly, the hip line tilts up on the side of the engaged leg (the leg holding the most weight), and the shoulder line tilts down. The opposite is true for the relaxed side of the body (Figure 5–4).

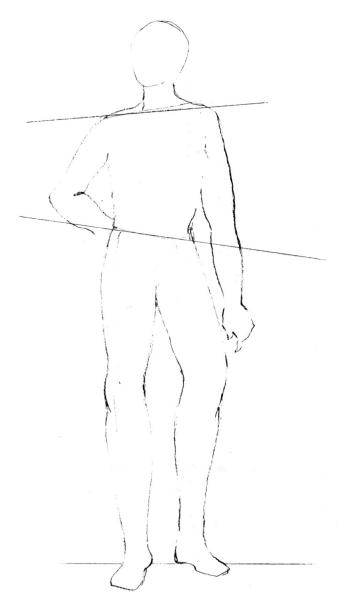

FIGURE 5–4
Shifting balance: shoulder and hip angles.

A straight line drawn from the base of the neck to the ground line (perpendicular to the ground line) serves to check the balance of the figure. Regardless of the angles of the shoulder and hip lines, the figure will appear balanced only when the feet fall on either side of this vertical balance line (Figure 5–5).

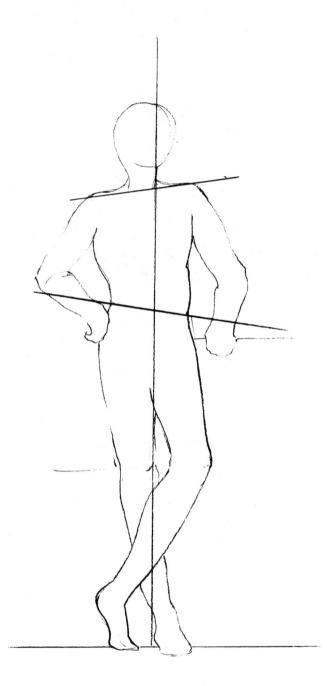

FIGURE 5–5
Vertical balance line.

Once the head proportion and balance lines are established, the designer should lightly sketch in the body parts as geometric curvilinear shapes. In this way the head is an oval, and the upper and lower arms become two tapered cylinders, as do the legs. The torso can be divided into two blocks, one representing the upper chest and another indicating the abdomen area. The space between the chest and abdomen (the rib cage) becomes a smaller block connecting the more independently mobile hip and chest areas (Figure 5–6).

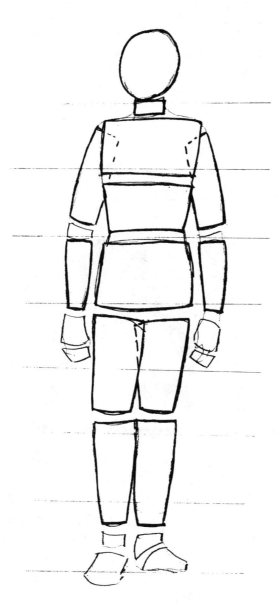

FIGURE 5–6
Dividing the body into geometric components.

Contours

Once the basic proportions and geometric abstractions of the figure have been laid in, the contours of surface flesh can be drawn over the structure. At this stage, regular practice drawing from live models and referring to the source-file can provide a wealth of information as to the complex series of curvilinear lines that comprise the contours of the human body.

A basic technique in learning to draw the human figure involves strict exercises in the art of **contour drawing,** a few of which are listed at the end of this chapter. The main objective of this method of drawing is to train the eye to see anew the curvature of the outer and inner surfaces of the flesh. Beginning students tend to draw what they think should be there, rather than seeing the body as it really is. Contour drawing is a way of retraining eye-mind-hand coordination. Extensive work in this particular form of drawing also allows the artist to impart a greater sense of reality to the finished drawing. Figure 5–7 illustrates a contour drawing of just the outlines of the body, resulting in a silhouette; Figure 5–8 illustrates both exterior and interior contour lines, suggesting three-dimensionality. Superimposing exterior and interior contour lines on the roughed-in geometric shapes and support lines of the figure can bring the drawing closer to the final result: a more realistic representation of the human form.

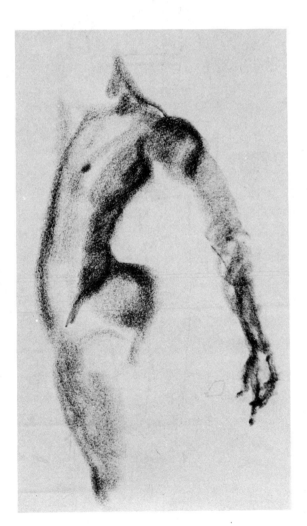

FIGURE 5–7
Contour drawing of the body outlines.

FIGURE 5–8
Contour drawing of interior body shapes and the body outline.

Drawing the Body

Head and Face

Facial features can be as complex to draw as the figure itself. It is important, however, for designers to learn to draw the relative proportions of facial features, at least in a shorthand manner. Study and practice can develop skills in creating highly detailed faces that will enhance drawings. The study of stage makeup is also recommended as a supplement to the art of drawing the face. The knowledge to be gained in such study will be of enormous value in acquainting the artist with the structure of the face, the principles of age and character, and the effects of highlight and shadow. A stage-makeup book with good illustrations is a handy reference for work on facial drawing.

The basic elements of the head and face can be sketched as follows:

1. Draw an oval, the shape of an egg resting on one end, for a frontal view of the head. Note that the chin area is the narrow part of the "egg," with the forehead creating the widest part at the top.

149

2. Divide this oval vertically and horizontally in half.

3. Center the eyes on the horizontal line and space them approximately one eye length apart (Figure 5–9).

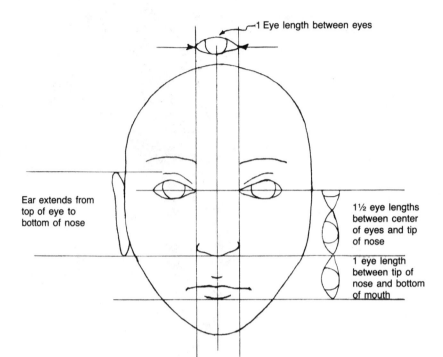

FIGURE 5–9

Spacing of facial features.

Ear extends from top of eye to bottom of nose

1 Eye length between eyes

1½ eye lengths between center of eyes and tip of nose

1 eye length between tip of nose and bottom of mouth

4. Place the nose on the vertical line. The tip of the nose should be located approximately 1½ eye lengths below the horizontal line dividing the face.

5. Position the mouth on a horizontal line. The bottom of the mouth should be one eye length below the bottom of the nose.

6. The ears should span the distance between the top of the eyes and the bottom of the nose.

The designer should practice these basic proportions until they become second nature. The designer will then be ready to use many variations of the basic formula to indicate personality, sex, race, and age. The picture source-file, drawing notebook, and a stage-makeup book can be invaluable references. Notice especially the differences of character that can be indicated by the shape of the eyebrows or by the length and shape of the mouth. Age can be indicated by the droop of the eyelids, the thickness of the eyebrows, gradual exposure of the skeletal structure that underlies sagging flesh, and many other muscle and bone details (Figure 5–10).

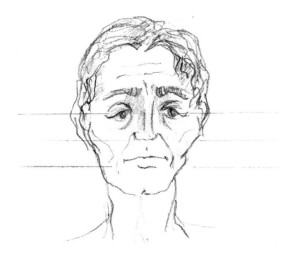

FIGURE 5–10
Indications of character and age on the facial features.

There are some subtle differences between male and female features which help in facial drawing (Figure 5–11). Some of the most obvious differences are the more angular jawline of the male versus the softened jawline of the female; the flatter, thicker eyebrows on the male versus the arched, thin eyebrows on the female; and the thin lip and wide mouth of the male, in contrast to the thicker lips and wider mouth of the female. The picture source-file is a help in making this differentiation as well as in practicing the facial features representative of different ethnic groups.

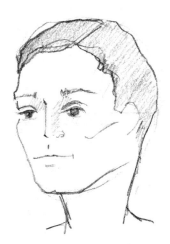

a.   **b.**

FIGURE 5–11
Differences between male and female facial features.

Hair

Hair styling is as much a part of the figure as the details of the face and is as significant a part of costume design as clothing. The hair style changes and softens the oval outline of the face (Figure 5–12) and is an important means of conveying character. Hair in itself is a shape as much as the silhouette of the figure is a shape. Establishing the basic silhouette of the hair is more useful to figure drawing, however, then spending hours detailing every strand.

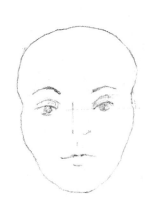

a.

b.

FIGURE 5–12

*Softening the shape of the
face oval with the addition of
hair.*

Using illustrations from the picture source-file, draw the outer
shape or silhouette of the hair. Note that the hair encroaches on the
forehead, thereby changing the shape of the top of the head oval. In
frontal poses, the height of the hair will extend above the head oval,
the exact height determined by the hair style. Hair is also visible on
the sides of the face. Again, the exact dimensions are determined by
the hair style. Quite often, the ear is either fully or partially covered
by hair.

Once the basic silhouette of the hair has been drawn, the curvature
and dimensionality of the hair can be established through undulating
patterns of light and shade (Figure 5–13). Now it is possible to go
back into the sketch and create individual groups of hair—wisps at
the forehead or nape, a shock of hair breaking the forehead line, or
special arrangements of hair such as a beard or moustache. A purposely

FIGURE 5–13

*a) Hair may be drawn sim-
ply as a silhouette, or b)
Hair can be made dimen-
sional with the addition of
highlight and shadow.*

a.

b.

"mussed" appearance can be conveyed by a number of individual strands breaking the silhouette of the hair (Figure 5–14).

Be sure to include photographs, paintings, and sketches of a variety of hair styles in the source-file. In addition, a book that illustrates period hair styles is another good reference to have near the drawing board.

FIGURE 5–14
Breaking the hair line with wisps of hair.

Hands and Feet

The effects of foreshortening and the complexity of detail necessary in figure drawing require careful treatment of hands and feet. For many drawing situations, a shorthand indication of hands and feet is adequate; however, it is very important to include some indication of these appendages in a finished sketch or costume rendering since the actor will usually possess all of these parts of the anatomy. Drawing the focus to or away from the hands, feet, or face becomes a crucial decision in creating a costume design.

The hand is often indicated in costume drawings merely by sketching two lines or a curved shape at the end of the wrist to form a "mitten;" however, it takes little extra effort to create a hand that is more realistic. Consider how in figure drawing, the body was divided into geometric or cylindrical shapes for simplification. The same can be done with each of the fingers on the hand (Figure 5–15). Each portion of the hand, palm, fingers, and thumb is simplified into an abstract form that indicates the presence of a complete hand on the body. It is also helpful to draw some guidelines for the hand. Indicate

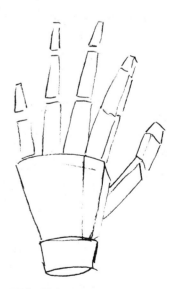

FIGURE 5–15
Geometric components of the hand.

153

the angle of the wrist, the angle of the knuckles, and a line that spans the hand across the broadest part lining up with the base of the thumb (Figure 5–16). It is sometimes helpful to draw a series of lines that lightly mark out the basic shape of the hand. Note how this method differs from contour drawing. After the hand has been detailed in

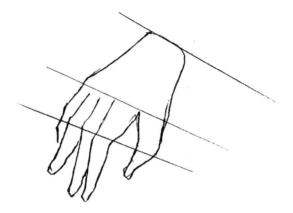

FIGURE 5–16
Basic angles of the hand are established by the position of the wrist and the angle of the knuckles.

geometric form (as in Figure 5–15), contour lines such as the curve of the inside of the fingers and the shape of the knuckle can be superimposed onto the basic structure for an even more realistic rendition of the hand (Figure 5–17). Sources for models of this type of contour drawing can be the artist's own hand, live models, photographs, and illustrations from the source-file.

The feet are as important as the hands in a costume sketch because they give vital information regarding footwear and its relation to the rest of the costume in terms of color, style, and proportion. As most costume sketches indicate the figure in a frontal or 3/4 position, the problems of foreshortening come into play, as they do in perspective drawing.

Figure 5–18 contains drawings of some possible shorthand variations of foot positions. If the costume designer does not feel that enough information has been provided in these shorthand sketches, it is important to provide supplementary information in the form of notes or detail drawings elsewhere on the sketch or in separate drawings.

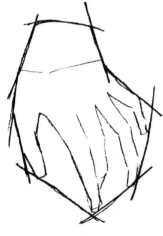

FIGURE 5–17
Guidelines can be used to establish the exterior form of the hand.

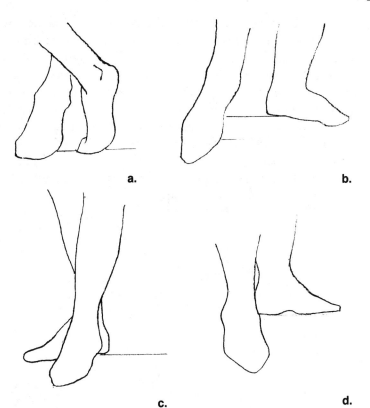

FIGURE 5–18
Four examples of shorthand drawings of the foot.

As with the hands, some structure lines are helpful in establishing the basic shape of the feet. The shape of the foot can be described as a trapezoid with the narrowest portion at the heel, the widest at the toe. The instep curves both horizontally and vertically, accompanied by a curve for the arch (Figure 5–19). The lesser toes curve away from the big toe, and the littlest toe is about one-half the length of the big toe.

The Figure in Motion

Although a static, full-front position can provide a surface on which to draw clothes, a more interesting figure drawing or costume sketch will result when the figure looks a bit more lifelike. The additional steps to create a more lifelike sketch might be as simple as turning the head of the figure slightly, shifting the weight of the body, or showing the body in a 3/4 position. Some designers can imbue their sketches with an even greater sense of motion, giving a sense of the fluidity to the clothing and imparting a great liveliness to the finished drawing. The actor onstage is, after all, rarely stationary for great lengths of time, and it can be very helpful as well as rewarding to try to simulate the sense of a real person wearing real clothing in the sketch.

Drawing the figure in motion requires referral once again to live models and supplementally to the picture source-file.

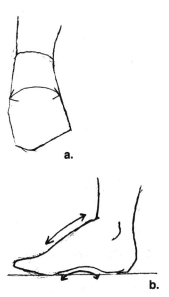

FIGURE 5–19
Instep and arch curves of the foot.

155

Establishing a gesture line for the body will be helpful in imparting this sense of movement to the figure. A **gesture line** is a sweeping line intended to capture the essence of the figure's motion (see Figure 5–20). Making sketches of live models, dancers, or athletes can aid the student in capturing this sense of movement in one or two strokes of the pencil. The use of gesture drawing gives a different kind of reality to the sketch than contour drawing: outward surfaces are temporarily ignored to capture the inner motion of the figure; the result is a certain believability in the final drawing. The use of gesture line combined with the elements of proportion, balance, and contour can create an even greater illusion of realism.

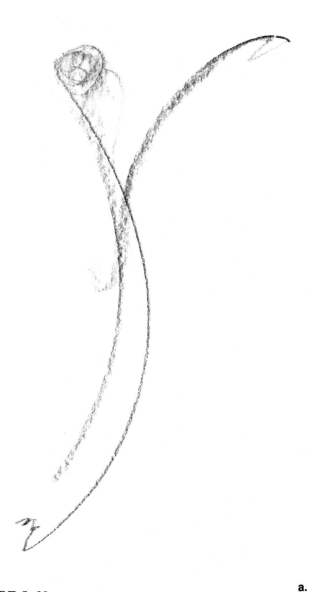

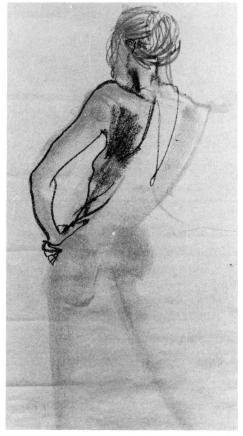

a.

b.

FIGURE 5–20
a) A gesture drawing, b) A gesture drawing and contour drawing combined.

When drawing the figure in motion, the gesture line *precedes* the creation of proportion and contour lines. The artist proceeds as if from the inner core of the body outward, establishing the essence of movement first, then adding layer upon layer until the outer surface is "discovered."

To Draw the Figure in Motion

1. Establish the head and gesture of the movement in light, broad, sweeping strokes. (Figure 5–21)

FIGURE 5–21
Establish the gesture of the figure.

2. Keeping in mind the "eight head" proportions, rough in the
geometric shapes of the body. (Figure 5–22)

FIGURE 5–22
Rough in the geometric
shapes of the figure over the
gesture drawing.

3. Add the outer contour lines over the established geometric shapes. (Figure 5–23)

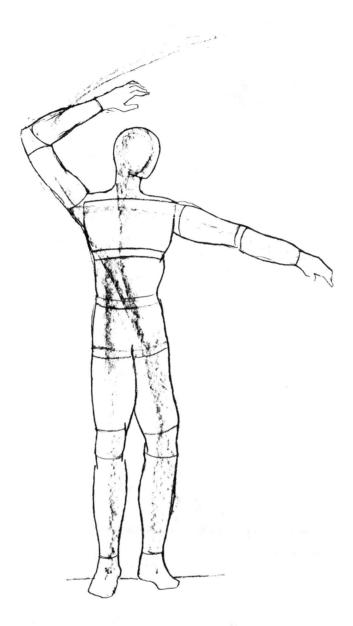

FIGURE 5–23
Add the contour lines to the geometric shapes.

4. Fill in the details of hands, feet, facial features, and hair. (Figure 5–24)

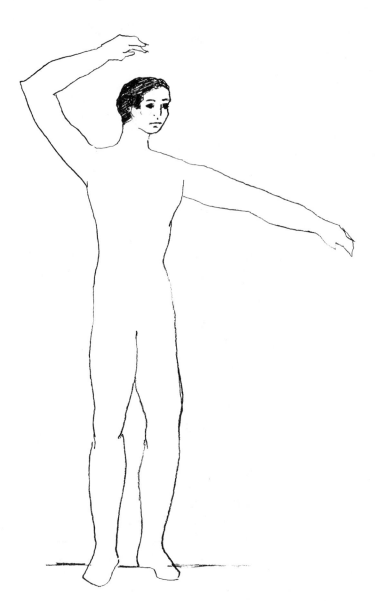

FIGURE 5–24
Add details to complete the figure in preparation for "dressing the figure."

The Figure Clothed

Drawing clothes on the figure is approached in the same way as drawing the figure; that is, from large forms proceeding gradually to inner line and detail. It must never be forgotten that there is a real body beneath the clothing, even when drawing the most artificial of period shapes. It is a good idea to begin the costume drawing by sketching in the figure first, using both gesture and contour drawing techniques. This step can be done on tracing paper, drawing the costume overlaying the figure drawing, or, the figure can be lightly drawn on the final paper or board and drawn over with progressively darker linework as the costume is added. Either way, the value of drawing the nude figure first will become obvious in terms of evaluation of proportion and stance.

Defining **period silhouettes** (outer form and shape) for a costume can be approached by drawing the geometric components of the costume in the same manner that the figure was initially defined. In this way the period silhouette is broken down into its related geometric shapes (Figure 5–25). Another approach is to establish the gesture the *garment*

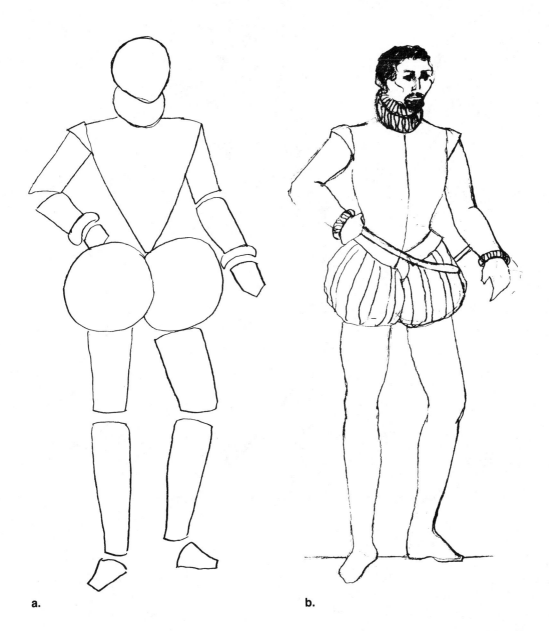

a.   b.

FIGURE 5–25
a) A period silhouette drawn in geometric components, and b) A detailed sketch.

makes when it is over the figure (garments move in a certain way
when on the body) and then successively add more contour details
until the finished garment emerges (Figure 5–26).

a.   **b.**

FIGURE 5–26

a) A gesture drawing of the
garment, *and b) The gar-*
met sketched over the gesture
drawing.

It is important to remember that there are very few straight lines
within the contours of clothing on the body. Even the seemingly
straight lines of a stiffened period bodice or a pant leg can be accurately
depicted only by a combination of concave and convex curves. In
Figure 5–27, note specifically the curvature of the bodice shape as it
molds the bust and proceeds to the waist. Note also the curve of the
waist seam on a period bodice and the way the shoulder curves on a
man's suit jacket. Carefully redrawing period shapes and silhouettes
in the drawing notebook with an eye to this complex combination of
curved lines will aid the designer considerably in duplicating the costume
in the finished sketch.

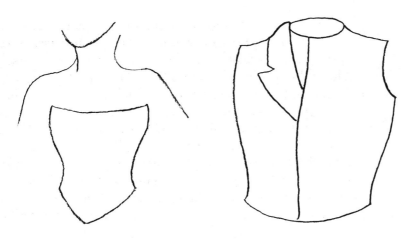

FIGURE 5–27
Even stiff, apparently flat garments are constructed with curved lines.

The weight of the fabric and the body position will determine which parts of the body push against the fabric, causing **fold lines.** Some of the more common places for fold lines are the knee in contemporary men's pants, the armpit, the bend of the elbow, the area below the pocket line if the hand is in the pocket, or areas where the fabric is controlled by pleating or gathering (Figure 5–28).

FIGURE 5–28
Fold-lines of fabric at shoulder, armpit, elbow, waistline, pocket, and knee add dimensionality.

Just as the costume designer should not ignore the figure beneath the clothing, the designer should not ignore the **understructure** of the garment. This can take many forms, from petticoats, corsets, and farthingales to bum rolls or padding. In many periods of clothing, for both men and women, the understructure makes a considerable difference in the skirt silhouette and in the angle, shape, and line of the skirt as it moves away from the waistline. Compare Figures 5–29a and 5–29b. The first is a sixteenth-century skirt silhouette supported from underneath, the fullness created by cartridge pleating. Compare this to Figure 5–29b, which shows a nonsupported gathered skirt from a more contemporary period. These subtle line changes will make a significant difference in the reality and credibility of the finished sketch.

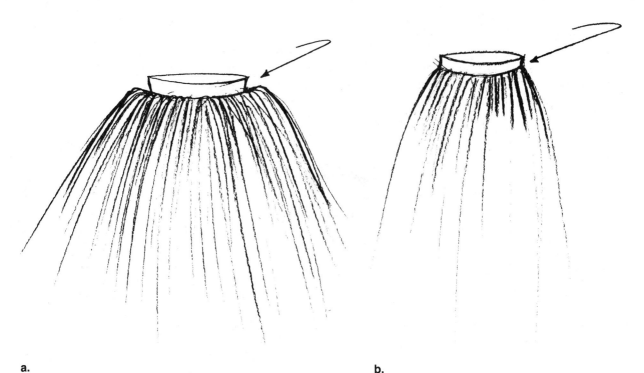

a.

b.

FIGURE 5–29

a) A cartridge-pleated skirt with undersupport, compared to b) A nonsupported contemporary gathered skirt.

For robed figures, consider the drawing of the train. A ground line is established in the sketch, allowing the literal **break of the line** as it reaches the floor (Figure 5–30). Whenever the fabric is forced to change direction, the line should break and change direction accordingly. This change in the line is similar to the **break** in a man's contemporary pant leg where it hits the shoe (Figure 5–31).

FIGURE 5–30
The "break" of fabric at the floorline of a train.

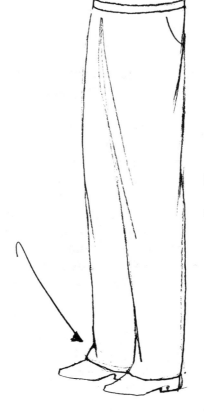

FIGURE 5–31
The "break" of fabric in men's pants over the shoe.

In drawing clothing on the figure, it is also helpful to establish a series of curved lines across the body—the bustline or chestline, the waist, the hips, the hemline (in a full-length garment), and, in some cases, the sleeves (Figure 5–32). These lines are similar in function to the basic proportional lines in the face. The curvature of the line helps to project the figure forward and to create an illusion of three-

FIGURE 5–32

Curvature of the body indicated at the bust, arm, waist, hips, and hemline.

dimensionality. Compare Figures 5–33a and 5–33b. Figure 5–33a utilizes curved lines across the body; the other uses straight lines. The result of the latter approach is a flat, "paper doll" look that should be avoided in most representational or "realistic" costume drawing styles.

When clothing the figure in a costume drawing, begin with the body beneath the clothes. Once the stance and proportions are established for the nude figure, superimpose the clothing on the form, paying particular attention to the exterior contour lines or the costume's silhouette, the curvature of the fabric against the body beneath, the break or change in direction of the fabric, and any additional understructure that will affect the shape of the garment above. Once the essential pieces of the garment have been superimposed on the figure, details of the trim and the interior line can be drawn, in addition to the highlight and shadow that will increase the three-dimensionality of the sketch.

a.   b.

As with all other aspects of figure drawing, making practice sketches from research and from illustrations compiled for the production will familiarize the designer with the forms, shapes, and interior line of a given period.

Highlight and Shadow

Highlight and shadow add three-dimensionality to what would otherwise be a simple line drawing. It is helpful to think of the shadowed areas as shapes or silhouettes in themselves. In this way, the designer can avoid drawing a hard edge and can more clearly denote the structure of the object being drawn.

Consider highlight and shadow on the human figure. Ideally, use a live model with a direct light source to see where the shadows fall. Notice how the shapes of shadows vary from curvilinear to angular, depending on the "fleshiness" or "boniness" of a particular area of the body. The same principles can be adapted for drawing the face (Figure 5–34). The principles of stage makeup are intricately interwoven with the principles of drawing the face, and a knowledge of one will automatically serve to improve the other.

In figure drawing without the advantage of a live model, a source of light must be assumed. Imagine a light source directed at a strong angle from above (as in stage lighting directions), and keep all highlights and shadows consistent with the light source. It is extremely important

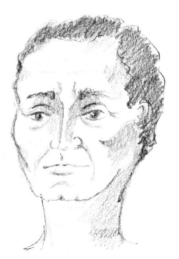

FIGURE 5–34
Highlight and shadow in the facial structure.

167

to remember that in highlight and shadow, consistency equals believability.

Highlight and shadow are also extremely useful in describing fabric or clothing on the body. Mastering the relatively simple process of quickly shading folds will enable the designer to give a sketch a sense of three-dimensionality and "realism." In Figure 5–35, notice how the folds of a standard cartridge-pleated skirt are denoted—the highlight picks up the top of the fold, and the lowlight or deepest shadow falls in the crevice. Notice, too, that in addition to the individual folds creating highlight and shadow, the entire shape of the skirt has highlight and shadow, as does the torso.

FIGURE 5–35

Individual folds of fabric are shadowed in addition to overall shadowing of the entire torso and skirt.

The use of highlight and shadow is one of the best ways to distinguish between differing weights of fabric. Velvet and other heavy fabrics tend to fall in larger, thicker folds. Light is absorbed more deeply by velvet (because of its darker shadows) than by a fabric that is more reflective, such as satin. The play of light on silk or satin (as in the paintings of Watteau or Fragonard) results in more diffusion and smaller areas of light and shadow. The surface of satin seems to be broken up by the movement of light and shadow, and the contrast between the highlight and the shadow is not as great as with a more light-absorbent fabric.

COSTUME RENDERING

Costume designers prepare both costume sketches and costume renderings. Although the terms are used synonomously, in general a **costume sketch** is a preliminary drawing that usually lacks color or complete detail. A given costume sketch may be revised and redrawn several times before being approved and subsequently rendered in detail. A **costume rendering** is the approved costume sketch, complete with color, fabric swatches, and all details to be used for presentation to the director and other designers as well as a guide to construction in the shop.

Functions of the Rendering

A costume sketch or rendering is more than a simple rendition of an idea. Its function is to provide information to a great many people involved in the production process. On the one hand, the sketch informs the director as to the resolution of ideas discussed during design conferences and reveals character, mood, and style in specific visual terms. The sketch provides a concrete means to ascertain if the designer and director are in agreement regarding the design. The rendering also shows the scenic and lighting designers how the costume's style and mood reflect the overall production concept.

The rendering also serves to inform the individual actor of the "look" and "feel" of the garment. In this case the actor will be less

FIGURE 5–36a
Costume sketch for Olga, The Three Sisters, *American Conservatory Theatre.* (Designer: Michael Olich.)

169

FIGURE 5–36b

*Costume design for The
Mother,* Six Characters in
Search of An Author,
*University of California,
San Diego.* (Designer: Lynn
McLeod.)

FIGURE 5–36c

*Costume rendering for Sir
Toby,* Twelfth Night,
*University of California,
San Diego.* (Designer: Deb-
orah Dryden.)

170

FIGURE 5–36d
Costume rendering for The Elephant Man, *Alaska Repertory Theatre*. (Designer: Michael Olich.)

interested in the number of buttons on a vest and more in how the fabric and weight of the costume will affect the actor's physicalization of the role. Perhaps equally important, the sketch suggests qualities the designer has incorporated in the costume that may be of use to the actor for business or character development.

The sketch also conveys specific information to the costume-shop staff regarding clothing to be purchased, pulled, or constructed. The staff should be able to find this information given very clearly in the sketch, aided also by notes and by verbal support from the designer. Viewing the sketch in this way helps the staff to determine the general silhouette and complexity of a costume and aids also in budgeting the entire production.

Finally, the costume rendering is of value to the costume designer. Although it may seem as if a designer should have a perfectly clear picture of what each character will look like, an amazing amount of detail is learned from putting a design idea down on paper. All kinds of decisions can be made on paper before construction begins, such as the kind of shoes, size of lapel, style of hair, and so forth. The more design problems that can be resolved during the drawing process, the more the designer can focus on construction problems encountered during the actual creation of the costumes in the shop.

Qualities of the Rendering

An effective costume sketch usually conveys some, if not all, of the following qualities:

1. An evocation of the mood of the play.
2. A sense of the character being portrayed.
3. A clarity of costume detail which gives the sense that the designer fully understands the design.
4. A feeling of liveliness or three-dimensionality in the figure.
5. A sense of connection between the sketches that implies an approach or attitude on the part of the designer towards the whole production. The sense of connection may come from something as simple as restricting the costumes to a historical period that binds the individual characters into the same unity, or it might be represented by a style decision; for example, to utilize only selected elements of a historical period or an overall style of abstraction. The possibilities for design unity are endless, and they can be among the more exciting and stimulating ways that the designer's imagination is utilized to support the production.

In the initial stages of the creative process, the costume designer must have a clear idea as to the theme and content of the production, a strong sense of each character, and an understanding of how this particular production will be made unique. All of this involves considerable research and numerous discussions with the director and other designers. Once the basic framework has been established, the designer can sit down at the drawing board and actually grapple with applying these ideas to paper.

The Size of the Sketch

Within reasonable limits, a costume sketch or rendering may be any size appropriate to the needs of the design. There are no perfect dimensions for all renderings. The choice of rendering size should be determined on the basis of several factors:

1. The sketch (not just the paper) should be large enough to accommodate both the written and pictorial information necessary.
2. The sketch should be a practical size for transporting to meetings and for use in the shop.
3. The size of the sketch is often dictated by the nature of the production. A small, delicate, refined production may suggest the need for a different size rendering than a production that

is broad or bombastic in style. This is a strictly aesthetic design choice.

4. The size of sketch may be determined by the rendering technique employed. Some rendering techniques require larger figures, while other techniques are conducive to smaller sketches.

5. The size of sketch may also be determined by the time available and the number of drawings that have to be completed within that time period.

The size renderings that currently seem to be most common range from 8½″ × 11″ to 18″ × 24″ for a single sketch. Although the size of the rendering may vary for different shows, it is important that all costume sketches for the same show be the same size. This is a point of convenience more than one of aesthetics.

The Rendering Process

Preliminary Drawings

While preparing the sketches for an entire show, it is sometimes advisable to work up a series of **thumbnail sketches.** These sketches are small drawings (thus the name "thumbnail") usually no larger than two to three inches high, and quite often existing together on one sheet of paper. The purpose of making these miniature costume sketches is for the designer to explore the relationships of the silhouette (the shape and form) of the clothes to each other before drawing them in larger scale and greater detail. Confining the drawing to such a small size prevents the designer from getting too involved with the inner details of the costume before establishing appropriate and harmonious silhouettes for each of the characters. These thumbnail drawings are a transitional stage between the quick sketches of research and ideas in the designer's notebook and the larger, detailed, "rough" sketches of the costume rendering. A series of thumbnails demonstrating the designer's ideas for each character are a useful visual tool in discussions with the director to determine if the design scheme is on the right track before the designer invests extended time and energy in making the full-size renderings. The thumbnails may also be photocopied in multiples and used by the designer to explore the color relationships and balance of the entire show. Such photocopies are an extremely useful step in the preparation of the final designs to improve the potential for continuity of form and color over the entire production.

The next step of the costume-design process is to make rough sketches. These can be done in pencil, on tracing paper or drafting vellum, or directly on the board or paper of the finished rendering. The advantage of drawing roughs on tracing paper is that overlays may be done on top of a sketch-in-progress to refine the drawing continually without starting anew for each new idea or variation. Once the rough is complete (without color) and approved, it can be easily transferred to a board or paper suitable for painting. Graphite paper (available in art stores) may be used, or the entire back of the tracing-paper sketch may be shaded with a soft lead pencil. The sketch is attached securely to the board, and the outlines of the figure are drawn

173

over with a hard, sharpened pencil or a fine-point pen to transfer the image to the painting surface. Some designers, however, prefer to draw the rough sketches directly on the painting surface. This method requires greater drawing confidence but at the same time gives a greater spontaneity to the final rendering. The choice of either method is a matter of individual preference, rendering style, and time.

Color

Once the rough drawings have been approved and revised, the addition of color is crucial. Beginning color schemes can be formulated by using color chips, locating swatches of fabric, or coloring thumbnails, as mentioned above. A general color palette should be agreed upon by the designers and the director before color is applied to the final rendering.

Color sources are often invaluable in broadening the imaginative possibilities for the costume designer. As with the previously mentioned pictorial research, the variety of colors gleaned from photographs, paintings, textile designs, and other sources will stimulate the designer's imagination. All too often a costume design is limited by a conventional palette. The use of one color source, such as a specific painting or illustration, for a whole show or a particular character can serve to expand the color possibilities and the available color relationships.

Media

Wet media are the ones most frequently used for costume rendering, including ink, gouache, watercolor, and acrylic paints. Some dry media such as colored pencil, colored pastels, and felt pens are also used. These media can be combined successfully to achieve interesting results. It is important to note that each medium possesses its own particular qualities which the designer may use to advantage. These are discussed in detail in Chapter 8.

Backgrounds

As with all other aspects of the costume-rendering process, it is important that the designer remember that the end product is the costume worn by the actor on stage. Anything the sketch can do to help clarify or reveal that final image is to be desired; anything that confuses or diffuses that final image is to be avoided.

Designers differ in their opinions about using backgrounds on costume sketches. If the paper or board is white, a vague shadow fully or partially surrounding the figure will help soften the contrast between the figure and the surface of the paper. Unless the setting is pure white, this kind of softening will help all those involved to see the colors within the costume more accurately.

For some productions, a choice of colored paper or board close to the actual color of the setting is helpful. Some designers give the hint of a doorway or a piece of furniture in the drawing to place the figure in a truer sense of the environment. In all cases, however, the costume rendering is a rendering of the costume, not of the setting. Time spent on overly elaborate backgrounds in costume sketches would be better spent elsewhere in the design process. Simulation of the background color is important; specific architectural detail less so.

Supplementary Information

The finished costume sketch may include a variety of supplemental information. Much of this is added as the costumes come closer to realization. Basic information should include the name of the character, the name of the play, the actor's name, and the scene or act in which the particular costume is worn. The designer's initials or name may appear on the sketch as well. There may also be verbal descriptions added and notes to clarify specific items. Either on the sketch or in separate drawings, the costume designer should provide pertinent information such as back views, details of trim and accessories, footwear, and wig styles. Also, fabric swatches should be affixed to the finished sketch. Some designers actually incorporate all of this supplemental information as part of the visual whole of the sketch. In a large show requiring multiple sketches, it is helpful to number the sketches in the upper right-hand corner for easy reference. Covering sketches with acetate will protect them during use in the costume shop.

Matting or framing the sketch is not usually necessary or even advisable for in-shop production use. However, matting should be done for exhibition of costume renderings or portfolio presentation.

Exercises

1. Practice **contour drawing.** Using a live model or an illustration, fasten your eyes on any one part of the body and place the pencil on the page. Without looking at the paper and without lifting the pencil, move your eyes gradually down the contours of the body, and allow the pencil to draw what you experience through your eyes. This should be an extremely slow process. Do not take your eyes off the subject. The resulting drawing is rarely "realistic" by conventional standards, but students are frequently surprised by the qualities and knowledge that result.

2. Once the strict form of contour drawing explained in Exercise 1 has been mastered, perform the same exercise, occasionally glancing at the paper to reposition the pencil. However, draw only when your eyes are on the subject; do not draw when your eyes are on the paper. Both Exercises 1 and 2 should be performed repeatedly as part of the on-going training for the eye to see and for the pencil to follow what the eye sees—not what the mind says.

3. Using the eight head proportions, draw the figure-establishing proportions wih the aid of a rule or scale. Repeat until the process can be accomplished by eye without the aid of a measure.

4. Using a mirror and your own face as a model, draw just the head, hair, and facial features using the strict method of contour drawing (no glancing at the page). Repeat, this time glancing at the page long enough to relocate the pencil occasionally.

5. While looking at a live model or at people participating in active movement, draw a series of quick **gesture studies** using the principle of the gesture line. These should take no more than ten seconds each. The people depicted may look much like active "stick" figures at first. Use a large pad of newsprint and the broad side of a soft lead pencil or charcoal stick. While drawing the "inner line" of the model's movement, try to experience the sense of activity in your own muscles.

6. Practice the basic shorthand principles for drawing the proportions of the face until you can sketch the head shape, eyes, mouth, and nose line without following a diagram and can do this in a matter of seconds.

7. Using examples from your source-file, draw a female head and a male head from a photograph, from a fashion illustration, and from another artist's drawing. (Portrait artists such as Holbein, Dürer, and Ingres are very useful. Try to find examples of their drawings or engravings, since these will be easier to follow at first than the paintings.)

8. Choose an illustration from your source-file depicting extreme age in male and female. Practice drawing their faces. Now put the sources away, and try to duplicate some of the features of age on your basic head from Exercise 6.

9. Draw your own face from observation in a mirror. Try to see your face as it really is, not as you perceive it. If this is difficult to do, try utilizing the contour method of drawing first, not looking at your paper until you feel you have subjected your face to the closest scrutiny.

10. Draw a face from a live model, a friend, a relation, or roommate. Do not be intimidated into thinking that you are drawing a portrait! This is an exercise in sketching for you alone and need not even be shown to the sitter, if you prefer.

11. Chose several illustrations of hair styles for men and women from your source-file. A good selection might be a 1920s male, an eighteenth-century male with full-bottomed wig, and a male in a contemporary advertisement. Choose an equally eclectic group of hair styles for women, some that utilize a "set" intricate hair style and at least one that is long and loose. Draw each of these, incorporating the silhouette of the hair shape, light and shadow, and some detailing of the hair within.

12. Practice drawing the hand, both left and right, in various positions, using just the geometric components.

13. Using your own hand as a model, use the contour drawing approach slowly and carefully to draw the exterior contours of the hand.

14. Combine Exercises 12 and 13, lightly roughing in the geometrics and structural shape and drawing over this with contour lines.

15. Collect a variety of other artists' "shorthand" drawings of hands—fashion illustrations and graphic designs are a good source. Practice these styles of hands and gestures until you have committed them to memory.

16. Using a photograph or a live model, make several sketches simply showing the hand in various positions.

17. Copy the shorthand versions of unshod feet in Figures 5–18 and 5–19. Collect more illustrations as source material, and copy these in your drawing notebook.

18. Collect a variety of period shoe illustrations. These will be easily found in costume history books. Draw silhouettes of these shoes in your drawing notebook until you can do so without using the sources.

19. Using live models, photographs, or paintings, try to draw the foot position in terms only of its basic structural components—the curve of the instep, the curve of the arch, the toes, and the foot's basic trapezoidal shape.

20. Now give special attention to period postures and stances that involve placement of the feet. Such historical postures are particularly evident in men's wear from the sixteenth through the nineteenth centuries. Note how the stance and subsequent placement of the feet affect the overall indication of historical period. Draw a selection of period postures in your notebook, depicting as a minimum, the legs and the feet of the models.

21. Using a mirror and a portable light source, draw your own face with highlight and shadow. Repeat this exercise on white, colored, and black paper.

22. Using a live model and a strong light source, create the form of the figure by drawing just the shadows—in other words, do not establish contour lines. Allow the figure to be defined by its highlight and shadow only.

23. Copy a line drawing (a drawing without highlight and shadow) from a costume-history book. Then assume a light source and draw in shadow accordingly.

24. Using a painting or drawing of a figure in period clothing (an original artwork from the period, not a redrawing), draw the form by establishing only the shadowed areas. This exercise is similar to Exercise 22. Do not draw in contour lines.

25. Collect in your picture file examples of other artists' renditions of fabric—look particularly for satins, velvets, and fur. Draw these fabrics with highlight and shadow until you have committed the different treatments to memory.

CHAPTER 6

Light and Shadow

INTRODUCTION

An orthographic projection consists of three or more views to describe the construction of a table. Drawn as an isometric projection or a pictorial drawing, the planes of the table are seen in an assembled view, and a perspective sketch shows the table as a three-dimensional representation. Each of these views is an outline drawing that utilizes only lines to describe shape. In life, however, outlines are seldom perceived independently. An object such as a pad of paper is not seen as an arrangement of four lines; instead, the pad is seen as a rectangular mass distinguished from its surroundings by highlights, shadows, and differences in texture and color. The lines forming the outline are incidental to our vision of the object. Although outline views provide a great deal of information, they are neither complete nor necessarily accurate. The outline drawing in Figure 6–1a appears to be a circle. As light falls on the surface of the circle in Figure 6–1b, it is apparent the form is a ball. The addition of highlight and shadow adds a sense of solidity, making the drawing more accurate and more interesting.

FIGURE 6–1

a) A ball receiving no illumination appears to be a black circle; b) A ball in both light and shade appears in its true form.

a.

b.

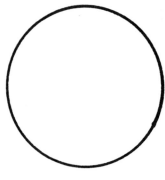

FIGURE 6–2

A ball receiving excessive illumination appears to be a white circle.

The human eye perceives external shape as the edges of mass against a background, but internal shape and texture are revealed as a result of highlights and shadows. Experience has taught us that surfaces located on different planes and forms with planes that change in direction reflect light in diverse patterns and degrees, dependent upon the shape of the surface and the direction, quantity, and quality of light striking it. We know that an absence of light makes it impossible to see. Equally true is that an excess of light washes out shadows and makes it impossible to discern detail. The intense illumination of the ball in Figure 6–2 obliterates all shadows and makes perception of the three-dimensional form impossible; it appears as flat as the circle in Figure 6–1a. Both light and shadow are necessary to identify shapes and textures clearly in life and in drawing.

THE TECHNICAL NATURE OF LIGHT AND SHADOW

An understanding of the effects of light and the causes of shadow can help the artist create meaningful drawings and paintings. The best way to achieve this understanding is careful observation of the world, both directly and by studying black-and-white photographs. These observations can be enhanced if the technical nature of light, reflection, and shadow is understood.

Light

Light has several qualities of which the artist must be aware. These qualities significantly affect the perception and representation of forms and spaces. Light may be diffuse, providing general illumination over an area, or it may be specific, projecting rays of light in patterns; it may be bright or dim, hard or soft, colored or colorless. Each of these qualities affects the way a surface or space is illuminated, the quality of shadow created, and the ability to distinguish form, texture, and color. These qualities determine the manner in which a setting is represented in a design drawing.

Reflection

Highlight is the presence of extremely intense light. It may be directly projected by the sun or a lamp, or it may be reflected by a surface. All surfaces absorb and reflect light. Highly textured materials such as rust and velour absorb most light striking them. In contrast, highly polished materials such as chrome, glass, or satin reflect almost all light they receive. Most materials occur between these extremes. The quality of light and the texture of a surface determine the nature and degree of light that is reflected. An intense beam of light striking a polished material is reflected in a tight, sharp pattern. This is what occurs when an image is reflected in a mirror. The reflectability of a material contributes to the strength of reflection, as does the intensity of light and the angle at which the light strikes the surface. This angle is called the **angle of incidence.** It is measured in relation to the **normal** for a surface (Figure 6–3). The normal is an imaginary line drawn perpendicular to the reflecting surface at the point light strikes it. The angle at which light is reflected by a surface is called the **angle of reflection,** which is measured between the normal and the reflected rays. *The angle of incidence always equals the angle of reflection.* The strength of reflection increases as the angle of incidence occurs closer to the normal. When light rays fall on the normal (when angle of incidence and angle of reflection equal zero), an extreme highlight occurs. On textured surfaces, the same rules apply; however, the

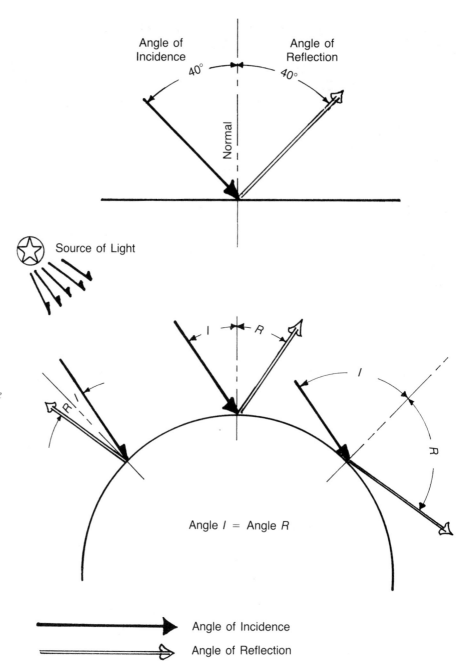

FIGURE 6–3

The technical nature of reflection. The normal is a perpendicular located at the point at which light strikes a surface. The angle of incidence always equals the angle of reflection.

reflections are broken into dispersed patterns (Figure 6–4a). The more coarsely textured the reflecting surface, the greater the dispersion of the reflected light (Figure 6–4b). Also, the more diffuse the light striking a surface, the more dispersed the pattern of reflection (Figure 6–5).

Shadow

Light is necessary for a shadow to exist. A **shadow** is the absence of light caused by the interception of light rays in an illuminated area. In other words, a shadow exists when there is both light and something

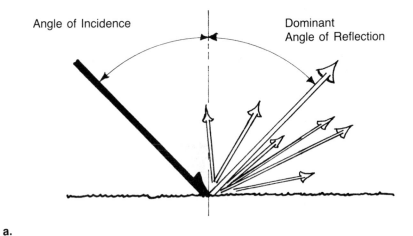

Angle of Incidence

Dominant Angle of Reflection

a.

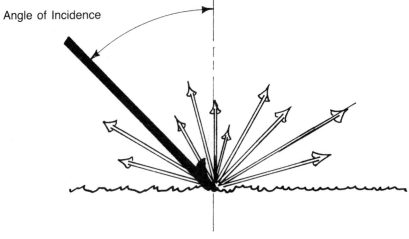

Angle of Incidence

b.

FIGURE 6–4
Reflection on a coarse surface behaves in a similar manner as reflection on a smooth surface; however, the texture of the surface disperses the reflected light.

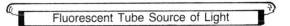

Fluorescent Tube Source of Light

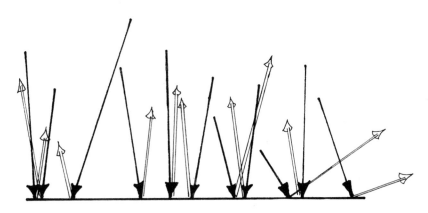

FIGURE 6–5
A diffuse source of light reflects in a dispersed pattern.

to block the light. The interceptor may be as slight as a protruding molding or as massive as a building (Figure 6–6). In the formation of shadows there is a perspective relationship between the source of light, interrupting forms, and the surfaces on which shadows fall. A shadow may be hard or soft, intense or dim. This quality is determined

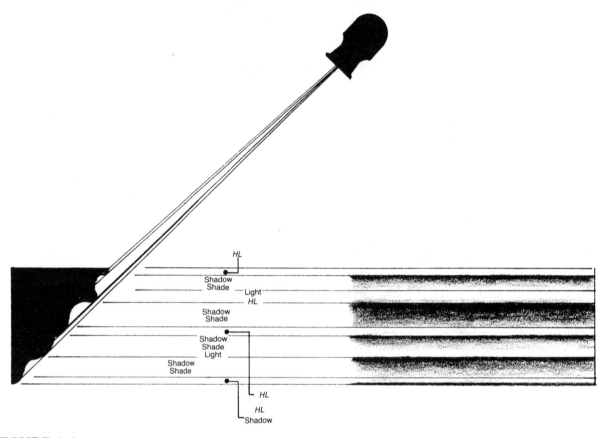

FIGURE 6–6

A molding can be drawn entirely with light and shade.

by the quality of light causing the shadow: bright, hard, directional light results in crisp, dark shadows (Figure 6–7a); dim, diffuse light results in soft, indistinct shadows (Figure 6–7b). When an area of shadow receives indirect illumination from reflected light, the intensity

a.

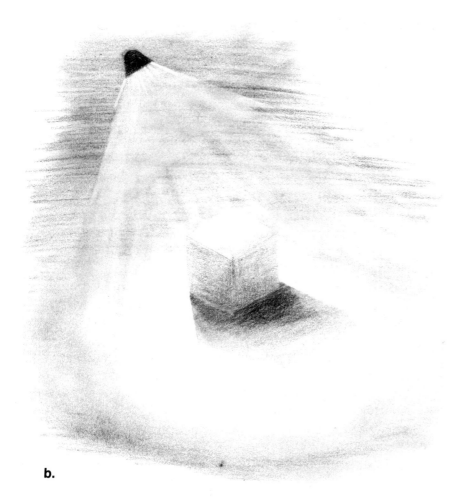

b.

FIGURE 6–7
a) Bright, hard, directional light casts a crisp shadow, but b) Soft, diffuse light casts a soft shadow.

of the shadow is diminished, and the area is in shade (Figure 6–8). A surface may receive illumination directly and be in **highlight** or **light,** it may be lighted indirectly and be in **shade,** or it may be cut off

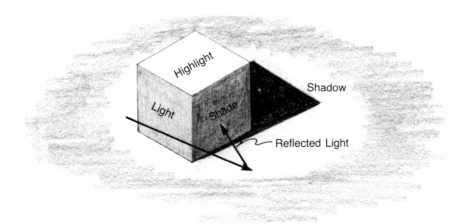

FIGURE 6–8
A surface can receive light directly and be in highlight or light; illumination can also be indirect, creating shade, or light can be blocked from a surface, leaving it in shadow.

from light entirely and be in **shadow,** depending upon the location, direction, and quality of light, the shape and texture of the surface, and the position of interrupting forms (Figure 6–9).

Principles of Light and Shade

1. Light striking a surface is reflected in direct proportion to the intensity of light and the reflectability of the surface.
2. Surfaces closer to the source of light are illuminated more intensely than surfaces farther from the source of light.
3. Surfaces lighted directly reflect more intensely than surfaces lighted indirectly.
4. Smooth materials reflect light more intensely than textured materials.
5. Surfaces turned away from the source of light but receiving indirect illumination are in shade. Surfaces facing the source of light but prevented from receiving illumination by intervening objects are in shadow.
6. The shape and direction of a shadow are determined by the location of the source of light, the shape of the object causing the shadow, and the shape of the surface on which the shadow falls.
7. The darkness of a shadow or the lightness of a highlight is proportional to the intensity and crispness of the source of light. A diffuse source such as a fluorescent tube or an ellipsoidal reflector flood (scoop) produces soft shadows; a hard source such as an ellipsoidal reflector spotlight produces crisp multiple shadows.
8. Multiple sources of light produce multiple shadows.

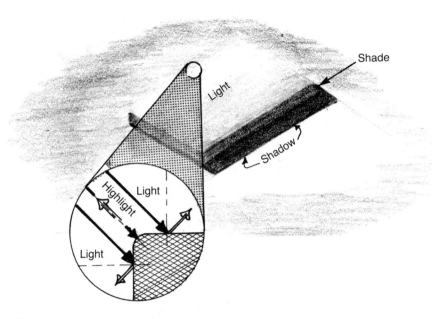

a.

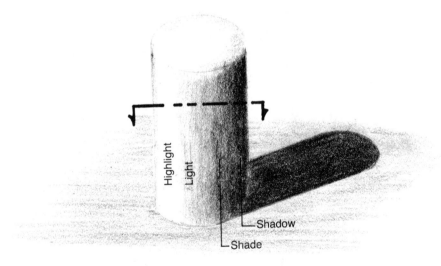

FIGURE 6-9
Analysis of highlight, light, shade, and shadow on a) A flat object, and b) A round object.

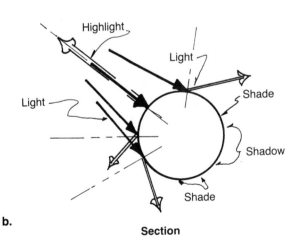

b.

Section

FIGURE 6–10

Multiple sources of light produce multiple shadows, each weakened by the presence of the other.

9. Equal sources of light located at conflicting angles weaken or wash out each other's shadow and increase the quantity of reflected light. The result is multiple shadows and shaded areas of lighter value.

10. The rendered value of a surface is influenced by its natural value, its texture, and the effect of light.

11. Highlights appear opaque, obliterating the natural appearance of a surface.

12. Shadows appear transparent, allowing the natural appearance of the surface in shadow to be visible but diminished.

13. Shadows gradate from extreme dark to lighter values as more reflected light enters the shadowed area.

14. Light passing through space appears to raise the value of surfaces behind the beam of light. Shadows passing through space appear to lower the value of surfaces behind the shadow.

RENDERING LIGHT AND SHADOW

The degrees of light and shade are infinite. For the sake of convenience they are represented on a nine-step scale (Figure 6–12) in mixtures of black and white. Step 5, medium, represents a neutral condition where there is neither highlight nor shadow. Steps 4, 3, and 2 are "shades" representing an increasing absence of light. Black represents total darkness. Steps 6, 7, and 8 are "lights" representing an increasing presence of illumination. White represents the most extreme illumination: either the source of light or strongly reflected light. In art work, these gradations of light are represented in tones of grey or in colors equivalent to those tones.

Drawings that show light and shadow may represent the color and texture of a surface relative to the overall design, or, more frequently, disregard the actual color and represent texture only in an abstract manner that emphasizes the effect of light. Pen-and-ink and pencil are

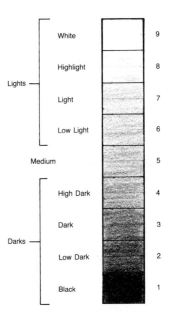

FIGURE 6–12
The value scale of light.

media especially conducive for this style of art work. Tones of grey may be created in linear form with rigid parallel lines (Figure 6–13a), hatch lines (Figure 6–13b), scribbles (Figure 6–13c), dots (Figure 6–13d), or graded shading (Figure 6–13e). The direction in which parallel lines and hatch lines are drawn may emphasize the natural direction

FIGURE 6–13
Drawing light and shade with monochromatic media.

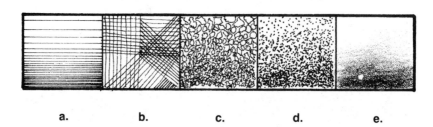

a.   b.   c.   d.   e.

of a plane or may have an arbitrary pattern. Figure 6–14 shows three approaches to expressing light and shade in a linear manner. The impression created in each sketch is similar, but subtle differences in

FIGURE 6–14
Three ways to render light and shade on a cylinder.

appearance distinquish the approaches. Representation of grained textures such as trees and wood are especially effective in this style of art work (Figure 6–15).

FIGURE 6–15
A line drawing using only light, shade, and texture.

SHADOWS IN PERSPECTIVE

Most productions for stage or camera are illuminated by lighting instruments throughout the acting area, but in design drawings the artist will frequently give the sense of directional light from a single source, to produce a dramatic sketch. The art work begins with a regular perspective drawing to which the designer adds textural and lighting effects. But first the designer must know the location and quality of light and the nature of materials contained in the drawing. From this information and an understanding of the causes of highlight and shadow, the designer may apply rules of perspective to create a credible representation of form and space.

The shape and position of a shadow is determined by a mechanical procedure. A shadow extends from the bottom of a form across its supporting surface, for example, a floor or platform, and continues up, down, or over any plane in perspective alignment with the source of light and the form casting the shadow. Two vanishing points are necessary for each shadow. One point is determined by the plan location of the **source of light;** the other is determined by the elevation of the source of light. *Each source of light has its own pair of vanishing points.* Drawings with several sources of light require multiple pairs of vanishing

191

points. The location on the plan of the source of light is called the **shadow vanishing point.** It is transferred to a position on the horizon line. The elevation of the source of light is placed on a vertical line extending above or below the shadow vanishing point. The vanishing point for a source of light located behind the picture plane is placed above the horizon line. The vanishing point for a source of light downstage of the picture plane is placed below the horizon line. These positions may be established arbitrarily or may be measured.

To Determine a Shadow When the Source of Light Is Located on a Plane Parallel to the Picture Plane

The shadow from a source of light located parallel to the picture plane will fall on the same plane as the source of light. It is only necessary to determine the position of the source of light; a shadow vanishing point is not needed to determine the direction of the shadow. The downstage and upstage edges of the shadow can be drawn with the aid of a T-square from the base of the object casting the shadow to the farthest distance of the shadow.

1. **Figure 6–16.** On the perspective sketch, determine the location of the source of light (SoL). The light may be placed arbitrarily, or its location may be determined with a protractor and scale. With a T-square, draw horizontal lines in the direction the shadow will fall. A line should attach to each bottom corner of the form casting the shadow.

FIGURE 6–16

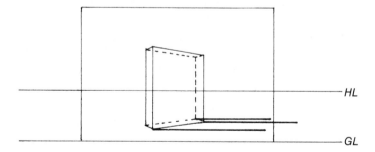

2. **Figure 6–17.** Draw lightweight lines from SoL to each top corner of the form casting the shadow. Extend these lines until they intersect the horizontal lines on the floor.

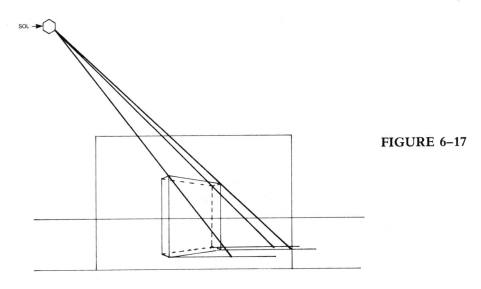

FIGURE 6–17

Note: Although lightweight lines are called for throughout these examples, **thick** lines are used for emphasis and clarity of each step in the process.

3. **Figure 6–18.** Attach the points of interception with each other to complete the outline of the shadow.

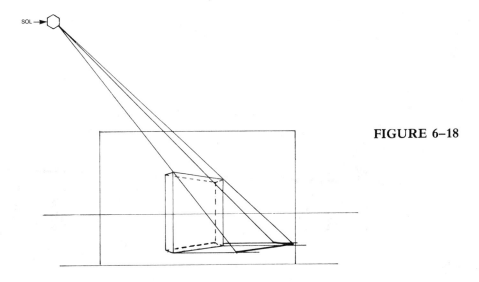

FIGURE 6–18

4. **Figure 6–19.** Erase all unnecessary lines, and complete the drawing with appropriate light and shade.

FIGURE 6–19

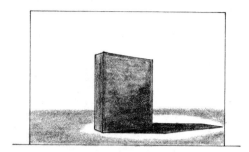

5. **Figure 6–20.** Were the wall shown in Figure 6–19 an archway, the light projected through the opening would be defined by drawing horizontal lines from the base of the opening into the shadowed area. A second pair of lines would be drawn from SoL to the top corners of the archway opening and would continue to the new horizontals. Again, the points where the horizontals and lines from SoL intersect would be connected to define the edges of the shadow and the light.

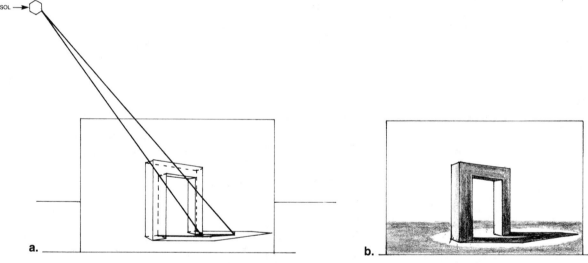

FIGURE 6–20

To Determine a Shadow When the Source of Light Is Located Behind the Picture Plane

1. **Figure 6–21.** Determine the location of the source of light in the plan. Drop a lightweight perpendicular from the source of light in the plan to the horizon line (HL) in the picture plane. Label the intersection of this line and the horizon line VPs (vanishing point—shadow).

2. Determine the vertical position of the source of light on the perpendicular above VPs. The height of the source of light may be measured with a protractor or scale, or it may be placed arbitrarily. Label this new point SoL (source of light).

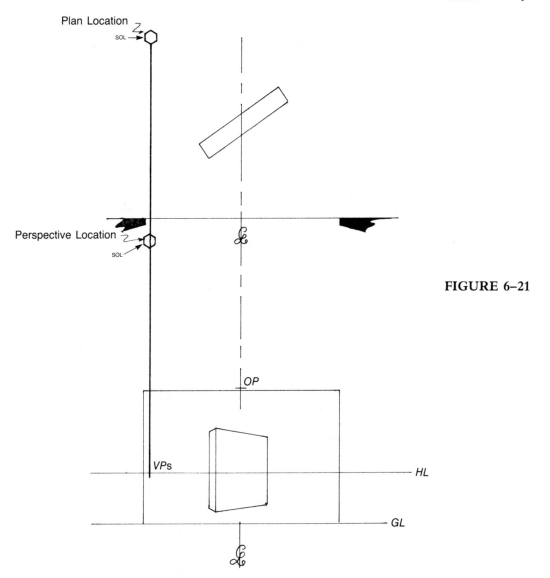

FIGURE 6–21

3. **Figure 6–22.** Draw a line fom VPs, in the direction the shadow will fall, through each bottom corner of the form that will cast the shadow.

FIGURE 6–22

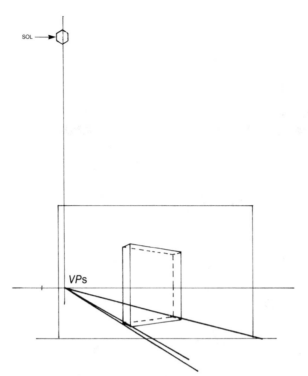

4. **Figure 6–23.** Draw a line from SoL through each upper corner of the form that will cast the shadow until the line intersects the lines from VPs.
5. Connect the intersections of the lines from VPs and SoL to outline the shadow. *Note:* Shadow line CD is parallel to line AB on the form, and both lines recede to the same vanishing point on the horizon line.

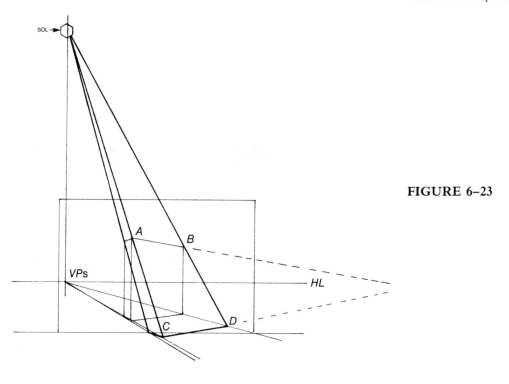

FIGURE 6–23

6. Erase all unnecessary lines, and complete the drawing by applying appropriate light and shade.

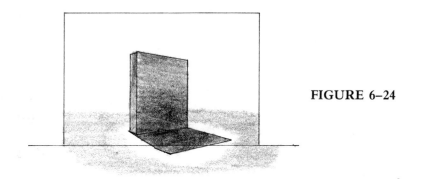

FIGURE 6–24

To Determine a Shadow When the Source of Light Is Located Downstage of the Picture Plane (Behind the Observer)—Measured Method

1. **Figure 6–25.** On the plan, determine the distance from the picture plane (PP) to the observation point (OP). On the perspective sketch, measure this same distance on the centerline from the groundline (GL) to establish a new observation point below the picture plane. Label this point OP′.

FIGURE 6–25

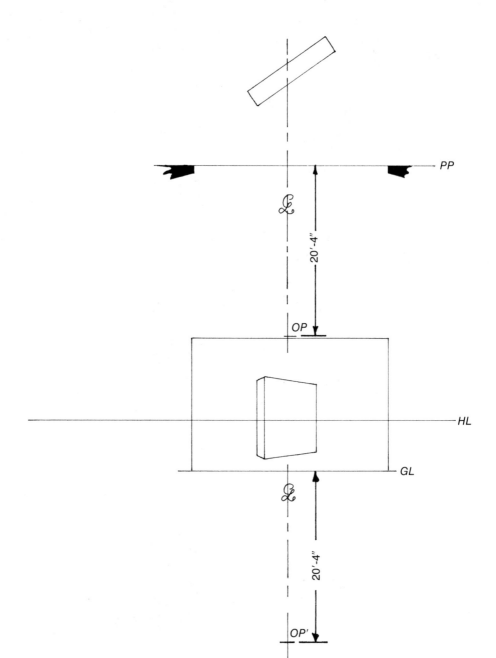

2. **Figure 6–26.** Determine the plan angle of the source of light. In the example, this angle is 50°. At OP′ measure this same angle on the side of the centerline opposite the source of light. Draw a lightweight line at this angle from OP′ to the horizon line (HL). Label the intersection of the horizon line and the lightweight line from OP′ as VPs (vanishing point—shadow).

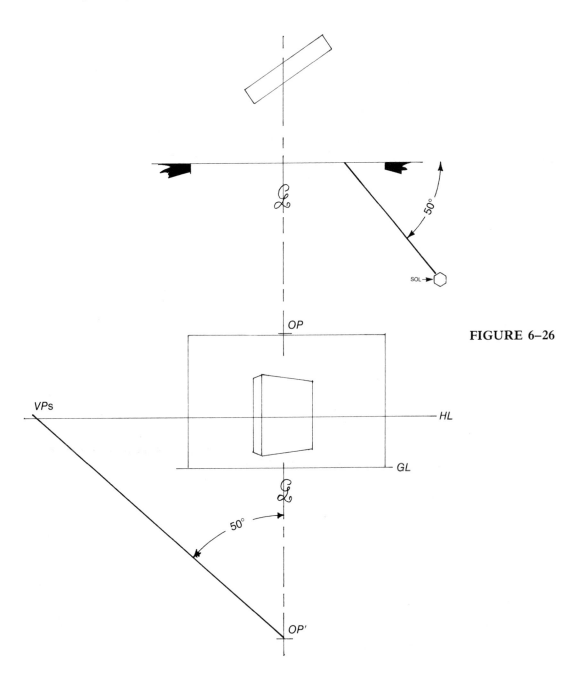

FIGURE 6–26

3. **Figure 6–27.** Measure the distance from VPs to OP′. Measure this same distance from VPs along the horizon line toward or past the centerline; label this point A.

FIGURE 6–27

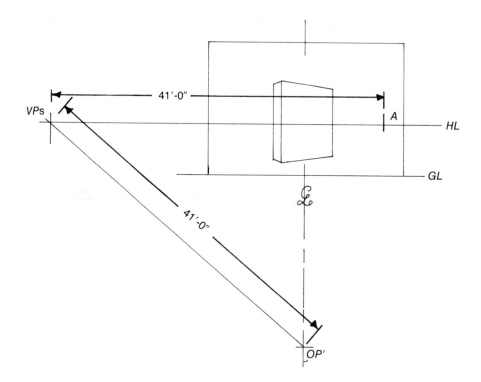

4. **Figure 6–28.** Drop a perpendicular from VPs below the picture plane. At A, measure the vertical angle to the source of light below the horizon line. In the example, the vertical angle to the source of light is 30°. Draw a line on this angle from A to the perpendicular below VPs. Label the intersection of the new line and the perpendicular SoL.

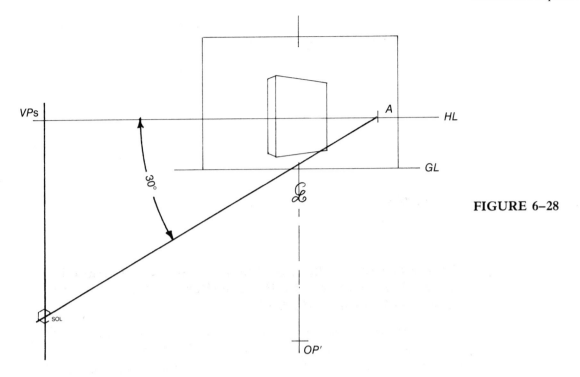

FIGURE 6–28

5. **Figure 6–29.** Connect the floor points of the form casting the shadow to VPs.

6. Connect the top points of the form casting the shadow to SoL.

7. Connect the intersection of the lines from VPs and SoL to each other to complete the outline of the shadow.

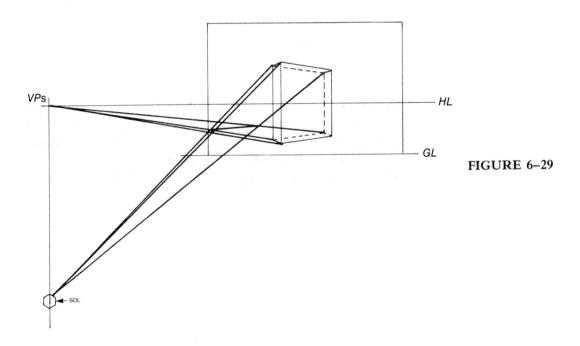

FIGURE 6–29

8. Erase all unnecessary lines, and complete the drawing by applying appropriate light and shade.

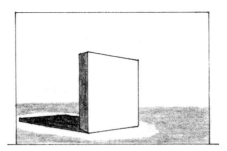

FIGURE 6–30

To Determine a Shadow When the Source of Light Is Located in Front of the Picture Plane (Behind the Observer)—Arbitrary Method

1. **Figure 6–31.** Arbitrarily draw the length and direction of the shadow for one major element of the picture.
2. Continue the arbitrary shadow line along the floor until it crosses the horizon line. Label the intersection of the extended shadow line and the horizon line VPs (vanishing point—shadow).

FIGURE 6–31

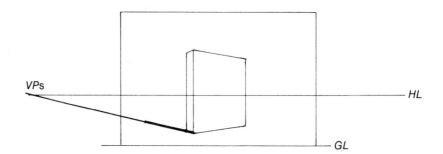

3. **Figure 6–32.** At VPs drop a perpendicular below the picture plane. Draw a line from the top of the form casting the shadow to the point where it crosses the end of the arbitrarily established shadow. Extend that line to the perpendicular dropped from VPs. Label the intersection of the perpendicular below VPs and the new diagonal SoL (source of light).

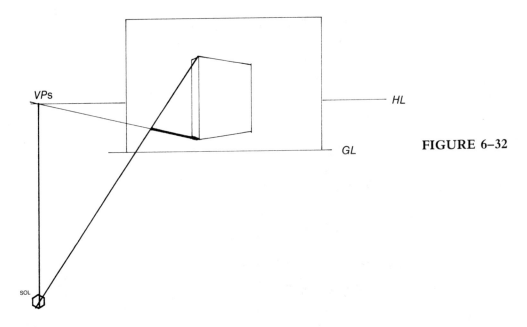

FIGURE 6–32

4. **Figure 6–33.** Connect VPs to all the floor points of the form casting the shadow.

5. Draw a lightweight line that connects SoL to the other top points of the form casting the shadow, thus creating new points of intersection for lines from VPs and SoL.

6. Connect the intersections of the lines from VPs and SoL to each other.

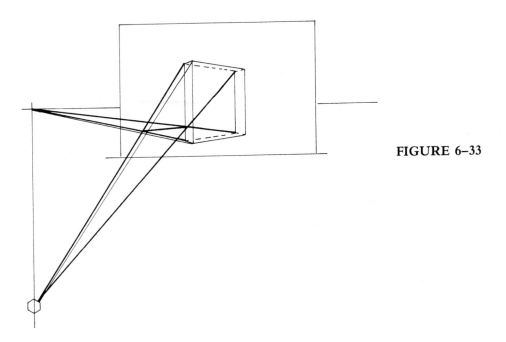

FIGURE 6–33

7. **Figure 6–34.** Erase all unnecessary lines, and complete the drawing with appropriate light and shade.

FIGURE 6–34

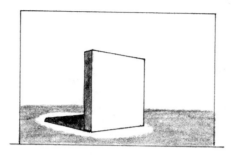

To Locate a Shadow on a Vertical Plane

1. **Figure 6–35.** Using one of the methods described above, determine the outline of the shadow on the floor as if it were not interrupted.

2. The shadow will change direction at any point where it is interrupted by a vertical or inclined plane. In the example, the shadow will change directions at points A, B, C, and D. Draw a vertical line from point A and from point B to the top of the vertical plane. Label the upper end of the lines C and D, respectively.

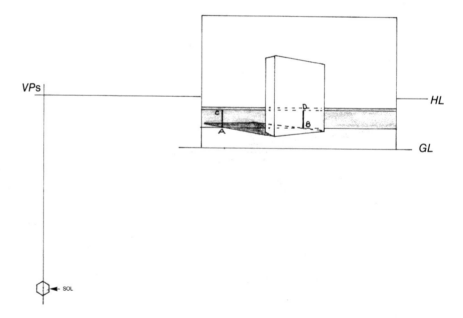

FIGURE 6–35

3. **Figure 6–36.** The top plane of the interrupting form will cause a second change in the direction of the shadow. Draw a line from C to VPs and a second line from D to VPs.

4. Connect the points where lines C–VPs and D–VPs cross the lines from SoL.

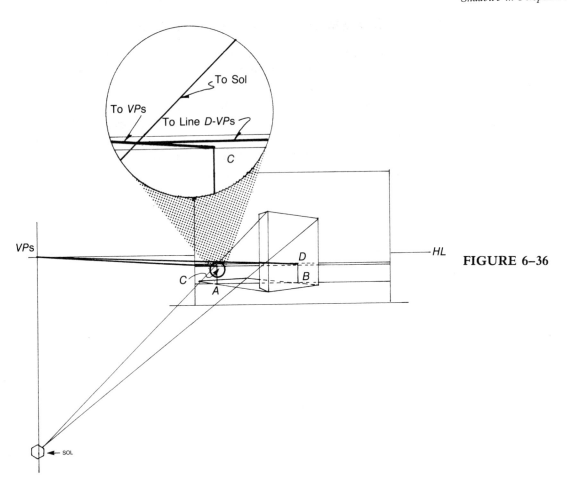

FIGURE 6–36

5. Erase all unnecessary lines, and complete the drawing with appropriate light and shade.

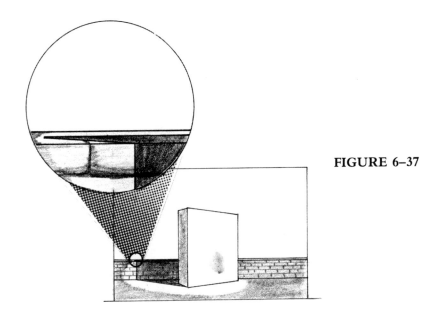

FIGURE 6–37

To Locate a Shadow on an Inclined Plane

The same process may be used to establish shadows on inclined planes. Rather than drawing vertical lines at A and B, place the lines on the same plane as the incline.

When the rendering has been completed with appropriate shading, the original sketch, which was composed of outlines, should have a solid appearance and a sense of texture, dimensionality, and light. The lines that guided the art work should be obliterated by the highlights, shadows, and textures of the final composition.

Exercises

1. Obtain several black-and-white photographs of various subjects from magazines or other sources. Include at least one exterior scene, one interior scene, a close-up photograph of any opaque three-dimensional object, a close-up photograph of any transparent three-dimensional object, and a human face. Each photo should be at least 4″ × 5″. Analyze each picture carefully.

   a. Using the following symbols, mark each area of highlight (H), light (L), shade (S), and shadow (X).
   b. Determine the cause of each shadow.
   c. From the location of highlights and the shape and direction of shadows, determine the location and quality of each source of light. Identify this location on the photo with an asterisk and a brief description.

2. Work on drafting vellum, and use an HB lead or other soft pencil to sketch a nine-step scale of light. Number and label each step of the scale.

3. For the following exercises you will need a single-filament high-intensity desk lamp. Any drawing paper will be satisfactory.

   a. Find a plain square or rectangular carton. Place the high-intensity lamp above and to the right-front of the carton. Lightly draw the outline of the carton with thin (4H) lines. Using a soft lead (2B) pencil, add appropriate highlight, shade, and shadow to the sketch. Be sure to include the shadow cast by the carton. When completed, the drawing should reveal the shape of the carton without the use of outlines on any portion of the work. Repeat the exercise until you feel the drawing correctly represents what you see.
   b. Repeat Exercise 3a, using a can or ball in place of the carton.
   c. Repeat Exercises 3a and 3b, with the source of light located above and behind each form.

4. Following the procedures accompanying Figures 6–16 through 37, sketch each "set" with a single source of light, and then apply the appropriate light and shade.

5. Repeat Exercise 4, but provide two sources of light, 90° apart.

6. Return to one of the perspective sketches you drew for Chapter 4. Complete the development of one of those sketches by providing a single source of light located downstage of the plaster line and drawing in all highlight, shade, and shadow.

CHAPTER 7

Color

INTRODUCTION

Color has significant influence on our lives. Although we may not be conscious of it, color contributes to our moods and attitudes and affects our choice of clothing, automobiles, and even the food we eat. Some colors evoke such strong sensations they instantly communicate attitudes or ideas: bright red suggests danger, white evokes a sense of purity or sterility, green implies nature, and black suggests death. These responses to color contribute to choices made by artists and designers. In the performing arts, color may be the most vital element of design. Not only do colors bear significant meanings, they contribute to the interest and attention of audiences. Properly employed, color can be used by the designer in the performing arts to control focus and to create psychological and emotional effects. It can create a sense of form, style, and mood and suggest the period or locale of a performance. With all of these attributes, color is one of the most important elements the designer can use.

THE COMPONENTS OF COLOR

Color is also one of the most challenging elements with which the designer works. Unlike other design elements such as line, mass, or texture, color is multifaceted. It consists of three interrelated components: hue, value, and chroma. The hue of a color is its name, distinguishing it from all other colors; the value is the whiteness or blackness of a color; and chroma is the brightness or intensity of a color. Each of these components may be treated individually or in relation to the others.

Hue

Hue is the term used to differentiate one color from another. In technical terms, individual colors are made from light. When a beam of light is passed through a prism, it produces stripes of color like a rainbow (Figure 7–1). Each colored stripe is composed of a different wavelength of light. A colored material reflects one or more of these wavelengths. Each hue is distinguished by the wavelengths of light it reflects. On this basis hues can be arranged in a logical pattern on a color wheel.

A basic **color wheel** (Figure C–1) is composed of three primary colors, three secondary colors, and six intermediate colors, equally spaced around the perimeter of a circle. The **primary colors**—red,

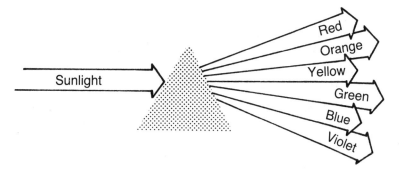

FIGURE 7–1
When sunlight is passed through a glass prism, the beam of light is divided into individual wavelengths. Each wavelength is seen as a different color of light.

yellow and blue—are essential to the formation of the color wheel. Primary colors may be mixed with each other in varying proportions to form other hues, but mixing two or more hues together will not create primary colors. This color system depends on the previous existence of the primary colors. **Secondary colors** are created by mixing equal proportions of two adjacent primary hues. The secondary colors are orange (red plus yellow), green (yellow plus blue), and violet (blue plus red). They occur halfway between the primary colors on the perimeter of the color wheel. **Intermediate colors** are mixed from equal amounts of neighboring primary and secondary colors. The intermediate colors are red-orange, yellow-orange, yellow-green, blue-green, blue-violet and red-violet. They occur halfway between each primary and secondary hue on the color wheel. An almost infinite variety of additional colors can be mixed by combining two or more hues, located in any position on the color wheel.

The position of a hue on the color wheel gives its characteristics and its relationship to other colors. **Analogous colors** are located next to each other on the color wheel (Figure 7–2). Thus orange and

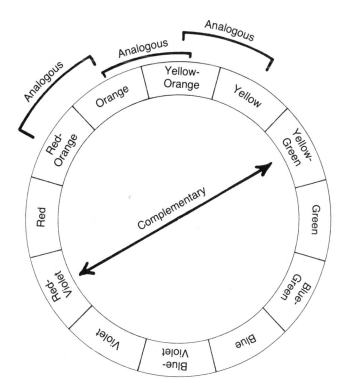

FIGURE 7–2
The color wheel. Colors located next to each other are analogous hues; colors located opposite each other are complementary hues.

red-orange are analogous; both colors contain a quantity of a common hue, in this case orange. Orange and yellow-orange are also analogous colors, with orange common to both hues. Continuing around the circle, yellow-orange and yellow are analogous colors, but yellow is the common hue rather than orange. Analogous pairs of colors can be listed all the way around the color wheel.

Also, two colors that are directly opposite each other on the color wheel—for example, orange and blue—have a specific relationship. Any hue directly opposite another color on the color wheel is its **complementary color.** In this way, blue and orange are complementary colors. A secondary color always occurs opposite a primary color, so that red/green and yellow/violet are pairs of complementary colors. Intermediate colors occur opposite other intermediate colors, so the complement of blue-violet is yellow-orange, the complement of yellow-green is red-violet, and red-orange is the complement of blue-green. These color pairings become important in the mixing of colors and selection of palettes.

Value

Hue describes only one characteristic of a color. In addition, a color may be bright or dull, light or dark. **Value** describes the lightness or darkness of a color. Lightness and darkness are qualities of illumination. In drawing and painting, these qualities are represented as white, grey, and black.

The scale of light and shade used to represent degrees of illumination in Chapter 6 may also be used in pigment as a **value scale** (Figure 7–3). Neither black nor white has any hue; they are described as **neutral** or **achromatic** (without hue) colors. When mixed together, they form a range of greys that are also neutral. An almost endless number of subtle gradations of grey can be mixed from black and white. Most artists limit the value scale to nine colors, with black at the bottom (Value 1), white at the top (Value 9), and medium-grey in the middle (Value 5). Medium-grey represents a totally neutral visual condition. It contains no hue and seems to consist of an equal quantity of white and black. Medium-grey occurs at the center of the color wheel equidistant from all hues (Figure 7–4). Values 1 through 4 are shades and fall below the wheel; values 6 through 9 are tints and rise above the plane of the color wheel to establish a perpendicular axis around which the hues are located.

Hues also have characteristics of lightness and darkness. Every hue has its own natural value relative to white, grey, and black. This may be seen when a chip of yellow pigment is placed next to a chip of blue and compared to black and white (Figure C–2). In this relationship yellow appears much lighter than blue; it is more similar to white than to black. On the other hand, blue appears to be more similar to black. These are differences in the natural value of these hues. Figure C–3 shows the hues of the basic color wheel arranged in order of relative natural value.

Hues and neutrals may be treated independently to render light and shade, or they may be combined to form new colors. A hue may

FIGURE 7–3

The value scale. This scale represents the range of grey colors that can be mixed by combining black and white. Value 1 is black, Value 5 is medium grey and Value 9 is white.

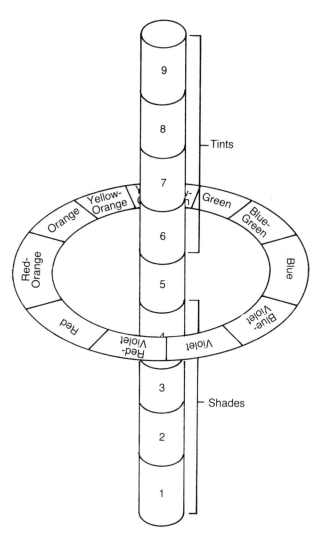

FIGURE 7–4
The value scale is a column located at the center of the color wheel. Value 5 is located on the same plane as the hues. Each value is equidistant from all hues on the color wheel.

be mixed with white or black to form a nine-step value scale of a color (Figure C–4). Black is at the bottom of the scale (Value 1), the base hue is at the middle (Value 5), and white is at the top of the scale (Value 9). All gradations below the base hue (Values 1 through 4) are shades of the base color; all gradations above the base hue (Values 6 through 9) are tints. These nine even gradations indicate the range of values to which a color may be mixed. Many subtle gradations between each tint and shade are possible.

Additional variety can be obtained by mixing a hue with *both* black and white *at the same time.* The seven gradations of greys that occur between black and white on the neutral value scale can be mixed in varying proportions with a hue to form **tones.** Unlike tints, which consist of a base hue plus white, or shades, which contain a base hue plus black, tones are mixed with the base hue plus white plus black. The ratio among the components of this mixture may vary widely. It may contain, for instance, one part orange, two parts black, and six parts white; or two parts orange, five parts black, and one part white; or any other proportion of hue and neutrals. These mixtures tend to subdue colors, resulting in soft, muted tones (Figure C–5).

Chroma

Hue names a color; value describes its lightness or darkness. The third component of color is **chroma.** This term refers to brightness or intensity of a color. Chroma is distinct from value. A color may be light, that is, a tint, but at the same time not be bright or intense. An example may help an observer identify chroma. Both a fire engine and a radish are red, but they are certainly not the same color. The color of the fire engine appears bright—it almost seems to glow. The radish, however, appears dull. Neither object is lighter or darker than the other; the difference in color is *brightness.* Although both objects are red, the radish has a weaker chroma. The red skin of the radish is dulled by the presence of a small quantity of green pigment, the complement of red. A color is at its strongest chroma in pure form— as it appears on the perimeter of the color wheel. The chroma of a color is weakened by the presence of its complementary hue. In this way, pure red can be made duller by adding a small amount of green pigment. Eventually, a sufficient quantity of green may be added to absorb the red color entirely; the color then becomes neutral. Any pair of complementary colors may be mixed in this manner to reduce the chroma-strength of one member of the pair, and ultimately in this way the color will be neutralized. Each hue on the color wheel requires a different quantity of additions of its complementary color to reach a neutral level. Stated another way, every hue has its own natural maximum chroma that is not equal to the maximum chroma of other hues. The twelve hues on the color wheel are listed according to strength of chroma in Table 7–1.

TABLE 7–1
Relative number of chroma steps for hues

Color	Number of Chroma Steps
Yellow	9
Yellow-orange	8
Orange	8
Red-orange	9
Red	10
Red-violet	6
Violet	6
Blue-violet	9
Blue	6
Blue-green	7
Green	7
Yellow-green	8

Summary of Color Terms

Color   the combination of hue, value, and chroma perceived as a result of reflected light.

Hue   the name of a color distinguishing it from all other colors, based on the wavelengths of light it reflects.

Chromatic   a color having hue.

Achromatic   a color lacking hue, including black, white, and greys mixed from black and white.

Color wheel   hues arranged around the perimeter of a circle according to the wavelengths of light each reflects.

Primary colors   hues that cannot be mixed from other colors but can be used to mix other colors. The primaries are red, blue, and yellow.

Secondary colors   hues mixed from visually equal amounts of neighboring primary colors and located halfway between each primary on the color wheel. These hues are orange, violet, and green.

Intermediate colors   hues mixed by combining neighboring primary and secondary colors. On a basic color wheel, these hues are red-violet, red-orange, yellow-orange, yellow-green, blue-green, and blue-violet.

Analogous colors   hues located next to each other on the color wheel, such as red, red-orange, and orange.

Complementary colors   hues located opposite each other on the color wheel, such as red/green or blue/orange.

Neutral colors   colors without hue. These include black, white, and all greys mixed from black and white.

Value   the relative lightness or darkness of a color in relation to black and white. Values are described as tints, shades, or tones.

Value scale   a nine-step scale of neutral colors located on a perpendicular axis at the center of the color wheel. A chromatic value scale may be constructed from each hue and includes a base hue plus tints and shades mixed from white, black, and the base hue.

Tint   colors mixed with white and located above medium (Value 5) on the value scale.

Shade   colors mixed with black and located below medium (Value 5) on the value scale.

Tone   colors mixed with grey.

Chroma   the brightness of a color, determined by its purity as a result of the presence or absence of its complementary color. "Intensity," "brightness," and "saturation" are frequently used as synonyms for "chroma."

COLOR MIXING

Pure hues as they appear on the perimeter of the color wheel are seldom used in design. They are usually modified in some way. Colors may be combined with other hues, adjusted in value, or reduced in chroma, or all three components may be modified concurrently. A color may be created or altered in one of the following ways:

A new color may be created by mixing two or more existing hues.

A tint may be made by adding white to a color.

A shade may be mixed by adding black to a color.

A tone may be created by adding grey to a color.

A color may be reduced in chroma by adding its complementary color.

It is helpful to think of color mixing as three-dimensional movement (Figure 7–5): 1) a change in hue causes a color to move around the perimeter of the color wheel; 2) a change in value causes vertical movement up or down the value scale; and 3) a change in chroma causes movement toward the center of the color wheel.

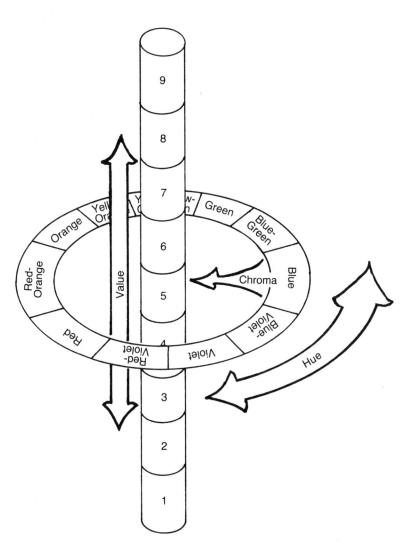

FIGURE 7–5

Color mixing can be visualized as three-dimensional movement. A change in hue will move a color around the perimeter of the wheel, a change in chroma will move a color toward the value scale, and a change in value will move a color up or down the value scale.

In the construction of the color wheel, secondary hues were formed by mixing equal proportions of two adjacent primary colors. In this way, green was made by mixing yellow and blue pigment. Intermediate colors were mixed in a similar manner. Variations of secondary and intermediate colors are mixed by adjusting proportions of the base colors that are combined. In this manner, a color falling anywhere between two hues on the color wheel can be created. For instance, an infinite variety of red-violets can be mixed by increasing or decreasing the proportion of red. Similarly, a variety of yellow-orange hues can be mixed varying the proportion of either hue contributing to the mixture.

Other colors may be mixed by blending hues located in any other position on the color wheel. For instance, yellow-orange may be mixed with red-violet to create a brownish color, or yellow-orange may be mixed with green to create a chartreuse color. The specific color created is dependent not only on the choice of hues but also on the proportion of the colors contained in the mixture. Thus, a yellow-orange, red-violet mixture might be dominated by one hue or by the other. The mixture could be further modified by increasing the proportion of violet, red, or yellow in the base colors. This mixture of yellow-orange and red-violet would result in a new hue; however, the new color will be weaker in chroma than either of the base colors (Figure 7–6). Such reductions in chroma occur whenever two nonanalogous hues (hues not located next to each other on the color wheel) are mixed

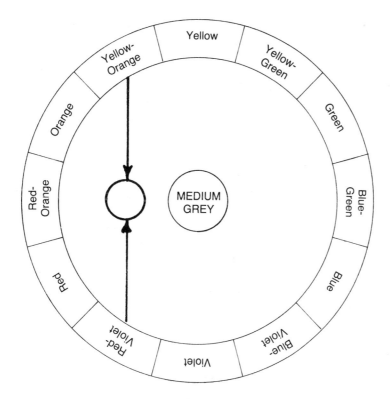

FIGURE 7–6
Mixing nonanalogous colors will result in a reduction of chroma that brings the new color closer to medium grey than the starting colors.

together. Further modifications of chroma can be caused by adding a small amount of a hue that is close to the complement of the new color. In this case, blue-green would be the appropriate complement (Figure 7–7). Large additions of the complementary color will totally neutralize the mixture and result in a muddy, neutral color.

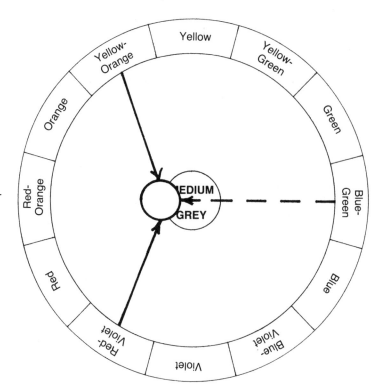

FIGURE 7–7
Adding the complement of the new color created by combining two nonanalogous hues will further reduce the chroma of the new color.

In addition to modifying chroma, an alteration of value occurs when nonanalogous hues are mixed together. It is apparent in Figure C–3 that yellow-orange has a fairly high natural value and that the value of red-violet is lower. When these hues are mixed together, the inherent value of yellow-orange is reduced in the new color, and the value of red-violet is raised. In other words, a mixture of yellow-orange and red-violet results in a new color with both a weaker chroma and a different value than either of the base colors contributing to the mixture. This principle of color mixing is true for all combinations of nonanalogous hues.

Creating a tint, shade, or tone is a much more direct process than mixing hues or adjusting chroma. Any color can be made into a tint by adding white or may be made into a shade by adding black to the base color. Mixtures of tones are dependent upon the addition of both black and white to a color. The quality of a tone created in this manner is dependent upon the proportions of white, black, and the base hue. A greater proportion of any one variable will dominate the new color.

TRADITIONAL COLOR PALETTES

The hues on the color wheel and the neutrals on the value scale can be combined to create several thousand different colors; therefore it would seem that anyone mixing paints should only need fourteen colors to accomplish the work: the three primary, three secondary, and six intermediate colors, plus black and white. Yet designer's paintboxes and studio paint rooms seem to be crammed with tubes, bins, and buckets of pigments. Over sixty oil colors and forty watercolor paints are available to the artist. This broad range of pigments is available for three reasons: a) to allow the artist to devote the greatest amount of energy to applying paints rather than mixing them, b) to make common colors and gradations of colors handily available in large quantities, and c) to make strong colors available in a broad range, since colors mixed by the artist are seldom as strong as those taken from the tube. Once a designer understands the broad range of colors that may be mixed from any two pigments, as many tubes or bins of paint as necessary should be available to the artist. This should not suggest that all forty watercolor pigments are mandatory in the designer's paintbox or that they should all be used in each design or rendering. The designer must exercise control of the palette to achieve desired effects.

Based on principles of harmony, contrast, and variety, a number of traditional color palettes have emerged. These should be considered only as guides by the artist. Production concepts, theatrical effects, technical limitations, and ever-changing audience taste should dictate the use of color, not traditions or rules.

Monochromatic Color Palette

A design may contain a multitude of colors, like a Harlequin costume, or may be limited to a single color, like a sepia photograph. The Harlequin is polychromatic (multicolored); the photograph is monochromatic (one color). A monochromatic palette may be used effectively by the scene or costume designer; the artist then uses tints, tones, and shades to create the design. Variety is achieved by manipulating line, form, texture, mass, and light rather than color. The design is automatically unified in color. From one point of view, a monochromatic palette is the easiest and safest utilization of color. From another point of view, a single color design requires highly creative use of line, form, mass, and texture to avoid tedium.

Analogous Color Palette

Closely related to monochromatic use of color is the palette of analogous colors. This approach expands the single color of a monochromatic palette to include the hues located to the right and left of a base hue on the color wheel.

An analogous color palette constructed around blue might include all variations of blue-violet and blue-green. In practical terms, a broader palette of analogous colors might extend from blue-green through violet. Using all variations of tints, tones, and shades, an almost infinite selection of colors is available to the designer to provide visual interest. For instance, a medium-value, strong-chroma violet piping might be used as trim on a high-value, weak-chroma blue-green dress decorated with low-value, high-chroma blue-violet flowers. Differences in hue, value, and chroma provide variety; the presence of blue in each color provides unity. The designer, however, must carefully control value and chroma if the desired effect is harmony. Should the designer wish to create an effect of dissonance, the strength of all chromas might be increased, but the costume would then appear garish.

219

Straight-Complement Color Palette

An alternative method to using colors related by proximity is using colors related by distance. Designs may be arranged around a palette of opposite or complementary colors such as green/red or yellow/violet. This does not mean that precise opposites must be used. A near-complement can be as effective as a direct complement. It is easy to imagine the discordant effects possible with such palettes; however, harmonious designs resulting in beautiful, lively effects can be created. The use of complementary colors usually requires one of the two colors to be dominant in chroma and value; the second color should be of weaker chroma but cover a larger area. Extreme care must be taken to select the appropriate value and chroma when using a palette of opposites. The designer must be further cautioned that lighting colors may significantly affect the appearance of one or both hues when they are separated by such great distance on the color wheel. Designers for the film or television camera must be aware that the camera lens may cause complementary colors placed in proximity to scintillate.

Split-Complement Color Palette

A split-complement palette offers greater variety than the straight-complement palette. The split-complement palette utilizes a base hue and the colors on each side of the complement of the base color; for instance, green with red-orange and red-violet (Figure 7–8). The same cautions for obtaining balance by controlling chroma and value apply here as with a straight-complement palette. With both the split and straight-complement palettes, a more balanced and harmonious design

FIGURE 7–8

The split-complement color palette consists of a base hue and the colors on either side of the complement of the base hue.

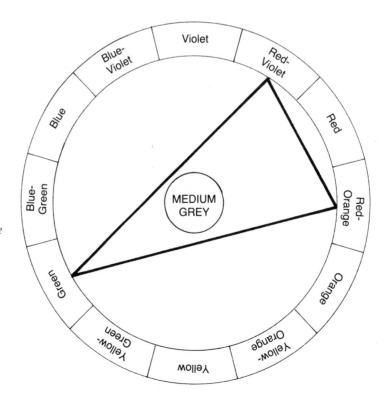

is more likely to be achieved when the stronger purer colors are used in the form of accents, such as molding or ornaments on sets or trim and accessories on costumes. This does not mean that in a yellow, red-violet, blue-violet split-complement palette that yellow must be restricted to door knobs and window frames. Instead, a tint, tone, or shade of yellow might be used to paint the major areas of the setting but their value and chroma must not be allowed to become too strong. The two violets could be used as accent colors. Alternatively, the violets could be subdued for use as the base color in the set and the yellow pigment at full chroma restricted to use as an accent color.

Color-Triad Palette

The greatest variety may be achieved by using a color triad. This palette uses colors equally spaced around the color wheel (Figure 7–9). A primary triad includes red, blue, and yellow; another example of a triad is blue-violet, yellow-green and red-orange. A harmonious design in each of the triads requires one of the three hues to be selected as the key color, which is available throughout its entire range of chroma and value. The other two colors are used at reduced chroma, which may be adjusted through tints, tones, and shades. The result will be a harmonious and exciting design. In contrast, a discordant and garish effect might be purposely created for a surrealistic or expressionistic production by using all three colors of the triad in pure form and in equal proportions.

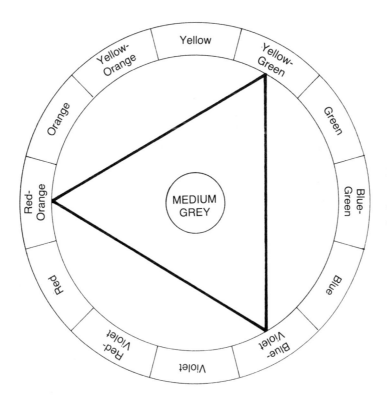

FIGURE 7–9

The color-triad palette consists of three hues equally spaced around the perimeter of the color wheel.

Although these are traditional palettes which have been found to yield harmonious compositions in art, the designer must be reminded that they do not imply rigid rules to be observed at all times. These palettes simply provide traditional guidelines for safe color choices. In the performing arts, production concepts, characterizations, lighting and the effect of the lens may dictate a conscious deviation from these guidelines.

COLOR PERCEPTION

Although a knowledge of the vocabulary and technology of color is important, it only serves to prepare the designer for the task of manipulating color in a composition. The choices that must be made are dependent upon some understanding of the human perception of color.

The way we see color is a physical phenomenon dependent upon light, pigment, and vision. People also respond to color as a psychological phenomenon. It is known, for instance, that colors communicate and sometimes cause a sense of warmth or cold, vitality, happiness, depression, melancholy, joy, anger, or tension. Colors also have a specific psychological meaning: red warns, white is pure, black represents death. Extensive research continues to be done in this area of psychology. For the designer, an awareness of these meanings can help determine appropriate color choices. These choices, however, should be made with further understanding not only of the technology of color but also of the effects of color perception.

Seen against a neutral background, a color seems to have inherent characteristics which are identifiable in terms of hue, value, and chroma. That same color is perceived differently when placed against a chromatic background. A color may be pleasant and soft, or harsh and sharp, depending upon its surroundings. In different environments, a color may jump out of the picture or recede into it; it may appear luminous, misty, glossy, metallic, transparent, or dull. It is the relationship of the color to its surroundings that causes these variations in appearance. The designer must be conscious of this effect, because it contributes not only to the selection of hue but to the determination of chroma and value. The effect can be described with some specificity in relation to warm and cool colors.

Warm and Cool Colors

Colors that have a red or yellow quality communicate a sense of warmth, and colors that have a blue or green characteristic communicate a sense of coolness, when either color group is seen against a neutral background. Any warm color, such as red-orange, appears warmer when placed against a cool background such as green; however, that same red-orange will appear cooler when placed against a warm background such as red (Figure C–6). The color does not actually change; only its appearance changes as the color is moved from background to background. This change in "apparent temperature" is a characteristic of color perception.

Color Perspective

The previous discussion of perspective showed that objects in the distance appear smaller than the same objects in the foreground. It is equally true that objects in the distance appear more neutral in color than objects in the foreground. The yellow school bus described in Chapter 4 would continue to be yellow as it travelled farther from the observer; however, the color of the bus would appear increasingly grey in the distance. This neutralization of color in the distance is called **color perspective**.

The contrast between the color of an object and the color of its surroundings contributes to perspective effects. For instance, a square of yellow on a light background will appear significantly larger when moved to a dark background (Figure C–7). There is no physical change in the size of the yellow square, only a change in perception by the observer. Also, in the first instance, the high-value, strong-chroma yellow square seems to remain fixed on the light background. Against the dark background, the yellow square seems to advance or jump off the surface. In contrast, a black square seen against a deep-violet background appears to remain fixed on the surface; but when the black square is moved to a yellow background, the black area seems to recede into the surface, creating a deep hole (Figure C–8).

For the designer in the performing arts, these effects play a part in the selection of values and chroma for any element of a production. The designer's challenge is to select appropriate colors and avoid creating "holes," distorting dimensions, or causing the loss of perspective relationships.

The use of color is a relative matter and a function of perceptions of the designer and the needs of the production. An understanding of how colors are created and the interrelationships of the components of color can facilitate the designer's work. Rules of harmony, contrast, and color mixing should be considered as guides to the use of color. Ultimately the designer must determine the appropriate combinations based on the effects desired. Success in reaching these goals is dependent on the designer's good taste and solid technical knowledge.

Exercises

1. Create a notebook on the use of color. Spend at least a portion of each day over a five-day period noting how color is used in advertising and on signs. Assign all the primary and secondary colors and white, grey, and black to separate pages of a notebook. On each page list ways in which you observe color used in television and magazine ads and on signs. If desired, expand the list to include the use of color in commercial buildings or any other obvious treatments of color. You might include "stop sign" under red, "caution sign" under yellow, "menthol cigarette pack" under green, and "restaurant booths" under orange.

For each of the following exercises use good watercolor paints and clean white paper. Mix each color required individually. Paint each color on separate pieces of paper. After the paint has dried completely, neatly cut out one-inch squares of the needed colors, and glue them onto a white, black, or grey surface such as illustration board.

*When mixing paints be sure to create **visually** accurate colors. Variations in pigment strength, dilution, and so forth cause mathematical or measured proportional mixtures that result in surprisingly inaccurate visual colors and gradations. In general, it is better to add small amounts of dark colors to lighter colors. After paints have dried, lay out all the swatches you plan to use. Place them next to each other to judge the appropriateness of the colors. Be objective. It may be necessary to replace some of the colors after you have seen them lined up next to each other. Glue swatches in place.*

2. Starting with only primary colors, make your own twelve-hue color wheel. Paste the swatches in the proper pattern on a board; then label the name of each color, such as "red-orange," and its identity as a primary, secondary, or intermediate hue.

3. Select a neighboring primary and secondary color, such as blue and green. Mix the two colors together in various proportions to achieve ten visual steps of gradation of hue between the two colors.

4. Using only lamp black and titanium white, create a nine-step achromatic value scale. Label each swatch as a tint or shade, and number each swatch from 1 through 9.

5. Select one primary, one secondary, and one intermediate hue from widely separated positions on the color wheel. Create a nine-step chromatic value scale for each of these three colors. Label each swatch as a tint or shade, and number each swatch from 1 through 9.

6. From Figure 7–10 select one secondary hue. Using only that color plus black and white, make a tone scale. Column A should be an achromatic value scale, and Column E should be a chromatic value scale. Columns B, C, and D should each be increasingly neutral tones of the base hue. Each row of the chart from top to bottom should make an even progression from white to black.

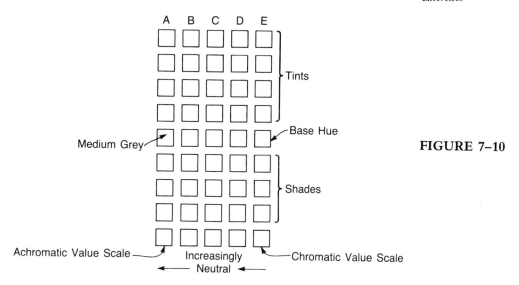

FIGURE 7–10

7. Select any primary color and its complementary color. Create the following chroma chart. Be sure each step of the chart is a visually equal change.

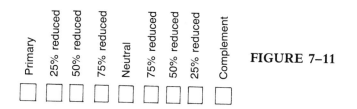

FIGURE 7–11

8. Select one primary hue from the right half of the color wheel and label it "Color 1." Select one intermediate hue from the left half of the color wheel, neither a color analogous to Color 1 nor a near complement. Label the intermediate hue "Color 2." Using Colors 1 and 2 plus black and white, create the color chart in Figure 7–12.

    a. Column A is to be a nine-step value scale of Color 1. Column K is to be a nine-step value scale of Color 2.

    b. Columns B through J are to be nine-step value scales of Colors 1 and 2, mixed together in visual proportions as follows:

Columns	Color 1	Color 2
B	90	10
C	80	20
D	70	30
E	60	40
F	50	50
G	40	60
H	30	70
I	20	80
J	10	90

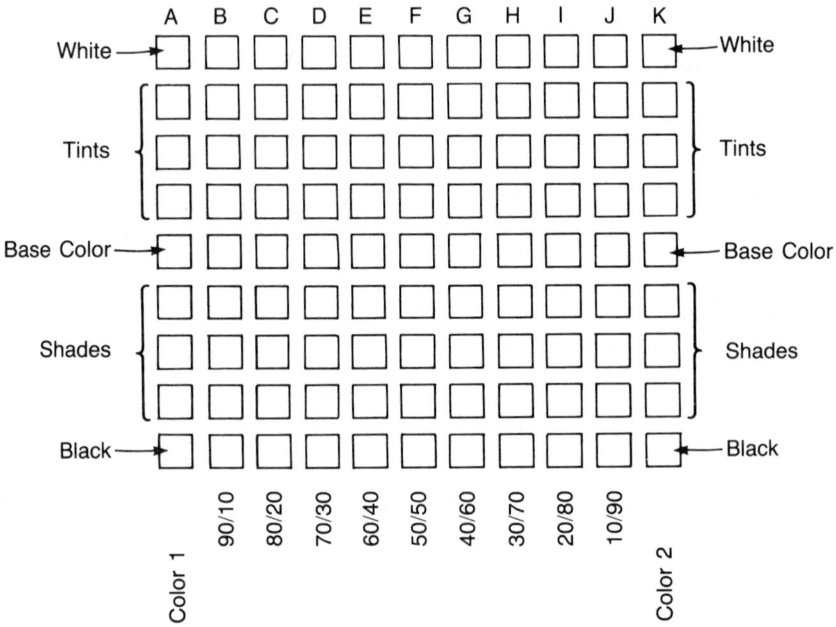

FIGURE 7–12

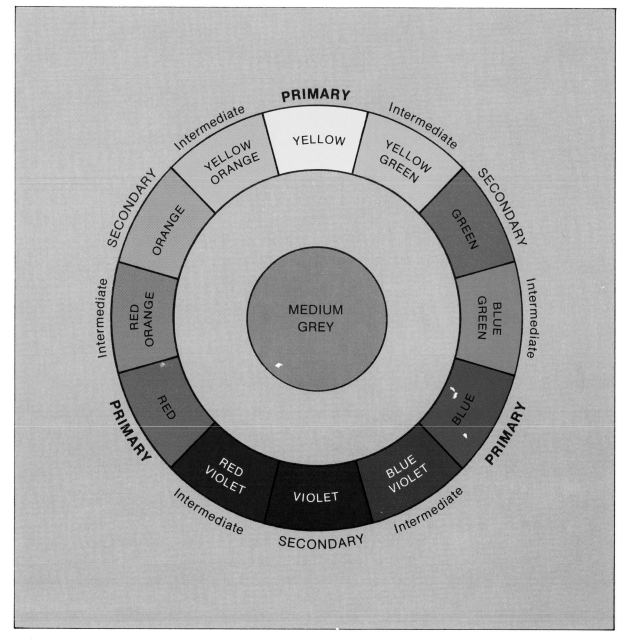

Figure C-1

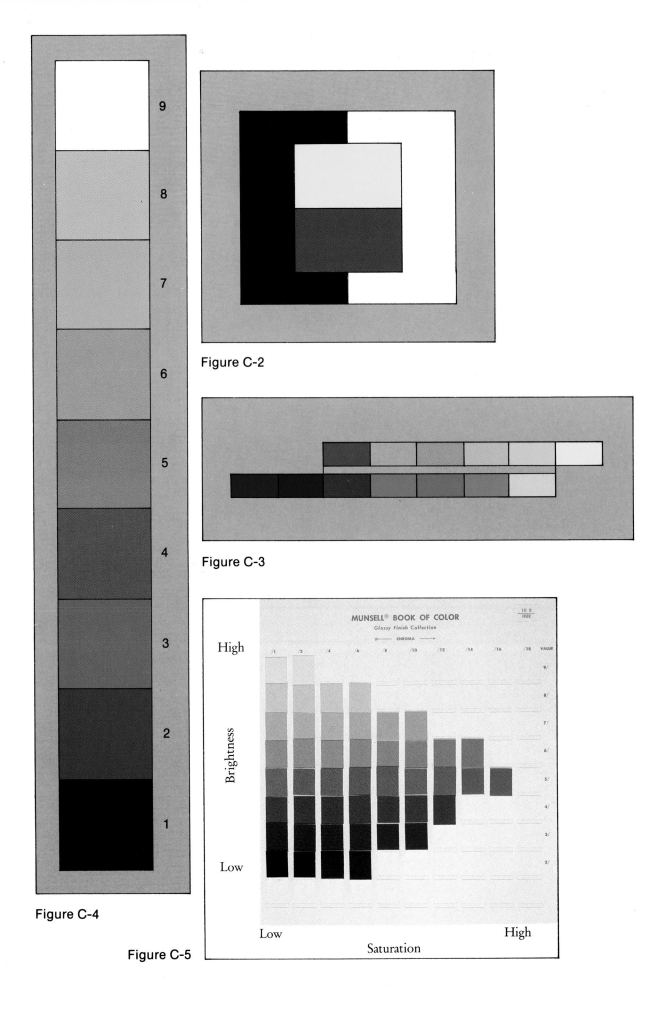

Figure C-2

Figure C-3

Figure C-4

Figure C-5

MUNSELL® BOOK OF COLOR

Glossy Finish Collection

CHROMA

/1 /2 /4 /6 /8 /10 /12 /14 /16 /18 VALUE

High

Brightness

Low

Low Saturation High

10 R
HUE

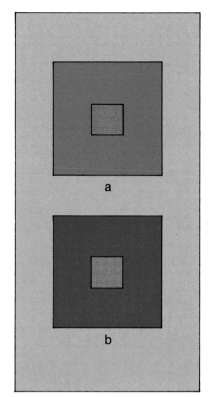

a

b

Figure C-6

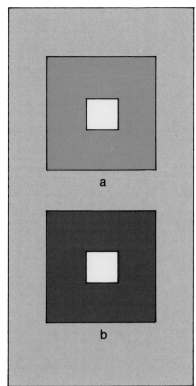

a

b

Figure C-7

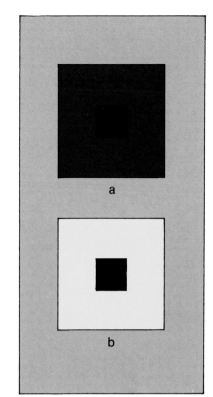

a

b

Figure C-8

Project design for *The Toilet* by Jay Jagim

Figure C-9

Figure C-10

Project design for *Saint Joan* by Katy Lyness

Figure C-11

Project design for *Lysistrata* by Katy Lyness

CHAPTER 8

Rendering Materials and Techniques

INTRODUCTION

In daily life we use photographs to show the appearance of people, places, and things. A photograph, however, can only reveal what already exists. A play, film, or television production in the planning stage is only an idea that has no physical form. An idea cannot be photographed, yet during the planning period of a production, it is necessary to know the intended appearance of the sets and costumes. This can be communicated most effectively by designers creating a graphic statement of the design idea. **Renderings** are sketches or paintings prepared by the scene or costume designer for this purpose. They are a means for the designer to show colleagues the vision in the mind's eye. A rendering is also a device a designer uses to solidify his or her design idea. In the period during which the rendering is developed, the designer tests concepts of form, style, line, mass, texture, color, trim, and decoration. The scene designer checks the effectiveness of the groundplan as a three-dimensional picture, and the costume designer translates silhouette into a vision of three-dimensional form. Upon completion, the rendering serves as a means of communication between the designers, producer, director, actors, and technicians. Renderings help the director begin to visualize the movements of the actors, they show the actors a guide to their characters' environment, and they help the lighting designer begin to interpret the stage environment. Scenic and costume renderings are thus essential elements in the production process.

Media

Almost any medium can be used for rendering. Four considerations contribute to this choice: a) the style of the design, b) the ability of the medium to appropriately express the design idea, c) the ability of the artist to manipulate the medium, and d) the rate and ease with which the medium can be worked.

Most productions are planned, constructed, and mounted in a relatively brief period. It is not uncommon for a designer to be allowed only four or five days to research and develop a design idea. Discussions during design conferences can result in the need to alter or revise a design. These changes must be completed with equal speed. To meet these schedules, a designer must work with a medium of expression that does not require extensive preparation of materials or a long drying time. Facility with a variety of media will enhance the ability of a designer to meet schedule requirements and to express the design idea effectively.

Whatever medium is selected, the designer must produce a rendering that will be able to withstand some physical abuse. Renderings are carried from meeting to meeting, passed from designer to director to choreographer, pinned up, stacked up, or tossed about a table. Certain fragile materials can be protected with adequate backings, coverings, or coatings, while other materials are too sensitive to be of practical value.

The most popular rendering media include pencil, colored pencil, ink, colored ink, watercolor paints, gouache, acrylic paint, or a combination of these and other materials. Each medium results in a distinctive quality of expression. A rendering may be impressionistic or photographic, monochromatic or multicolored, textural or smooth, two-dimensional or three-dimensional. The inherent characteristics of a medium may emphasize form, texture, color, or light, or a combination of several of these qualities.

Papers and Boards

The choice of a design medium contributes to the selection of papers or boards that may be used. A dry medium such as pencil requires a surface that abrades lead and holds granules of graphite. Surfaces for wet media such as inks and paints must be able to accept moisture without distorting the image. Art work done with pens generally requires a smooth paper, but painted designs are more effective on coarser material. The surface used for paints must be able to hold fine particles of pigment and absorb a certain amount of color in its fibers without blotting, bleeding, or warping. Any rendering medium may be applied on white or colored paper. Opaque media are unaffected by colored papers; however, the color of the working surface will make a substantial contribution to art work done with transparent paints or art that leaves a portion of the paper exposed, such as pen-and-ink drawings.

The designer must consider several characteristics when selecting a paper or board: tooth, texture, absorbency, color, strength, and weight. These factors are controlled by the composition of the paper, the manufacturing process, and the finishing treatment.

Paper is made from a combination of natural or synthetic fibers and water. This pulp may be modified by the addition of a number of chemicals, bleaches, or dyes to control color and finish. The pulp is laid on a screen or passed between rollers to squeeze out the moisture. The rollers may be hot or cold, smooth or textured. Heated rollers produce **hot-press** paper that has a relatively smooth surface. A coarser surface is produced by cold rollers and results in a paper called **cold press**. Paper with a **plate** finish is produced by smooth rollers, and a slightly dimensional surface is created with textured rollers. Finally, a paper may be treated with a variety of coatings to modify opacity, absorbency, or stability.

Paper may be thick, thin, or laminated to a cardboard base. The thickness of a paper is described by its weight, usually pounds per 500 sheets. Extremely heavy papers are measured in other quantities. Paper of any weight may be laminated to cardboard. The thickness of the board is determined by the number of layers from which it is made. Standard-weight board is single-ply; two- and three-ply boards are also available.

Although certain materials are preferred, a designer may use any variety of paper or board to render with any medium. If appropriate, even lunch bags or paper towels may be used. A common art paper for rendering is **bristol board,** which is a thick paper that can be finished in a variety of textures. It may be used with almost any medium, depending upon the finish. The surface may be glazed, smooth, coarse, or textured. Hot- and cold-press illustration board is composed of bristol board that has been laminated to a cardboard core. Drawing and layout papers are designed primarily for pencil work and have a great variety of finishes. Watercolor paper reacts well to moisture and holds or absorbs pigment with ease. Several grades of each type of paper and board are available. In general, better work is performed on better papers.

Equipment

The equipment used for rendering will vary depending on the medium used. Ink can be applied with a variety of pens or brushes, and paints can be applied with pens, brushes, or a palette knife. Each medium and each style of rendering creates its own requirements. As is the case with all other materials and equipment, rendering tools of different grades can be purchased. Once basic techniques are learned, better equipment will usually yield better results. Paint brushes are perhaps the greatest investment necessary. Good brushes are expensive, but when cared for properly, they can last many years and will provide better results than poor brushes. Cheap or worn-out brushes can be used with harsh or destructive materials but are otherwise useless.

Brush maintenance is important. *A brush should never be allowed to rest on its bristles and should never be soaked in water or any other kind of solution.* After a painting session, brushes should be washed in luke-warm—*never hot*—water to remove all traces of pigment. The clean bristles should be shaped to their proper form and the brush turned upside-down so that it will dry without touching anything which might cause the bristles to bend. Some artists prefer to dip the bristles in a solution of mild soap after washing and allow the soap to dry in the bristles. The soap acts as a starch to maintain proper brush shape; however, it must be rinsed from the brush before use. The bristles of any brush should be moistened in clean water before they are dipped in paint.

Many of the materials designers use react to moisture or can be rubbed off the surface. This damage can be reduced or prevented by using a fixative. **Fixative** is a liquid such as glue, varnish, shellac, or lacquer that is put as a coating over drawings and paintings to protect the art work. A **workable fixative** not only protects the surface but also allows drawing or painting to be done over the coated area without disturbing previous art work. Fixatives are available in aerosol cans and in matte or gloss finishes. Some care must be taken in the selection and use of a fixative. Although they are available for all art media, not all fixatives may be used on every material, nor are all fixatives workable. Container labels must be checked and the fixative tested on a small area of a rendering before a general application is made. Fixatives tend to discolor pigments, and excessive coatings may dissolve some media or create an undesirable gloss on the surface.

Preparing to Render

Designers usually develop preliminary drawings on newsprint, tracing paper, or drafting vellum. A final sketch in preparation for rendering can be drawn directly on the art paper or be transferred to the rendering surface. If the rendering surface is a transparent material such as drafting vellum, the artist may tape the vellum over the preliminary drawing and develop the final rendering using the underlying sketch as a guide. When a rendering is created on an opaque paper, the artist can transfer the original sketch to the rendering surface without redrawing it. The back of the original sketch is coated with soft lead (4B). The preliminary drawing is then placed right-side-up over the art paper, and the lines on the original sketch are retraced to transfer the drawing to the rendering surface. Care must be taken not to dent the art paper when drawing over the lines. Also, the coated sketch should not be rubbed all over during the transfer process, or loose graphite may smudge the art paper.

PENCIL

Pencil is a monochromatic medium that produces renderings emphasizing light, shade, texture, and form. Visually exciting designs in which color is of secondary importance or for which color will be determined at a later time can be developed fairly quickly with standard mechanical drawing pencils or special art pencils.

As a design medium, pencil offers some distinct advantages over most other media:

1. Every adult is familiar with basic techniques for manipulating pencils.
2. Pencils are readily available.
3. Almost any paper or board can be used as a drawing surface.
4. Pencil leads can be shaped to create distinct line qualities.
5. Pencils can be used with a light or firm touch to control tone and density of lines.
6. Pencils can be used for line drawings, constructed primarily with the point, or tonal drawings, constructed with blended lines.
7. Pencil drawings can be made permanent with fixative.

There are two major limitations to pencil as a design material: tedium during the drawing process and lack of color. It is easy for an artist to draw intricate detail in a precise or delicate style in small areas of a rendering, while neglecting large areas or treating them only in a coarse manner. This can lead to conflicting styles and qualities of workmanship. Also, the lack of color in drawing-leads restricts the art work to a monochromatic medium. If a clear indication of color is needed, a different medium should be considered.

Equipment

Standard office pencils and softer grades of drafting leads, especially HB, 2B, and 4B, may be used for rendering in addition to special art pencils. These include large-lead layout and sketching pencils; pencils with soft rectangular leads similar in appearance to a carpenter's pencil; carbon pencils and sticks that provide a very soft, dark, matte appearance; vine charcoal; compressed charcoal sticks and charcoal pencils that are even softer and darker than carbon pencils; and lithographic pencils, which are soft and waxy but effective for drawing on smooth surfaces such as acetate films. Pencil media are available in several forms: refills for mechanical lead holders, leads with a wood casing, or ¼″ or ½″ square sticks. Leads may be sharpened to a tapered, blunt, or chiseled point. Each point produces a slightly different quality of line (Figure 8–1).

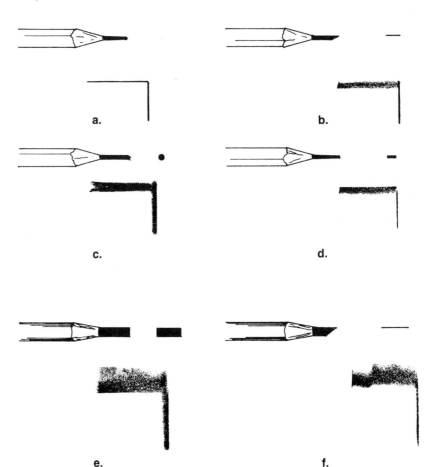

FIGURE 8–1

Lead points for drawing. a) Conical point, b) Chisel point, c) Blunt point, d) Double bevel, e) Rectangular-lead blunt point, f) Rectangular-lead chisel point.

Other equipment needed for pencil rendering would be drafting art gum, and kneaded rubber erasers; an erasing shield; a dusting brush; a sanding block; a knife or razor blade; fixative; and a supply of stomps.

A **stomp**, also called stump or tortillon, is a short, soft paper roll that is pointed on both ends. These disposable paper sticks are used on the drawing surface to blend dry media, such as pencil or charcoal.

Papers and Boards

Although a material with tooth is preferred, almost any paper may be used for pencil work. Hot- and cold-press illustration board and sketch papers have an excellent tooth, drafting vellum and tracing paper are satisfactory, and even newsprint or typing paper is adequate for pencil rendering. Generally with very smooth papers, pencil marks tend to rub off; smooth papers are not sufficiently abrasive to hold the particles of graphite. Art papers and boards the designer might consider are coquille board, charcoal paper, media paper, and Ross board. These art materials have distinctive textures that can contribute to the effectiveness of a rendering. In addition to a choice of textures, the artist may select a variety of colors. Most pencil work is done on white stock, but a broad range of grey, buff, tan, soft green, and blue drawing papers is available. Colored papers tint a rendering and give a sense of warmth or coolness to a composition. They also limit the value range of a rendering by reducing the maximum degree of highlight. No matter which paper or board is selected, the designer should test its ability to accept pencil and resist erasures without damage.

Rendering Techniques

Pencil rendering is a freehand technique performed without benefit of triangles or T-squares. The artist must practice drawing smooth, evenly spaced lines of consistent quality. In general, a pencil is held for detail drawing in the same manner it is held for writing: the wrist and fingers manipulate the tool. Long, broad strokes can be made most easily when the pencil is held about one-third of the distance from the point, letting the forearm and wrist control movement. Rapid, loose sketching can be most easily performed by allowing a sizable length of the pencil to extend beyond the fingers and using the entire arm to draw strokes. Although these are standard positions in which to hold the pencil, each artist will find an approach that is comfortable and provides the desired quality of line.

No matter which pencil technique is used, the artist should place a piece of clean, smooth paper under the drawing hand to prevent smudging or other damage from hand movement or perspiration.

Strokes

A combination of factors: type of pencil, softness and shape of lead, hand position and pressure, rate of work, texture of paper, and style of line determines the appearance of a pencil rendering. While there is no fixed vocabulary of strokes for pencil rendering as there is for mechanical drawing, there are a number of commonly used strokes (Figure 8–2). The quality of line produced by each stroke is altered whenever a variable is changed.

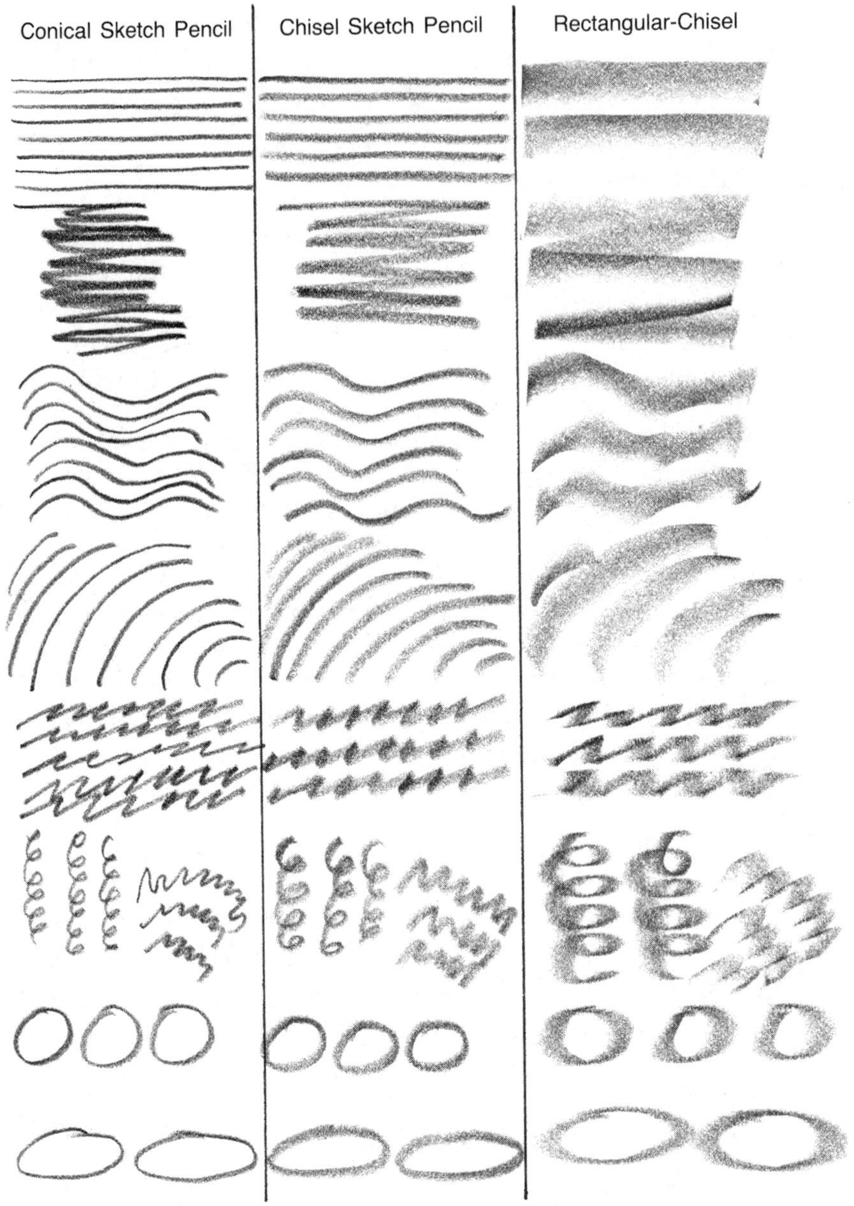

FIGURE 8–2

Pencil strokes. Column A uses a round lead sharpened to a conical point; Column B was drawn with a round lead sharpened to a chisel point; Column C was drawn with a rectangular lead sharpened to a chisel point.

Conical Sketch Pencil   Chisel Sketch Pencil   Rectangular-Chisel

Strokes are combined in a variety of patterns to create textures (Figure 8–3). A texture is the product of the direction and shape of strokes, the width of lines, and the hardness of lead. The texture or pattern of the paper or board contributes significantly to the overall effect, but if pencil work is sufficiently heavy, it will fill in the texture of the drawing surface.

Tone or value is controlled by the density of texture (Figure 8–4). The texture may be graduated in value from dark to light by controlling the density or by lightly rubbing a finger, facial tissue, or stomp over the darker areas to blend values. Should a value become too dark, the artist has a number of means to adjust the drawing. Some relief can be obtained by pressing a kneaded rubber eraser on the drawing. The eraser should be *only pressed* on the surface, *not rubbed* because rubbing will cause smudges. If a small area of a rendering needs to be repaired, an eraser can be rubbed through an opening in

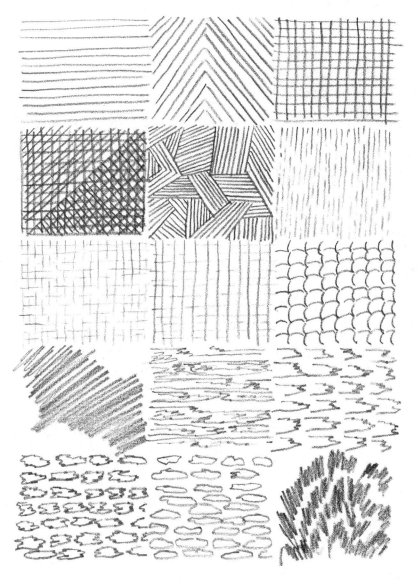

FIGURE 8–3
Pencil textures drawn with a round lead sharpened to a conical point.

a.   b.   c.

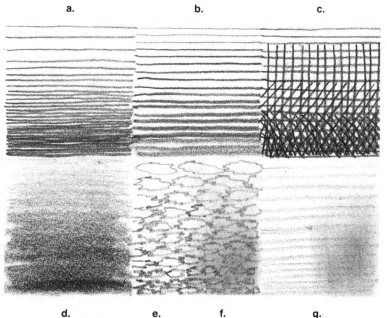

FIGURE 8–4
Tones constructed with a pencil. a) Controlling frequency of lines, b) Controlling thickness of lines, c) Using cross-hatching, d) Controlling darkness of shading, e) Controlling density of texture, f) Rubbing over the texture, g) Rubbing over lines.

d.   e.   f.   g.

235

an erasing shield. Care must be taken to use a clean eraser and not to bruise or mar the drawing surface. Drafting vellum can be cleaned thoroughly in this manner, but cleaning textured papers and boards is less successful. Fragile papers may tear as a result of erasing, and excessive erasing in one area will damage any paper.

A knife or razor blade can be used instead of an eraser. The edge of the blade is scraped across the surface to remove the graphite. Again, this technique can easily damage the paper and should only be attempted with care. A final repair method is also available: after all loose graphite has been erased or scraped from the surface, highlight can be drawn into an area with white pencil or chalk. This must be done judiciously, since the addition can be quite startling—creating a scar on the surface rather than blending with the pencil work. Colored pencils tend to get waxy if built up too heavily; chalk tends to dust off the surface if it is not sprayed with fixative. The introduction of colored pencil or chalk should be a last resort.

Rendering Procedures

Once the preliminary sketch of a costume or set has been completed, the location and quality of the light source determined, and the transfer to the art paper made, the rendering can be initiated. The normal approach to pencil rendering is to work from dark to light. That is, all the darkest areas of shadow are sketched first, with the appropriate texture and value. The next lightest value is then filled in, followed by each successively higher step of value. This method establishes the heaviest pencil work as the lowest value and the paper as the highest value of the rendering. All other tones will be between and relative to these gradations.

Dark values can usually be made darker, but it is almost impossible to lighten the highest value, the paper, satisfactorily without changing media. Each step of value is drawn over the entire surface of the rendering at one time. It is easier to obtain a visually balanced composition in this manner.

An alternative approach is to begin once again applying the darkest value first but then drawing the middle value. The artist then works up to the highest value of the paper and down to the lowest value that was first drawn on the surface. Extreme highlight and shadow are detailed last. As awareness of the medium grows, each artist will discover an approach most conducive to his or her own style of drawing.

With the variety of leads, papers, and strokes available, the artist is faced with a multitude of decisions. Each of these choices must be appropriate to the style of the design and the nature of the production. In addition, the pencil work should clearly represent the objects, spaces, and textures intended. Any texture may be drawn with any stroke. Some strokes result in more "realistic" compositions than others. The direction of a stroke may be determined by the actual texture of the object, the angle of the surface being rendered, or the direction of rays of light. For instance, a wall could be rendered as a series of horizontal brick rows built up with horizontal strokes of a wide lead (Figure 8–5a) or could be given greater interest by suggesting the texture of each brick individually with a sharply pointed lead and separating each brick by open areas to suggest joints (Figure 8–5b).

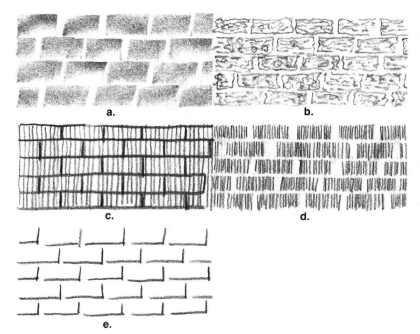

FIGURE 8–5

Five ways to render a brick wall with pencil. a) Using a rectangular lead, each stroke forming a brick; b) Using a conical point and building the form and texture of each brick individually with squiggles; c) Using parallel lines and drawing the joints with thick, dark lines; d) Using parallel lines and erasing the joints to form highlights; e) Drawing only a partial outline of each brick.

The same wall could be rendered as a dark flat surface by using an overall vertical, horizontal, or diagonal stroke to represent a general texture or the direction of light. Joint lines can be drawn as a pattern of horizontal and vertical shadows (Figure 8–5c) or drawn and then erased to form a pattern of highlights (Figure 8–5d). The wall could also be drawn as a partial outline of individual bricks (Figure 8–5e). A board fence, wood-paneled room, or any other surface can be treated with as much variety (Figure 8–6).

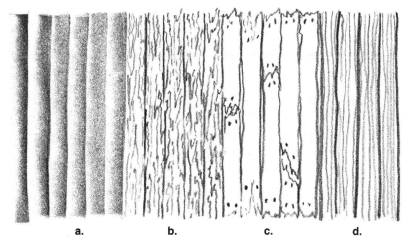

FIGURE 8–6

Four ways to render a wooden fence with pencil. a) Using a rectangular lead, each stroke forming a separate board; b) Using a conical point and building the form and texture of each board individually with squiggles; c) Drawing only the outline of each board; d) Using parallel lines to draw the boards and heavy lines to indicate the joints.

Burnishing is a shorthand technique to create textures. Drawing paper is placed over an existing three-dimensional surface such as a coarse fabric or a section of window screen. Lead is rubbed over the paper to transfer the underlying texture to the drawing (Figure 8–7). A stomp loaded with graphite can be used instead of a pencil to create a very soft effect. Templates with standard architectural designs such as brick, wood paneling, or shingles are available for use in this manner.

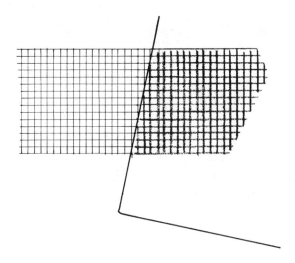

FIGURE 8–7
Burnishing.

A very soft effect can be created on any part of a drawing by rubbing an area with a stomp, tissue, or soft rag that has collected a great deal of graphite. This technique may be used to fill in large areas of a rendering with a soft, graded tone, for instance, a sky (Figure 8–8). A stomp can also be used to soften detail. An object or area can be drawn in detail with carefully developed textures and then reduced in strength of contrast by rubbing with a stomp to soften the appearance of an object in the background.

FIGURE 8–8

Filling areas with a loaded stomp or tissue results in a very soft effect.

Should rubbing with a stomp not sufficiently soften the appearance of pencil work, the graphite marks may be lightly coated with a solvent, such as carbon tetrachloride or turpentine. The solvent softens the appearance of the graphite and darkens it. This is an unusual technique that should be reserved for special applications or repairs. Any art work to be treated with solvent should be tested before a general application is made. Every paper and drawing medium will react differently, depending upon the solvent used.

COLORED PENCIL

Colored pencils are manufactured in more than seventy-two shades. They can be purchased individually or in sets. All colored leads tend to be much firmer than layout and sketch pencils. Thin-lead colored pencils are the firmest. They need to be used with heavy pressure to produce deep colors. Frequently this pressure will seriously dent the paper. On the other hand, the softer, thick-lead pencils crumble easily under pressure but build up deep colors on the surface. Heavy applications of colored lead may become waxy and create a glossy appearance that is inconsistent with other areas of a rendering. Colored pencil is difficult to erase from almost any drawing surface.

Techniques for using this medium are essentially the same as the techniques for renderings made with drawing pencils. Textures and tones are constructed with the same kinds of strokes; however, the hard lead makes it very difficult to blend colors into tonal gradations with a stomp or tissue.

Although the range of colors available is extensive, for any medium it is almost always necessary to mix colors to adjust hue, value, or chroma. Modifying colored pencil is only possible on the surface of the paper. Leads cannot be puddled together on a palette in the manner of paints. Any color-mixing with leads must be planned carefully and tested on scratch paper before attempted on the actual rendering. Colors can be drawn over each other, or the individual strokes used to construct a texture can be alternated in a pattern that produces a proper mixture. It is difficult to achieve satisfactory blends of complementary colors without the work becoming muddy. The most successful approach to create form, texture, and a good mix of colors with colored pencils is to apply each stroke so that it makes a clean impression. Black can be graded over almost any color. It is difficult to lighten a color with white or any high-value lead.

Colored pencils give their most satisfactory results on lightly tinted or black paper. The color of the paper mixes visually with the color of the pencil work and must be taken into consideration when selecting this medium.

Because of the hardness of the leads, it is usually not necessary to coat colored-pencil renderings with fixative. This characteristic is valuable, since fixative easily alters these colors.

PEN-AND-INK

Renderings done with pen-and-ink have some similarities to renderings done with pencil. Both media are monochromatic and linear, emphasizing light, shade, and texture. Unlike pencil, where the degree of darkness can be controlled by the hardness of lead and firmness of stroke, ink produces one consistent shade of darkness. Also, ink cannot be blended into smooth textures the way pencils can, nor can ink be easily erased. Rendering with pen-and-ink, however, does allow the artist to draw intricate detail and to state qualities of texture strongly. The medium can also be used effectively for outline drawings and can be easily combined with other media. In addition, renderings done just in pen-and-ink have a distinct style that can enhance certain design modes and periods.

Two types of pens are used for art work. Pens with replaceable nibs can be used for lines of varying width, and technical pens can create lines of fixed width. Technical pens were discussed in Chapter 1.

Art pens consist of an inexpensive holder and can be equipped with a variety of nibs or points. These points include lettering nibs, with straight, square, round, or oval tips; mapping; lithographic; and cartooning nibs; and a variety of quill pens which are hollow tubes tapering to very fine points (Figure 8–9). All of these pens are dipped into containers to let ink come between the blades of the pen. As a line is drawn, ink flows down the slit in the point and deposits a solid line the width and shape of the tip. When heavy pressure is exerted on the point while drawing, the portions of the nib separate to make a wider line. Although an extreme technique, in this way, the artist has some control of the width of a line while it is being drawn in addition to when the point is selected. Many art and lettering points are available on fountain pens. These pens provide a continuous supply of ink, eliminating the necessity to dip the pen every few strokes. Fountain pens require special inks.

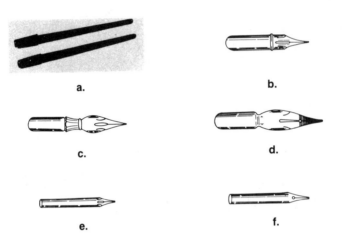

FIGURE 8–9

Artist's pens and holders. a) Pen holder, b–d) Artist nibs, e–f) Quill nibs. (Courtesy Hunt Manufacturing Company.)

The size of the pen point used affects the appearance of a rendering significantly. Ultrafine nibs yield thin, lightweight lines; broad points result in coarse lines. The size of point used is dependent upon the size of the rendering, the delicacy of detail, and the effect of aerial perspective. Objects in the distance can be rendered as a nearly solid mass or may read better as an open texture rendered with fine lines. A small rendering drawn with a broad point will have a very coarse appearance; in contrast, a large rendering drawn with a fine point will appear washed out. The pen point selected should provide the appropriate texture, sense of scale, and sense of distance.

Inks

India ink is used for most art work. This is an opaque, very black, waterproof ink that is available in three densities: thin, medium, and thick. The thinnest ink is most commonly used. It dries relatively slowly and is least likely to clog pens but is less opaque than the thicker inks. The thickest ink cannot be used in pens because it dries too quickly and clogs points. Thick ink is applied with a brush which creates the blackest, most opaque covering. The middle density ink can be used in pens. It is of medium opacity and rate of drying. Special formulations of india ink are used in technical and fountain pens. These pens should be used only with inks recommended by their manufacturers. Other special inks or ink additives are needed when drawing on plastic films.

Inks come in small bottles that have a quill or dropper in the top. The droppers are used to fill ruling pens and the inking tips of drafting equipment. Open ink bottles should be securely positioned to prevent spills. A bottle holder can be a small box, or a holder can be made by cutting a hole in a piece of fabric and thumbtacking it over the bottle to form a secure tent. Ink from one bottle only should be used on a drawing. Due to changes in density during the life of an ink bottle, alterations in drying characteristics and opacity occur that affect the appearance of the final rendering. When not in use, ink bottles should be kept tightly closed to prevent spills and to reduce evaporation.

Papers and Boards

In contrast to pencil, pen-and-ink renderings are more effective on smooth papers. Papers and boards with a coarse tooth may create interesting textures but result in distorted lines and also catch the pen point, causing ink to spatter. The primary criteria for selecting papers to be used with pen-and-ink are smoothness and strength. Papers should allow erasing with a minimum of damage to the drawing surface.

Preferred media for pen-and-ink renderings are smooth bristol board, hot-press drawing papers and boards, parchment, high-quality drafting vellum, tracing cloth, and acetate film.

Erasing

Special erasers with a coarse grit are used to remove ink. Although these erasers work fairly well on drafting surfaces, they are likely to mar very smooth papers. Ink solvents and solvent-imbibed erasers can also be used to remove ink, but they require a great amount of care to prevent damage to the drawing surface. When erasing is not feasible, dried ink can be scraped off the drawing surface with the tip of a knife or the edge of a razor blade. Again, care is required to avoid damaging the drawing surface.

Rendering Techniques

Pen-and-ink rendering is a freehand technique. Lines that are much more interesting and varied are created when they are drawn without the aid of a straightedge. Almost all pen-and-ink rendering is done slowly. Quickly rendered lines usually have a sloppy, inconsistent appearance and uneven spacing. However, drawing straight lines without the aid of a guide requires practice.

Pens are held for drawing in the same manner in which a pencil is held for writing. The grip should not be so tight that it produces nervous, jerky lines nor so loose that it prevents control of the instrument. Lines are drawn with a pen just as they are drawn with a drafting pencil: the pen is angled slightly so the tip flexes away from the body of the point, and the instrument is pulled in the direction of the line. Drawing horizontal and vertical lines requires different modes of control. Body position may have to be changed to draw some strokes conveniently.

Strokes

An innumerable variety of strokes are possible with a pen. Any stroke the artist considers appropriate can be used; each stroke produces a different effect. Pressure on the pen may be light to create thin lines only the width of the point, or pressure may be heavy, causing the blades of the nib to split and produce thicker lines. Consistent pressure throughout a stroke results in a line of even width (Figure 8–10a); inconsistent pressure produces a line of varied width throughout its length (Figure 8–10b). Changing the orientation of the point and direction of movement of the pen also alters the shape of a line (Figure 8–10c).

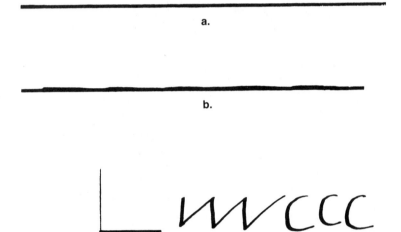

FIGURE 8–10

Basic pen strokes. a) Consistent pressure throughout the length of a line, b) Varied pressure throughout the length of a line, c) Change of direction while drawing a line without reorienting a wide pen point.

Any object can be rendered in a variety of ways. The artist must choose the style of line, textural effect, and the treatment of light.

There are three basic styles of drawing with pen-and-ink: hatching, stippling, and outlining which may be used with great variety. Frequently a rendering is developed by combining all three styles.

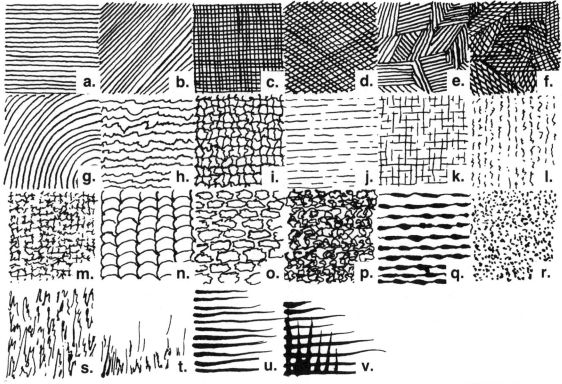

FIGURE 8–11
Pen-and-ink textures.

The vocabulary of styles for pen-and-ink can be extended by including brush techniques. Heavy outlines can be painted and large areas of a rendering filled in with a brush rather than a pen. The vitality and visual interest of a rendering will be greatly enhanced by a combination of different pen and brush strokes (Figure 8–11).

Although pen-and-ink renderings are usually monochromatic, color can be added in a number of ways. A convenient approach is to apply a watercolor wash over an entire sketch. If good paper is used and the paints are transparent, the results will be quite effective. This approach is used frequently by costume designers. Detail is carefully drawn with a pen, and then color is washed over the rendering to provide a sense of the color range of fabrics. Alternative approaches to color include the use of tinted papers, colored pencils, or felt-tip pens in combination with pen-and-ink. A rendering can be drawn entirely with colored inks. These designs are quite attractive if the art work is well controlled.

TRANSPARENT WATERCOLOR PAINTS

Watercolor paint once was the most popular medium used by designers. It requires minimum preparation, can be applied rapidly, and dries quickly; it is also polychromatic. Watercolor paint is available in three forms; transparent, gouache, and tempera. **Transparent watercolor** paints allow layers of transparent color to show through each other; the colored layers mix together visually. **Gouache** is a mixture of transparent watercolor paint with Chinese white pigment which creates an opaque medium. **Tempera,** also known as poster paint, contains

243

more opaquing matter than gouache. Tempera colors appear quite solid and lack the richness and luminescence of the other watercolor media. Tempera is used primarily for poster layouts.

Transparent watercolor paints have some features that continue to make them an attractive medium. They have strong, rich colors that give a sense of luminescence, suggesting qualities of light as well as the actual color of objects. The paints can be applied as rich, deep colors, or they can be diluted to create a light, atmospheric quality. Transparent watercolors can be worked rapidly to cover large areas or treated more delicately for details. Watercolor paints have a relatively short drying time, which makes them a practical medium to cope with tight production schedules. Transparent watercolors can be effectively combined with pencil, ink, or other media. Work with this medium requires careful planning. Since the colors are transparent, each brush stroke is critical. Multiple layers of paint can build up rich, controlled tones or can turn into a muddy mess as the layers blend with each other and with the color of the paper.

Transparent watercolor paints are a combination of very finely ground pigment plus a minimum amount of binder, such as gum arabic, and a moistening agent, usually glycerin. The paints come in three forms: tube, liquid, and cake. There are approximately forty different **tube colors** available. These pigments are diluted with varying amounts of water. Dilution makes the paint easier to spread, reduces the strength of colors, and alters both chroma and value as the pigment blends with the paper or with an underlying color.

Liquid watercolors are a diluted form of these paints. The colors are very intense. They can be used directly from the bottle with brush or pen, or they can be diluted for a less intense coloration. They tend to become absorbed in the fibers of the paper more quickly and deeply than the other forms of watercolor paints.

Cakes are a dry form of this medium. The cakes are manufactured from the same pigments and binders as other watercolors but have to be brought to liquid form by adding water. Most people are familiar with these cakes from children's paint sets. Artist watercolor cakes can be purchased in sets containing from eight to forty colors. **Semisoft cakes** are also available. These paints are somewhat easier to bring to dilution than the dry cakes. Most designers prefer to use tube or liquid watercolor paints.

In all three forms, the pigments from which the paints are manufactured are derived from one of the three sources: clay, known as **earth colors**; metal oxides, called **cadmiums**; or synthetic dyes infused in inert solids, called **lakes.** When earth colors or cadmiums are mixed with lakes, chemical reactions sometimes cause the paints to lose brilliance, to blacken, or to become gritty on the painting surface. There are times when these effects can be used to advantage; however, it is generally preferable to avoid these problems.

Significant differences in quality between brands of watercolors affect the artist's choice. The less expensive "scholastic" or "academic" paints are usually not as pure or strong in color and may have been made from more coarsely ground pigments than artist colors. Even among the artist colors, there are differences in quality between brands.

These differences affect the strength and purity of color and the permanency of the pigments. Every artist should experiment to find preferred brands with which to work.

Papers and Boards

The paper used for watercolor painting has a major influence on the appearance of a rendering, due to the transparency of watercolor paint. Essential characteristics for the paper are strength, the ability to hold fine granules of pigment on the surface, and the ability to absorb color into the fibers. Good watercolor papers are available in weights up to 500 pounds; 300-pound paper is considered to be medium weight, and thinner papers are lightweight. The thinner, lighter papers are more inclined to warp, buckle, and stretch when moistened, and for this reason heavier papers are preferred. Cold-press illustration board can be used with satisfactory results. Care must be taken to minimize warping which will make painting difficult. Should paper or boards warp, they may be flattened when completed by placing the rendering face down on a flat surface, covering it with a few layers of newspaper, and pressing the rendering with an iron set to the coolest temperature. Since the paper used seriously affects the final appearance of watercolor paints, a white painting surface is preferred to preserve the integrity of the colors. Tinted papers can be used, but the artist must remember that transparent watercolor paints mix visually with the color of the paper.

Brushes

Good brushes are required for any artistic painting. Watercolor brushes should be absorbent, finely textured, flexible with good spring, and able to maintain their shape when wet. The best watercolor brushes are made with **red sable** bristles. They are very expensive. An alternative to red sable is **sabeline** brushes, which may be made from any variety of hairs. Some sabeline brushes are very good; others are quite poor. A highly satisfactory and less expensive alternative to red sable is a synthetic bristle called **white sable.** The better white sable brushes are similar in feel to good red sables, although they tend to be somewhat stiffer and to have more spring than red sable. No matter which variety of bristle is selected, each brush will have its own characteristics and should be checked before purchase to be sure that individual bristles lie flat and maintain their shape when moistened. Bristles are mounted in a block of glue or plastic that is attached to the handle by a rustproof metal band called a ferrule. The handle should be smooth and comfortably shaped.

Most watercolor painting is done with flat and round brushes. Flat brushes are used to paint washes and wide glazes; round brushes are used for most other painting. A round brush has a large body that tapers to a fine point. One high-quality round brush should be capable of meeting all the needs of the experienced watercolor painter. The long bristles and large body are capable of laying-in washes, and the sharp point can be used to paint detail. Many designers are more comfortable using smaller brushes for fine detail. Round brushes are sized by number from 000000 (the smallest) to number 36 (the largest). These designations are relative, since sizes are not standardized among manufacturers. In general, scene designers use a one-inch flat brush and three or four different round brushes; costume designers use several smaller brushes for painting details. The final choice of brushes is a matter of personal preference.

Among other equipment needed for watercolor painting would be two large water bottles, one for clean water and one for rinsing brushes. Quart-size mayonnaise jars are excellent. A palette is also necessary; this can be any nonabsorbent surface that will hold paint. Manufactured trays with an aluminum or porcelain finish can be purchased, or else a muffin tin or saucer can be used.

Rendering Techniques

Very heavy papers and boards that are able to withstand extensive wetting can be used without mounting. These can be taped or tacked to a work surface and used directly. Medium-weight papers and boards should be firmly taped in place with one-inch masking tape or butcher's tape. Lightweight papers must be stretched on a drawing board. To do this, soak the paper by heavily brushing water onto the surface. Apply a thick mixture of wheat paste to a one-inch border around the edge of the paper and to the drawing board where the wheat-paste will lie. Place the paper on the board, bringing the two wheat-paste layers into contact. Tape the paper around the perimeter with butcher's or Kraft paper tape. The paper will warp and buckle but finally shrink to a smooth, tight working surface while it dries. Don't begin to paint on the paper until it has dried completely, don't remove it from the board until the painting is completed.

Watercolor paints can be applied as washes or as glazes. **Washes** are wet colors applied to a wet surface. They generally produce a smooth, soft effect. Color strength can be controlled by the density of paint and the wetness of the surface. Deep colors require more pigment; weak colors require less pigment.

Initial painting is usually done on a flat surface that has been brushed with clear water. After the layer of water has started to be absorbed, the paper will have a velvety appearance. Diluted paint is brushed over this damp paper to create a wash. An even wash of consistent color can be obtained by premixing the pigment to the appropriate dilution and then stroking a wide, flat brush over the paper. If the surface has been well saturated, the paint will flow on easily and dry without any indication of brushwork. Washes are usually applied from side to side: work the brush in a consistent rhythm of long, overlapping strokes. Over large areas, the brush is controlled by arm movement rather than hand movement. Excessively wet surfaces or surfaces with standing water will accept very little pigment. Washes are generally used to cover large areas with a smooth coating of paint. They have a soft, luminous quality, suggestive of a lighted cyclorama.

Paint must be quite moist to flow smoothly. The placement of paint can be controlled by wetting a limited area of the paper and applying the paint only to the area that has been moistened. The paint will flow only over the wet area or where the brush travels. Two colors of wash can be applied adjacent to each other, but as soon as the wet colors come into contact, they will begin to bleed together. A stylized painting techinique is used by some watercolorists to resolve this problem. They leave narrow areas of white paper between masses of color (Figure 8–12b).

A **graded wash** (Figure 8–12a) is an application of pigment in increasing or decreasing density. To paint a graded wash, moisten the surface of the paper with clear water. After the water has started to become absorbed, brush on the pigment in overlapping strokes. Proceed from the darkest to the lightest areas by adding more water to the pigment with each stroke across the page. Dilution of the pigment will reduce the strength of color.

A **glaze** (Figure 8–12b) is the application of wet paint on a dry surface. Most detail painting is done with glazes. Depth of color is controlled entirely by the density of pigment mixed on the palette. Glazes are used to build up layers of color and to render details.

a.

FIGURE 8–12

a) Graded wash; b) Adjacent washes applied with a white streak between colors to prevent bleeding: (1a) shows where colors intermingled during application, (2b) is a glaze painted over the washes after they dried; c) Lifting—the cone-shaped white area was lifted while the paint was still damp.

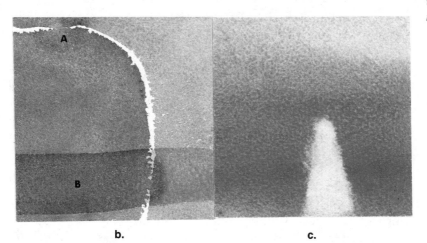

b.   c.

Lifting Color

Most watercolor paints that have been applied to a previously moistened surface can be removed by means of a lifting technique. The simplest approach, one frequently used when painting a wash over large areas, is to blot the wet paint off the surface with a piece of absorbent paper. As the wash dries, it becomes increasingly difficult to remove. Essentially the same lifting procedure can be performed with a clean, damp brush (Figure 8–12c). The moistened brush is wiped or scrubbed over an area where color is to be removed; the brush is wiped clean between each stroke. This approach will work even on many dried watercolor paints. Seldom will the paper return to a pure white condition. These lifting techniques allow the artist to paint a smooth wash over a background and then to remove paint from areas where transparent overlays of color would cause an inappropriate mixture of pigment. For instance, a blue sky would distort a yellow object in the foreground causing it to turn green. By lifting the blue pigment in the area where the yellow object is to be placed, a smooth wash can be painted over the entire sky and the yellow object can be painted on a clean surface after the wash has dried. Most lake colors and some other pigments will leave some residue of color after they have been lifted. These paints can be removed with a mixture of househod bleach diluted with water (which damages some papers) or with a liquid color remover. Liquid color remover is a commercially available product that is applied over dry paint. Eventually the color remover will fade the paint beneath it, leaving a relatively clean surface for additional painting. No matter which lifting technique is used, care must be taken to avoid damaging the surface of the art paper. Also, some papers used for blotting leave deposits of lint on the rendering surface. The lint must be removed before further painting.

Texturing Techniques

Watercolor washes are usually smooth or graded areas of transparent color. Glazes are also smooth, affected only by the texture of the paper. Watercolorists can create rich textures in a variety of ways.

Wet blending (Figure 8–13a and 8–13b) creates striations, puddles, or stars of color. While a wash or glaze is still wet, a clean brush is loaded with clear water or a dilute mixture of pigment and dragged along the edge of the wet paint to lay a stripe of water or paint that just overlaps the wash. The new application of water or pigment will bleed into the paint. Some dramatic effects can be created by tipping the rendering to create streaks of the new color. This technique results in a background that may suggest anything from a rain-streaked sky to a water-stained wall. The same technique can be used in a slightly different manner. Rather than brushing the wet blend into the paint, drop the water or pigment in puddles. The added water or pigment will lift the original color near the center of the puddle and bleed into the wet paint on the paper.

Dry brushing (Figure 8–13c) is used in watercolor painting in a manner similar to its use in scene painting. A damp—not wet—brush is dabbed in slightly diluted pigment. The brush loaded with relatively dry color is lightly dragged over a dry painting surface,

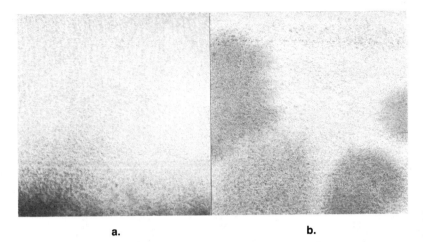

a.   b.

FIGURE 8–13

a) Wet blend of washes, b) Wet blend with one color dropped into the other color, c) Dry brushing, d) Scumbling.

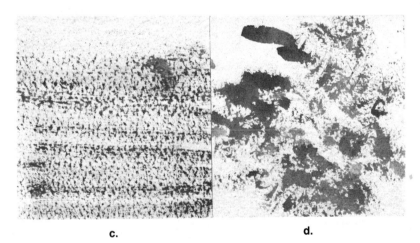

c.   d.

leaving several narrow streaks of the new color. A similar effect can be created by dragging the tip of a clean, dry brush through previously applied paint that is nearly dry. The brush will lift streaks of pigment to create a grained effect.

Scumbling (Figure 8–13d) creates a coarse pattern as a result of the brush movement. The tip of a round brush is loaded with a small charge of paint. The whole side of the brush is then worked back and forth on the painting surface, leaving the imprint of the brush, or the brush is slapped and dabbed against the paper, leaving a broken imprint of the bristle pattern. Using this technique with a small brush can imply a wallpaper or foliage pattern.

Sponging (Figure 8–14a) creates a texture by dappling the surface with pigment. The sponge can be loaded with pigment to apply paint or can be pressed on the surface to remove paint. A natural elephant-ear sponge is used. After the sponge has been moistened in clean water and wrung out, it is dipped into a pool of diluted paint and partially wrung out again. The paint-charged sponge is lightly pressed onto the rendering in the area to receive the texture. Between each application, the sponge should be rotated or turned so that no consistent pattern is developed. The same technique can be used in reverse by pressing

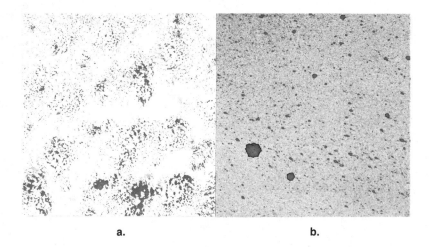

a.   b.

FIGURE 8–14

a) Sponging, b) Spattering, c) Salting, d) Scraping.

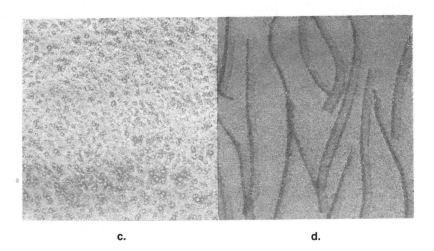

c.   d.

a clean, damp sponge over nearly dry paint to lift pigment from the surface. Either technique requires a great deal of practice.

Spattering (Figure 8–14b) creates a more regular texture. Instead of a paintbrush, a toothbrush is used. The bristles of a toothbrush are loaded with paint, and then a finger is passed over the bristles to throw a mist of paint on the rendering. The quality of spatter is governed by the quantity and dilution of paint and the proximity of the brush to the painting surface.

Salting (Figure 8–14c) creates a parchment-like effect. Ordinary table salt, rock salt, sand, or cornstarch is sprinkled over moist paint. Each particle of these materials acts like a little sponge, soaking up a portion of the wet paint. When the paint and texturing medium are completely dry, the rendering is brushed clean. When the salt or cornstarch is sprinkled over a single layer of paint, the paper will read through the texture; if a glaze has been laid over a previously painted surface, the salt will cause the first application of color to read through.

Scraping (Figure 8–14d) creates a bold, striated effect. This texturing technique works best on a smooth paper. Before painting, the blade of a pen knife is used to scrape striations into the paper. The striations must be in the direction of the desired texture and must not cut through the paper. Paint is then applied to the entire surface. The scraped area absorbs the paint in a completely different manner than the rest of the paper and dries darker, emphasizing the texture.

Masking is not really a texturing technique but a way to protect portions of the rendering. Areas are coated with a **frisket,** a masking material similar to rubber cement. The frisket is painted on the surface and allowed to dry. After the frisket has dried throughly, the rendering may be painted without concern for the masked area. When the paints have dried, the frisket is removed by rubbing a finger over the material to reveal clean paper beneath. Friskets can be used to block out areas that will be treated in detail at a later time, or it can be spattered over a surface to create a texture.

The Painting Process

Various approaches can be taken to painting with watercolor, but the logic underlying any approach must acknowledge the transparent quality of the paint and the effect of laying one transparent color over another. The general rule for watercolor painting is to apply light colors first and then darker colors. This order of work allows maximum control of blending on the painting surface. In scenic or costume design, applying light colors first is not always possible since the artist may desire a dark, smooth background or wish to paint foreground details without the distortion that a wash would create. In such instances, lifting or masking with a frisket could be helpful. In general, watercolor rendering is a technique of rapid application. For this reason careful planning must be done.

A typical rendering process begins by transferring the sketch to the art paper. Areas of wash are then painted. If the background is a single color, the wash can be applied in one step. If several colors are used for the background, each color must be applied separately after the preceding coat has dried, or a narrow margin of dry paper must be maintained between colors to prevent bleeding. It may be desirable to paint an initial wash on the entire rendering and allow it to dry before transferring the sketch to the painting surface. The sketch can then be drawn or traced onto the dried wash. Either approach is valid; the choice is governed by the amount of information necessary to paint the wash and the need for clarity of detail in the sketch to paint later glazes. While a wash is drying, textures can be created, areas lifted, or secondary washes applied. Drying time can be reduced by passing a hand-held hair dryer over the wet paint, although many watercolorists disdain this procedure. After the initial wash has dried completely, details can be painted on the rendering. Once again, care must be taken to prevent areas of wet pigment from bleeding into each other. Washes and glazes can be built up in layers to show details or to tone the entire rendering. At any time during the painting process, areas can be lifted or textured. Extreme highlights and shadows can be added to the rendering as a final step.

Rather than painting layers of colors, many scene designers prefer to work from the background to the foreground of a rendering. This usually requires masking lightly colored details or accepting some distortion of colors in foreground objects. Other artists prefer to paint detail first and then fill in the background with a wash around foreground objects. This technique leads to some problems, since washes applied over previous art work can cause paint to smear or bleed. A frisket cannot be used over previously painted areas because it will destroy the art work. If the artist paints washes around previously rendered foreground details, the brushwork tends to appear in the final rendering.

The normally rapid rate of watercolor painting can lead to fortuitous accidents or serious difficulties. When the accidents produce unsatisfactory results, it may be necessary to start the rendering over. At times a lifting or texturing technique can resolve the problem. One difficulty the artist may experience is excessive brightness or intensity in a rendering. It may be possible to solve this problem by painting a very diluted glaze over the completed composition. The dry rendering is placed on a flat surface, and a very dilute mixture of a modifying color is applied with a flat brush. The bristles must not touch the surface, or the glaze may disturb previously applied paints. Allow the glaze to dry completely. It is preferable to apply several dilute glazes to achieve the desired reduction of intensity than to attempt complete modification in a single coating.

ACRYLIC PAINTS

Acrylic paints have many similarities to transparent watercolor paints and have replaced that medium for many designers. Acrylic paints have the transparency, luminescence, and brilliance of transparent watercolor plus ease of handling and permanence.

Acrylic paints are manufactured from the same pigments as transparent watercolors, but they are combined with a plastic binder that makes the acrylic paint totally waterproof when completely dry. Over fifty acrylic colors are available—either as a thick liquid in jars or as a heavy paste in tubes. Acrylics can be used in exactly the same manner as transparent watercolors by diluting the paint with water to reduce the heavy viscosity and natural opacity of acrylic paint, or the paints can be used directly from the tube, diluted only slightly, to produce an opaque style.

Several materials are available to modify the viscosity, gloss, and drying time of acrylic paint. The simplest modifier is water, which dilutes acrylics in exactly the same way it dilutes transparent watercolor paints. **Gloss medium** reduces the strength of a color but maintains the paint at a creamy consistency. A sufficiently large addition of gloss medium makes the paint transparent and results in a shiny finish, similar to oil paints. **Matte medium** dilutes the paint in the same manner as gloss medium but dries to a satin finish. Either medium allows acrylic paint to maintain a heavy viscosity while diluting the color. **Gel medium** is an even thicker modifier, intended to prepare the paint for use with a palette knife. **Modeling paste,** which contains marble dust, is thicker than the gel and is used to construct three-dimensional painting surfaces by building up layers of paste. The paste can be mixed with tube colors to create a colored three-dimensional base for painting. **Retarder** is available to slow the drying time of acrylic paints.

Papers and Boards

Any paper or board can be used for acrylic painting. Most artists prefer a stiff working surface, such as cold-press illustration board, or tempered hardboard that has been treated with **acrylic gesso,** an opaque plasterlike material which is especially receptive to acrylic paints. When acrylics are used in the manner of transparent watercolor paints, watercolor papers will be most effective. The texture and tone of the paper affect the rendering in the same way the paper affects transparent watercolor paints. When acrylics are used as an opaque medium, the color of the paper or board will have little effect on the rendering.

Brushes

Although acrylic paints can be applied with the same brushes as watercolor paints, it is usually preferable to use a stiffer brush. Synthetic white-sable brushes are especially effective for acrylic painting, since they tend to have more spring to deal with the stiffer paint. Because acrylic paint becomes permanent when dry, brushes must never be stored with paint in them. While in use, the brushes should be rinsed thoroughly and after a painting session must be washed completely clean. As with watercolor brushes, good brushes well cared for will have a long servicable life.

Painting Technique

When used as a transparent medium, acrylic paint can be treated in exactly the same manner as transparent watercolors, with only one exception: once they have dried, acrylic paints cannot be lifted. This can be a disadvantage when lifting is desirable, but it can also be a major advantage since washes and glazes can be painted over completed art work without disturbing previouly painted layers.

As an opaque medium, acrylics can be used directly from the tube or diluted slightly with water or one the modifying agents. All of the technique of application and texturing discussed under transparent watercolors can be utilized, with the exception of lifting dried paints. In addition, the artist may paint layers of color over previous art work without concern for the new paints intermingling with dried colors. If desired, three-dimensional effects can be created on the painting surface by building up thick layers of paint or by preparing a three-dimensional base with modeling paste. Also, since acrylics are an opaque medium, the artist can approach the work in any convenient order; that is, work can progress from light to dark colors as in watercolor painting or may be reversed, with the dark colors painted first. All of these features make acrylic paints one of the most versatile media available to the designer. They can be applied with the same techniques as transparent watercolors, opaque gouaches, and oil paints, or even be used as a colored modeling medium.

MIXED MEDIA

Pencils, inks, watercolor, and acrylic paints can be used individually or in combination to achieve exciting results. Pencil, pen-and-ink, or charcoal sketches can be drawn on a surface that has been washed with watercolor paints, acrylic paints, or colored inks, or these paints and inks can be glazed over a sketch drawn with pencil or india ink. Acrylic paints can be used to apply colored detail to a pencil or pen drawing or to prepare a background for transparent watercolor painting. Alternatively, transparent watercolor paints or diluted acrylics can be glazed over an acrylic rendering with no effect on the underlying art work. The designer should experiment with these media individually and in combination, working over fixed and unfixed bases. The possibilities for combining media are endless.

PRESENTATION

A completed rendering has a rough, incomplete appearance until it is framed or mounted in some manner. Usually scenic renderings are matted rather than placed in a decorative wood or metal frame. A **mat** serves several functions: it protects the art work, hides the edges of the paper or board, and creates a frame that enchances the design's overall effect. A mat gives a finished appearance to the rendering.

Almost any material can be used to mat a design. Mat board, a single-thickness cardboard with a decorative paper attached, is available from art supply stores. The paper may have deep, rich colors; a bold texture; or a metalized, polished, brushed, or pebbled finish. One supplier manufactures mat board with over a hundred different finishes. If an adequate color or texture cannot be purchased, a mat board can be created, in any color or texture, by washing illustration board with acrylic paint or indelible ink. Textured mat boards can be made by gluing wallpaper, gift wrap, string, fabric, or any other material to the illustration board.

The best mat enhances a design. It draws the viewer into the picture and does not distract from the rendering. The mat can be in the same color range as the rendering, emphasize an accent color, or be in contrast to the rendering. There are no specific rules for the choice of matting materials.

The opening in the mat can be cut to almost any shape. Some designers prefer to use an equal border all the way around a rendering, others prefer a large border at the bottom, and still others artists use a wide border at the bottom and a narrow border at the top (Figure 8–15a–c). The opening in the mat can be square, rectangular, round, or shaped in some special pattern, perhaps in the design of an elaborate proscenium arch or a television screen. The simplest mat is a single layer with a rectangular opening. Mats can be quite elaborate, with double or triple layers of framing, and decorative lines, ornamentation, or designs around the opening. The edge of the opening on a mat is traditionally beveled at a 45° angle. The board can be cut with a mat knife or a commercial mat board cutter. A number of styles of cutters are available, from a very simple handheld device to an elaborate system with built-in cutting guides.

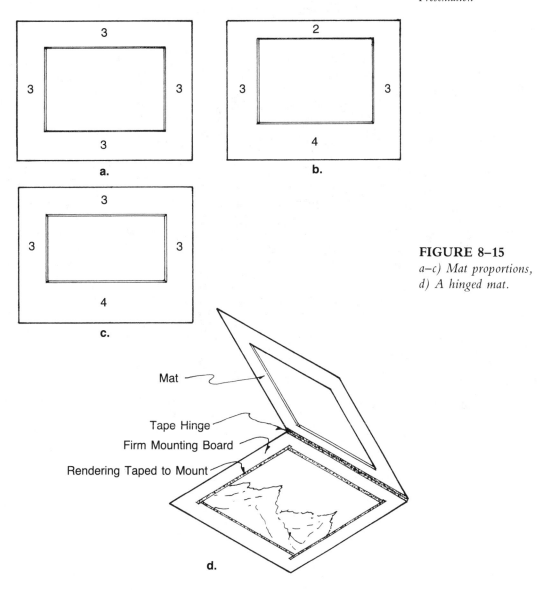

FIGURE 8–15
a–c) Mat proportions,
d) A hinged mat.

The rendering is attached to the back of the mat with butcher's, Kraft paper, or masking tape. Alternatively, the rendering can be attached to a stiff cardboard base that is hinged to the back of the mat board (Figure 8–15d).

A rendering may be mounted instead of matted. This can be particularly effective with renderings drawn or painted on illustration board, which will be dimensionally separated from the mounting surface by the thickness of the board. The rendering is attached to the mount with dry-mount tissue, polyvinyl glue, or a permanent spray cement. If desired, a mat can be placed around the mounted rendering, or the mount can be left plain.

Scene designers usually label renderings on the back with a neatly lettered or typed tag. The label identifies the production, scene, director, date of production or project, and the designer. A one-quarter-inch scale plan can also be attached to the back of the rendering.

Exercises

Perform exercises 1 through 7 on any paper that has a moderate tooth. Newsprint, drawing paper, and drafting vellum are excellent choices.

1. Divide two sheets of paper into six squares, each measuring 3½″ × 3½″. Number the squares 1 through 6. On the first sheet, use a 2B lead, sharpened to a conical point; on the second sheet, use a wide, rectangular-lead sketching pencil, sharpened to a chisel point.

    a. In Square 1 draw a series of horizontal lines the full width of the square. Try to make each line straight, evenly spaced, and equal in lineweight.

    b. In Square 2 draw a series of vertical lines the full height of the square. Try to make each line straight, evenly spaced, and equal in lineweight.

    c. In Square 3 draw a series of wavy, horizontal lines across the entire square. Make each line follow the same curves. Keep the lines evenly spaced and equal in lineweight.

    d. In Square 4 draw a series of straight, evenly spaced, diagonal lines to both the right and the left, creating a hatched texture similar to that in Figure 8–3d.

    e. In Square 5 draw a series of broken hatch lines with a texture similar to that shown in Figure 8–3g.

    f. In Square 6 create the texture shown in Figure 8–3l.

2. Divide a sheet of paper into six squares, each measuring at least 3½″ × 3½″. Number the squares 1 through 6. Reproduce the six tones shown in Figure 8–4, using a 2B lead or a round sketching pencil.

3. Choose a tree outdoors. Draw a pencil sketch of the tree showing its form and the texture of the bark and foliage.

4. Find an old wooden house or dilapidated brick building. Draw a pencil sketch of the house or building, emphasizing form and texture. Experiment with a variety of strokes to show the brick or wood.

5. Have a friend model for you, or use a good photograph of someone. Draw a full-figure drawing of the person that reveals the shape, texture, and tone of his or her garments. Again, experiment with a variety of strokes to construct textures and tones.

6. Working from a photograph, draw a portrait of an elderly man or woman.

7. Find a photograph of a portrait drawn or painted by a "Great Master" artist. Reproduce that portrait in pencil.

Perform Exercises 8 through 13 on a smooth paper. Drafting vellum is satisfactory, but a plate-finish bristol board is excellent.

8. With pen-and-ink, reproduce each of the strokes and textures shown in Figure 8–11.

9–13. Repeat Exercises 3 through 7, using pen-and-ink instead of pencil.

Prepare a 16″ × 20″ piece of watercolor paper for Exercises 14 through 17. Use transparent watercolor paints for Exercises 14 and 15.

14. Divide the paper into four 8″ × 10″ rectangles with masking tape. Number the squares 1 through 4.

    a. In Square 1 paint a smooth wash.

    b. In Square 2 paint a graded wash, progressing from dark at the top to light at the bottom.

    c. In Square 3 paint a graded wash, progressing from light at the top to dark at the bottom.

    d. In Square 4 paint a graded wash that is light on your left and dark on your right. This step will require vertical strokes.

15. Using masking tape, divide a clean piece of paper into three equal horizontal sections, each measuring approximately 5″ × 20″.

    a. Paint an even wash of primary yellow in the top section, primary red in the center section, and primary blue in the bottom section.

    b. While the washes are still damp, paint a ½″-wide stripe of each of the primary colors the entire height of the paper. Do not allow the stripes to come in contact with each other.

    c. While the washes are still damp, lift a ½″-wide stripe the entire height of the paper.

    d. Allow the washes and stripes to dry thoroughly. Remove the masking-tape dividers between the sections. Again, paint a ½″-wide stripe of the primary colors the entire height of the paper. Do not allow the stripes to come in contact with each other.

    e. Attempt to lift a ½″-wide stripe the entire height of the paper.

    f. After the paints from steps d and e have dried, select any five additional colors (which can include white and black), and paint ½″-wide stripes the entire height of the paper. Use at least four different dilutions of each color. Do not allow the stripes to come in contact with each other.

    g. After the paints from step f have dried, make at least four dilutions of each color, and use each to paint a narrow horizontal stripe across the width of the page.

16. Repeat Excercise 15, using acrylic paints.

17. Select four texturing techniques for watercolor painting and experiment with them.

APPENDIX A

Design and Technical Drawing

FIGURE A-1
Scenic rendering for a production of Bus Stop.

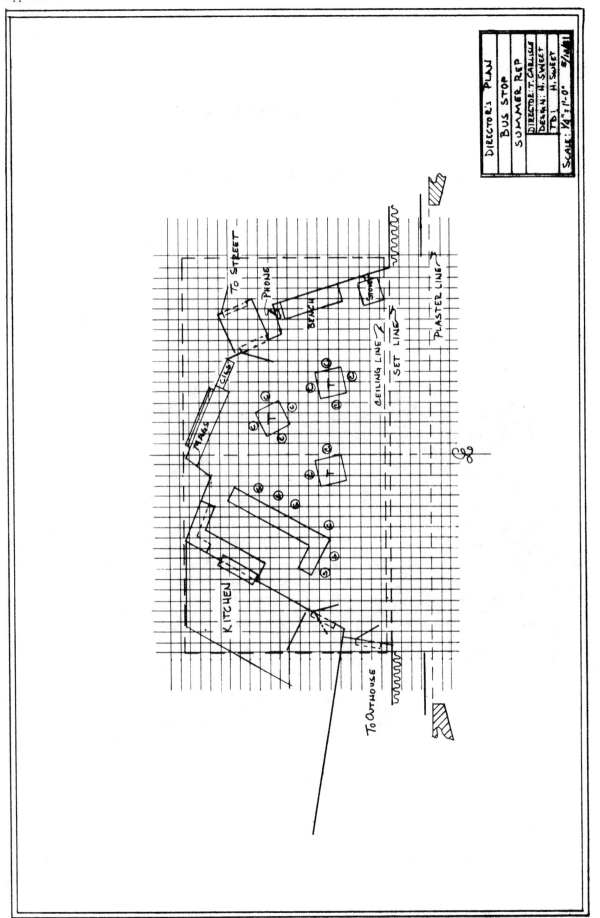

FIGURE A-2
Director's plan/properties plot.

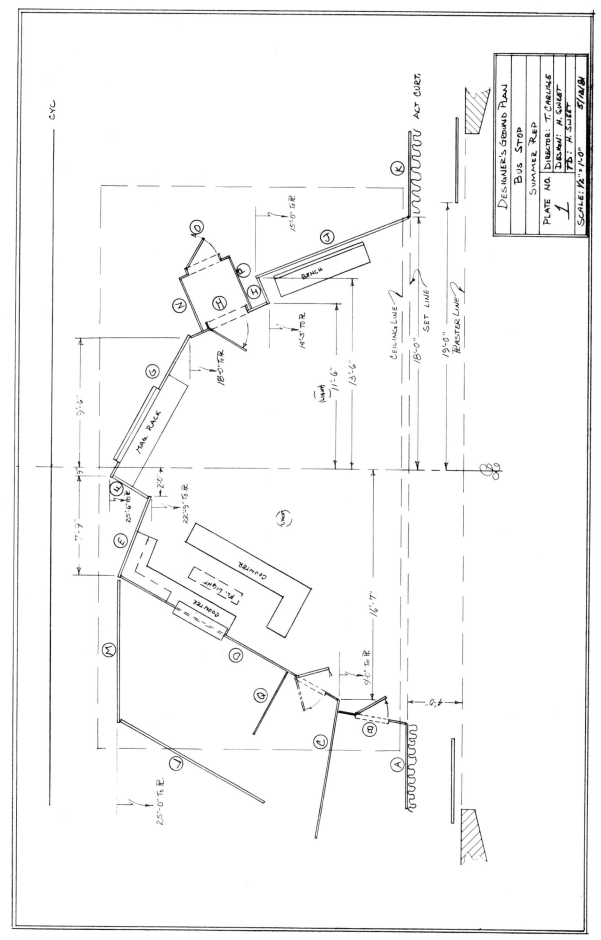

FIGURE A-3
Designer's ground plan.

261

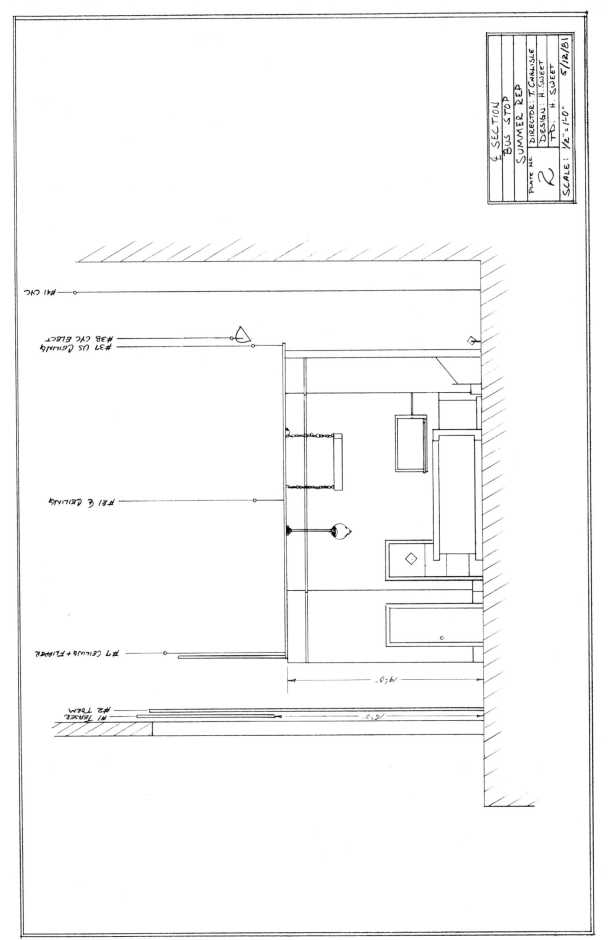

FIGURE A-4
Centerline section.

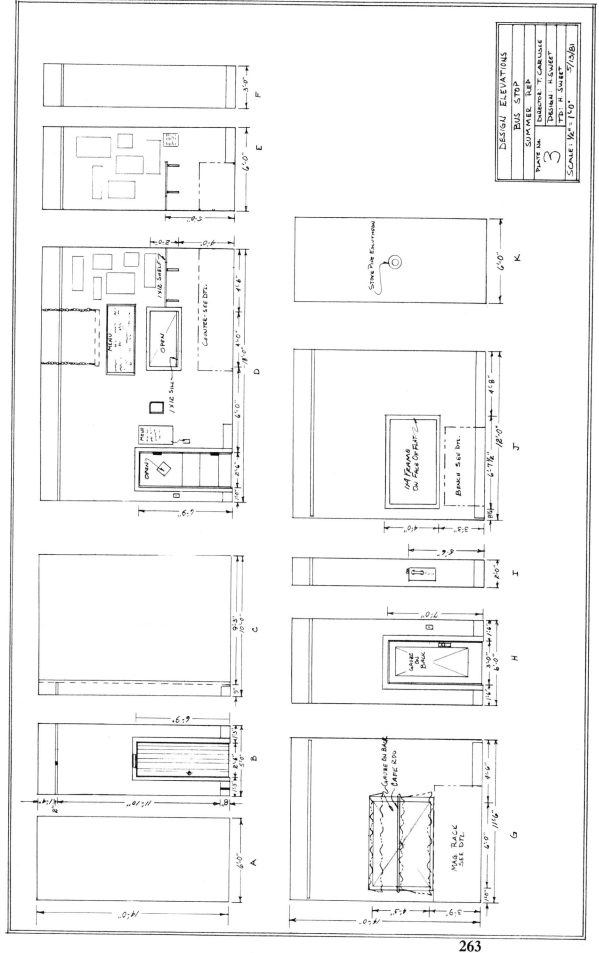

FIGURE A-5
Design elevations.

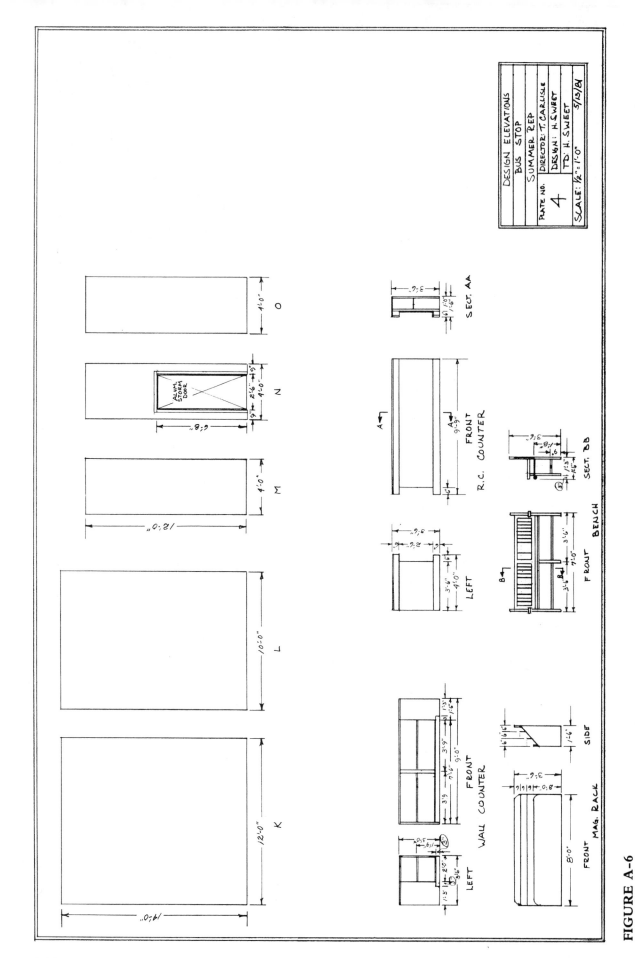

FIGURE A-6

Design elevations and details of furniture and other units to be constructed.

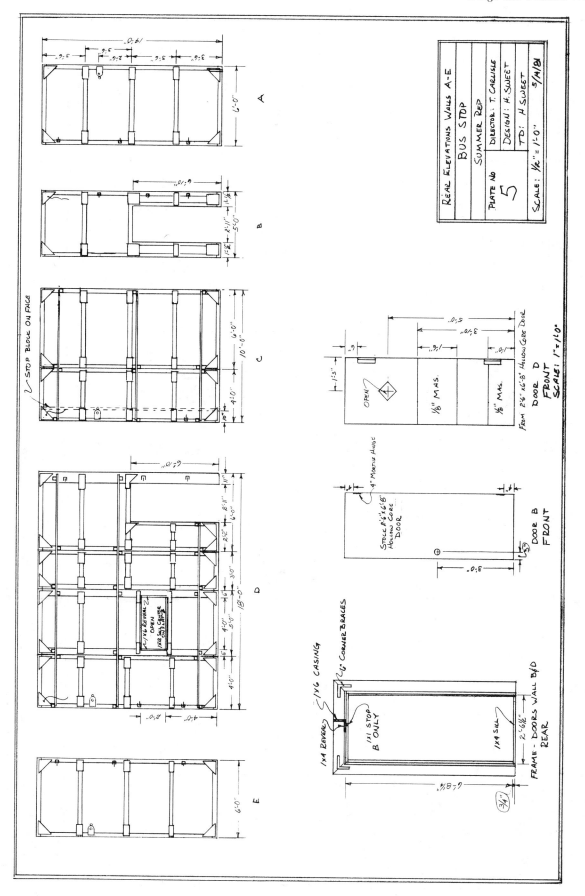

FIGURE A-7

Working drawings. This plate exemplifies working drawings with complete details for construction, including the placement of cornerblocks and keystones and all hardware. In addition, the doors and door frames are drawn in detail.

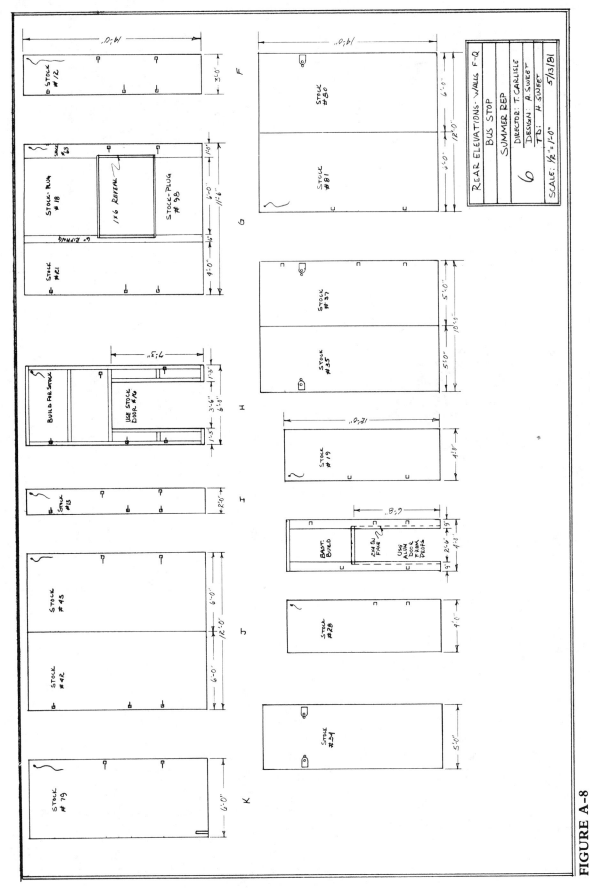

FIGURE A-8

Working drawings. This plate exemplifies working drawings for a shop familiar with standard construction practices and one that uses stock scenery. Only nonstandard constructions are detailed. Stock numbers are used to indicate the flats, doors, and so forth to be used.

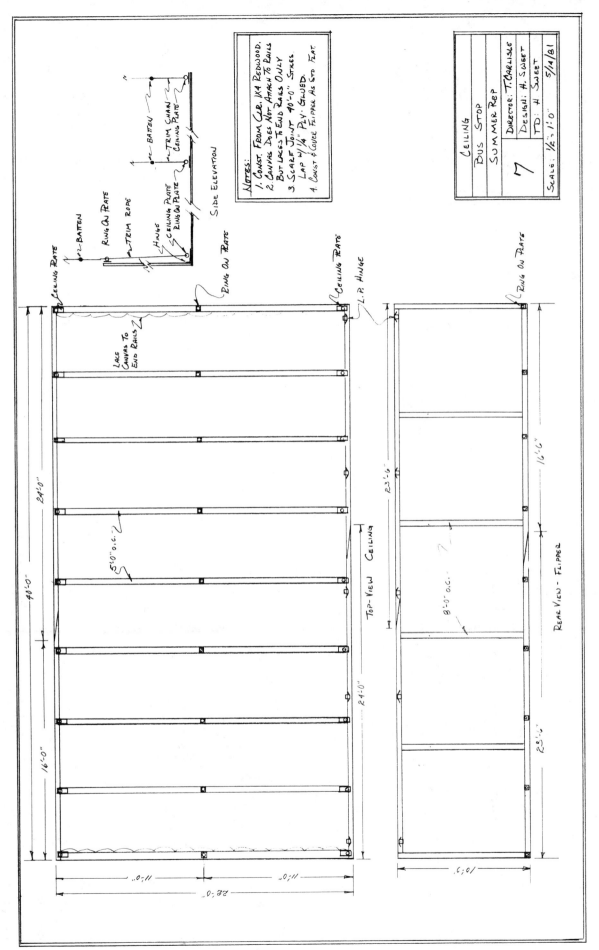

FIGURE A-9

Working drawing of the ceiling for this set. A side elevation has been included to demonstrate the use of hardware and assembly details.

267

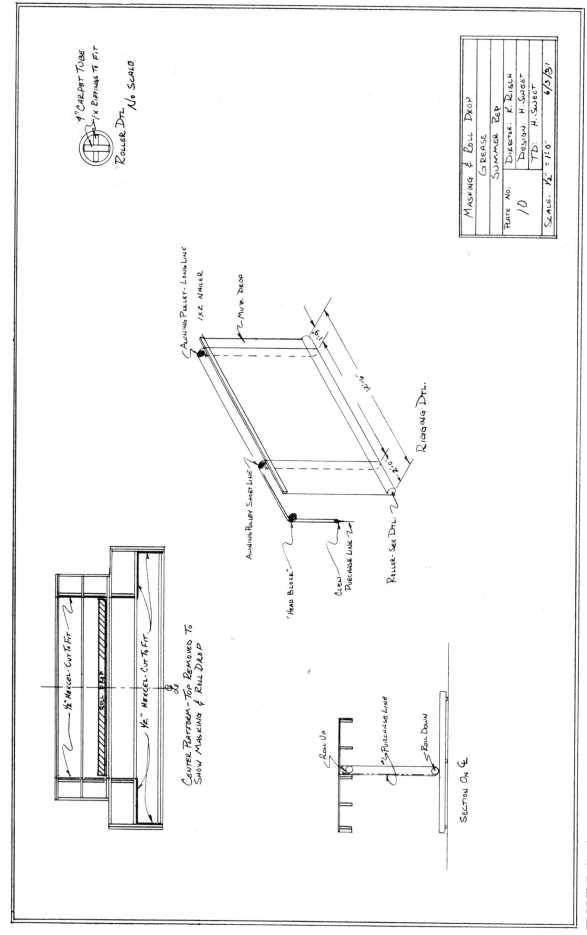

FIGURE A-10

This plate is from a different production, Grease, but is included to show the use of sections and isometric views to demonstrate the rigging for this roll drop.

FIGURE A-11
Production photo of Bus
Stop. (University of
Northern Iowa. Director:
Thomas Carlisle. Scenic
Designer: Harvey Sweet)

Graphic Standards Board Recommendations for Standard Graphic Language in Scenic Design and Technical Production

General Description

The concept of a standard must evolve from a logical basis. In this case, that basis is rooted in the only inflexible rule of technical drawing: that any graphic communication must be clear, consistent and efficient. While these recommendations will not include specific guidelines for the spacing of objects on each plate, any graphic presentation should adhere to the general recommendation of clarity — do not crowd nor unevenly space individual items on a plate. Equally important, all line weight, line types, symbols, conventions and lettering should be consistent from plate to plate and in a given set of drawings. This does not mean that everyone will be expected to letter in the same manner, nor draw their arrowheads in precisely the same way. It means that each drafter should be able to establish his "style" within the guidelines of the recommended standards and conform to that style throughout the drawings for a particular project or production. Finally, the standards and symbols used in any recommended guide should be efficient — both in ease of drawing, and in ease of comprehension for the reader.

Ground Plan

A great deal of drawing in technical theatre, both in presentation and symbology, is directly related to the drawing of the floor plan or ground plan. The specific definition of the ground plan is as follows: A floor or ground plan is a horizontal offset section with the cutting plane passing at whatever level, normally a height of 4'-0" above the stage floor, is required to produce the most descriptive view of the set.

Line Weights

The USITT recommends a modified ANSI standard two thickness line system. The approved line weights are as follows:

Pen: Thin: .010" to .0125" width. (ANSI standard .016")
       Thick: .020" to .025" width. (ANSI standard .032")

Pencil: Thin: .3MM
        Thick: .5MM

Source: Reprinted by permission of the U.S. Institute for Theatre Technology Graphic Standards Board, Education Commission, and Board of Directors.

In either pen or pencil, an extra thick line, .035″ to .040″ (.9MM) may be infrequently used, as necessary, for emphasis (plate border, suitable section cutting plane line, etc.)

Conventions

There are a number of standard theatrical units such as chandeliers, shelves and fireplaces that, because of their varying styles and sizes, should not be represented by standard symbols, but need to be easily and repetitively drawn.

The drawing of these items should subscribe to the general guideline offered under the definition of the ground plan. Shelves, fireplaces and similar items should be drawn using a sectional cutting plane of 4′-0″ unless another view would be more descriptive. Chandeliers should be indicated by a circle utilizing a hidden line as they are not at the 4′-0″ cutting plane. The circle should be drawn, in scale, the diameter of the chandelier at its widest point. The graphic should be placed in its proper position on the floor plan. Other suspended objects such as beams, drops not in contact with the stage floor (e.g., an Act II drop on an Act I floor plan, etc.) would be drawn in their appropriate outline using the hidden line type.

When flats are drawn in section view, as in a ground plan, they should be in scale thickness, and should have the space darkened between the two visible lines which are outlining the thickness of the flat.

Lettering

Lettering should be legible and the style should allow for easy and rapid execution. Characters which generally conform to the singlestroke gothic style meet these requirements. Only upper case letters should be used on drawings unless lower case letters are needed to conform with other established standards or nomenclature.

Title Block

The title block should be in the same location on all drawings of a single project. The title block should be located in either the lower right hand corner of the drawing or in a strip along the bottom of the drawing. In either case, the block should include the following information:

1. Name of producing organization and/or theatre
2. Name of production, act and scene if appropriate
3. Drawing title
4. Drawing number
5. Predominant scale of the drawing
6. Date the drawing was drafted
7. Designer of the production
8. Drafter, if different from the designer
9. Approval of drawing, if applicable

Dimensions

1. Dimensions must be clear, consistent, and easily understood.
2. Dimensions should be oriented to read from the bottom and or the right hand side of the plate.
3. Metric dimensions less than one meter are to be noted as a zero, decimal point, and portion of meter in numerals. All measurements

271

one meter and greater shall be given as a whole meter number, decimal point, and portion of meter. (0.1m, 0.52m, 1.5m, 2.35m)

4. Dimensions less than 1'-0" are given in inches without a foot notation, such as: 6", 9½", etc.

5. Dimensions 1'-0" and greater include the whole feet with a single apostrophe followed by a dash and then inches followed by a double apostrophe:

7'-0½"   18'-9¼"   1'-3"

6. Dimensions that require more space than available between extension lines are placed in proximity to the area measured, parallel with the bottom edge of the sheet, and directed to the point of reference by means of a leader line. [Figure B–1.]

FIGURE B-1

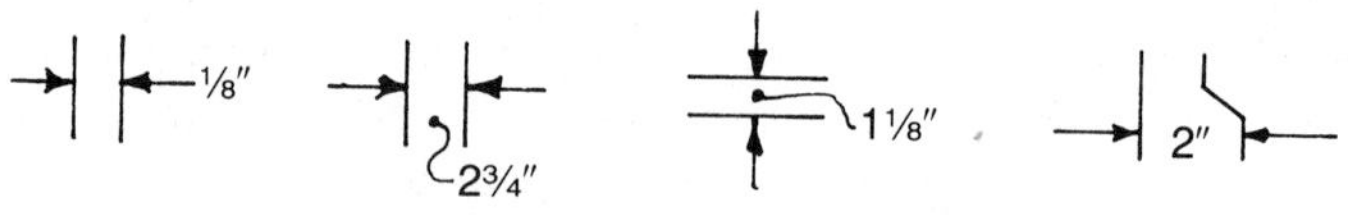

7. Platform and tread heights are given in inches above the stage floor. Such heights are placed in circles at or near the centers of the platform or tread. [Figure B–2.]

FIGURE B-2

8. Direction of arrows (when used to indicate elevation change on stairs, ramps, etc.), points away from the primary level of the drawing.

8. Radii

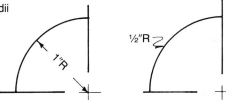 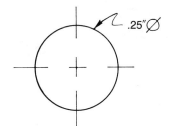 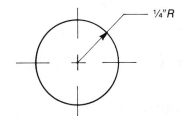

9. Diameter

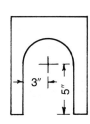 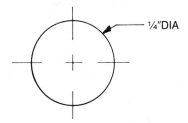

10. Centers

FIGURE B-3

 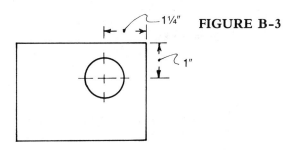

11. Angles

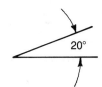

45°

20°

LINE TYPES

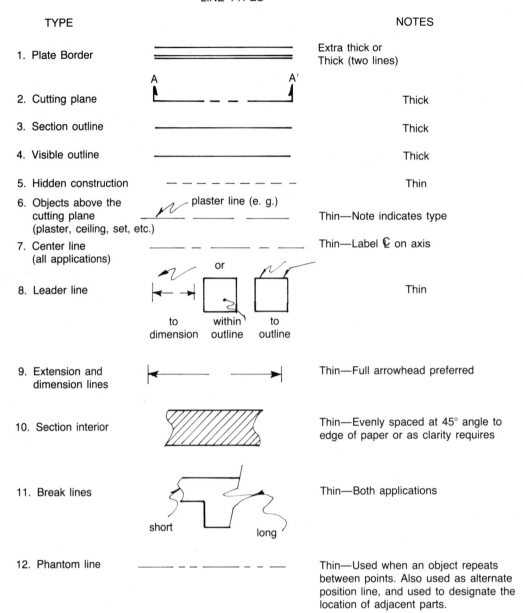

TYPE		NOTES
1. Plate Border		Extra thick or Thick (two lines)
2. Cutting plane		Thick
3. Section outline		Thick
4. Visible outline		Thick
5. Hidden construction		Thin
6. Objects above the cutting plane (plaster, ceiling, set, etc.)	plaster line (e. g.)	Thin—Note indicates type
7. Center line (all applications)		Thin—Label ℄ on axis
8. Leader line	to dimension / within outline / to outline	Thin
9. Extension and dimension lines		Thin—Full arrowhead preferred
10. Section interior		Thin—Evenly spaced at 45° angle to edge of paper or as clarity requires
11. Break lines	short / long	Thin—Both applications
12. Phantom line		Thin—Used when an object repeats between points. Also used as alternate position line, and used to designate the location of adjacent parts.

13. Any "special" lines not listed above should be noted in the legend of each sheet.

FIGURE B-4

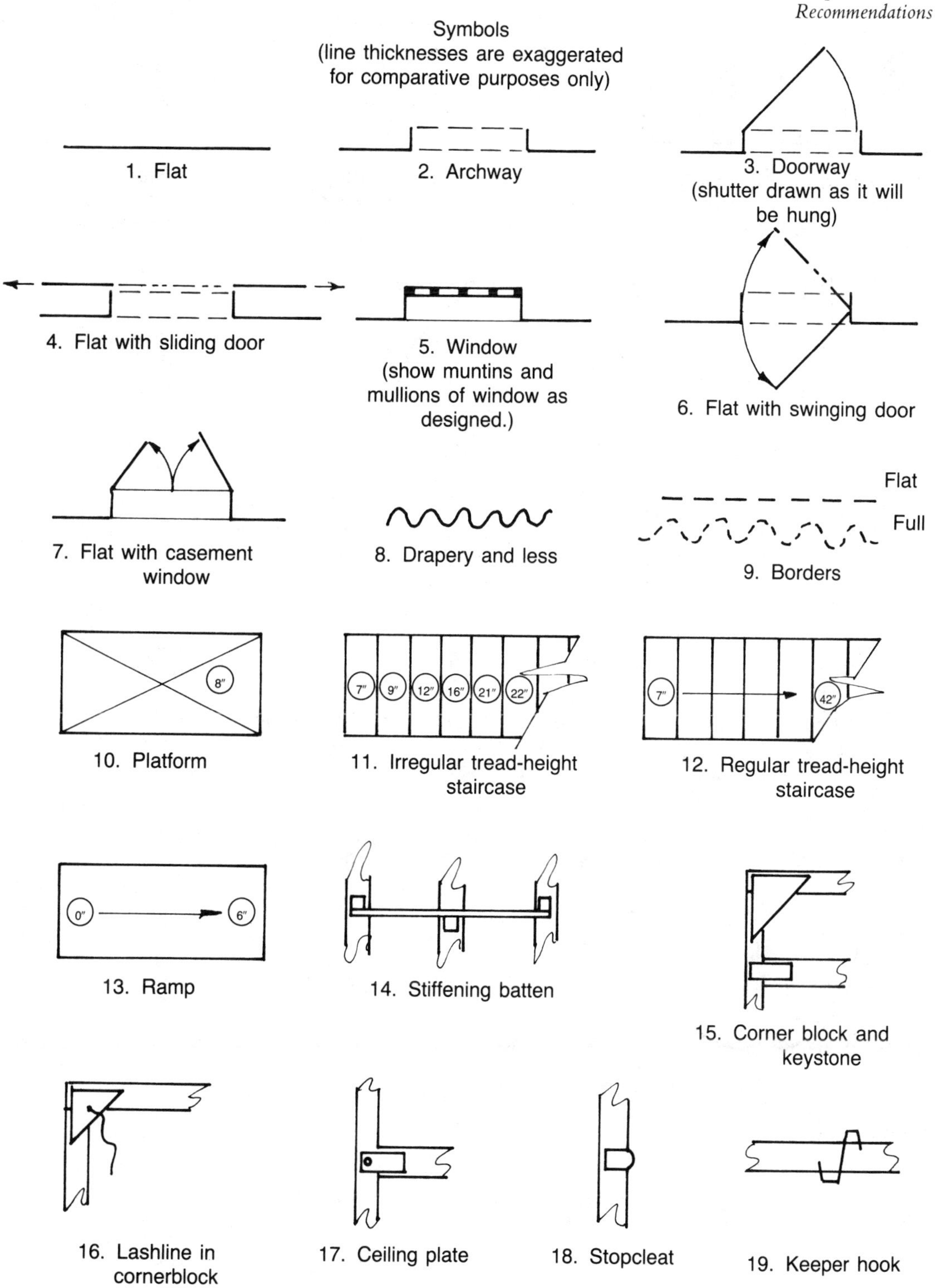
Symbols
(line thicknesses are exaggerated
for comparative purposes only)
1. Flat
2. Archway
3. Doorway
(shutter drawn as it will
be hung)
4. Flat with sliding door
5. Window
(show muntins and
mullions of window as
designed.)
6. Flat with swinging door
7. Flat with casement
window
8. Drapery and less
Flat
Full
9. Borders
8″
10. Platform
7″
9″
12″
16″
21″
22″
11. Irregular tread-height
staircase
7″
42″
12. Regular tread-height
staircase
0″
6″
13. Ramp
14. Stiffening batten
15. Corner block and
keystone
16. Lashline in
cornerblock
17. Ceiling plate
18. Stopcleat
19. Keeper hook

FIGURE B-5

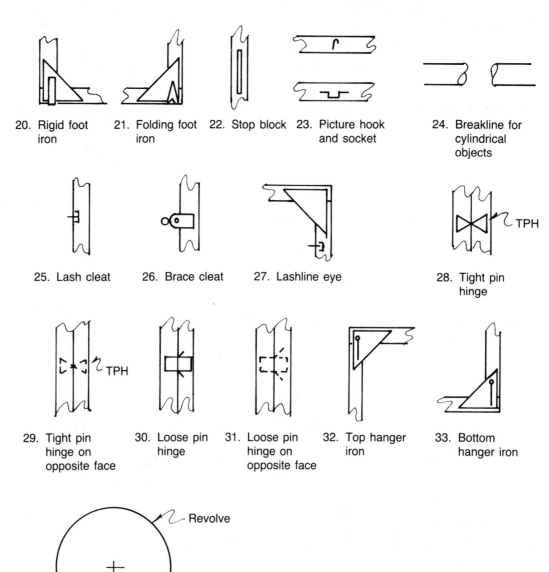

20. Rigid foot iron
21. Folding foot iron
22. Stop block
23. Picture hook and socket
24. Breakline for cylindrical objects
25. Lash cleat
26. Brace cleat
27. Lashline eye
28. Tight pin hinge
29. Tight pin hinge on opposite face
30. Loose pin hinge
31. Loose pin hinge on opposite face
32. Top hanger iron
33. Bottom hanger iron
34.

FIGURE B-5 continued

Bibliography

Birren, Faber. *Creative Color*. New York: Van Nostrand Reinhold, 1961.

Blake, Wendon. *Acrylic Painting*. New York: Watson-Guptill, 1979.

D'Amelio, Joseph. *Perspective Drawing Handbook*. New York: Leon Amiel, 1964.

Derkatsch, Inessa. *Transparent Watercolor: Painting Methods and Materials*. Englewood Cliffs, N. J.: Prentice-Hall, 1980.

Earle, James H. *Engineering Design Graphics,* 3rd ed. Reading, Mass.: Addison-Wesley, 1977.

Edwards, Betty. *Drawing on the Right Side of the Brain*. Boston: Houghton-Mifflin, 1980.

Fabri, Ralph. *Color: A Complete Guide for Artists*. New York: Watson-Guptill, 1967.

French, Thomas E. and Charles J. Vierck. *Engineering Drawing and Graphic Technology,* 12th ed. New York: McGraw-Hill, 1972.

Gray, Henry. *Gray's Anatomy,* 35th ed. R. Warwick and P.L. Williams, eds. Philadelphia: Saunders, 1973.

Guptill, Arthur L. *Pencil Drawing: Step by Step,* revised ed. New York: Van Nostrand Reinhold, 1959.

———. *Rendering in Pen and Ink*. Susan E. Meyer, ed. New York: Watson-Guptill, 1976.

Lohan, Frank. *Pen & Ink Techniques*. Chicago: Contemporary Books, 1978.

Martin, C. Leslie. *Design Graphics,* 2nd ed. New York: Macmillan, 1968.

Morgan, Harry. *Perspective Drawing for the Theatre*. New York: Drama Book Specialists, 1979.

Munsell, Albert H. *A Grammar of Color*. Faber Birren, ed. New York: Van Nostrand Reinhold, 1969.

Nikōlaides, Kimon. *The Natural Way to Draw*. Boston: Houghton-Mifflin, 1941.

Parker, Oren. *Sceno-Graphic Techniques,* 2nd. ed. Pittsburgh: Carnegie-Mellon University, 1969.

Ramsey, Charles G. and Harold R. Sleeper. *Architectural Graphic Standards,* 6th ed. New York: Wiley, 1970.

Richmond, Leonard and J. Littlejohns. *Fundamentals of Watercolor Painting*. New York: Watson-Guptill, 1978.

Snyder, John. *Commercial Artist's Handbook*. New York: Watson-Guptill, 1973.

Index

2067

2067